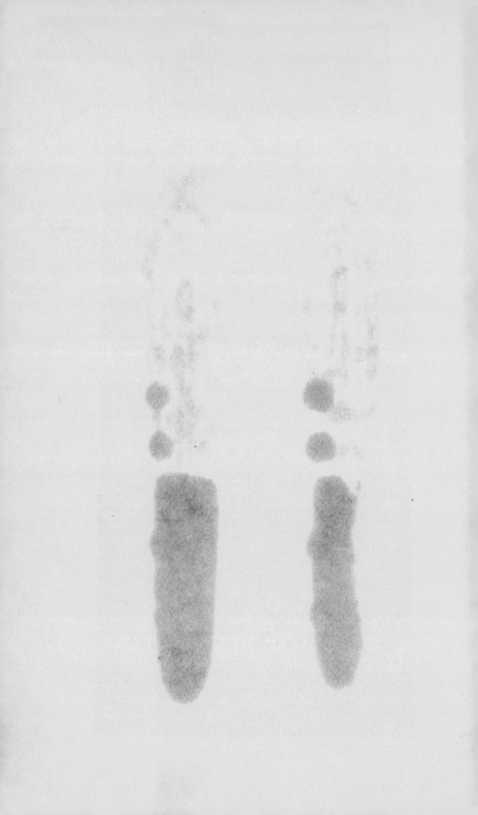

MODERN JERUSALEM

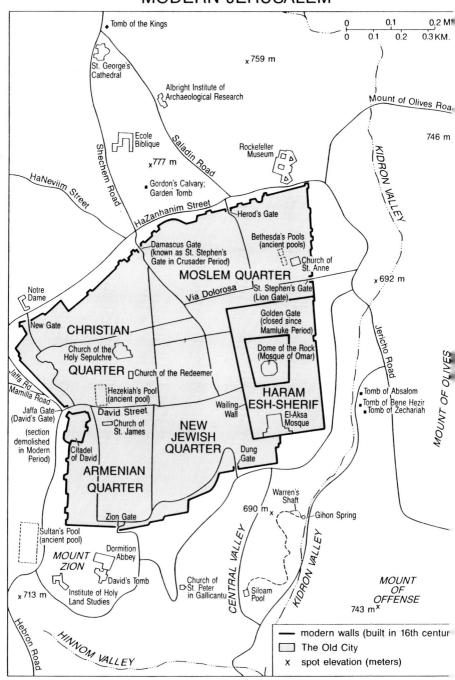

Tomb of the Kings

x 759 m

0   0.1   0.2 M
0   0.1   0.2   0.3 KM.

St. George's
Cathedral

Albright Institute of
Archaeological Research

Mount of Olives Roa

Ecole
Biblique

Rockefeller
Museum

746 m

x 777 m

Shechem Road

Saladin Road

KIDRON VALLEY

HaNeviim Street

Gordon's Calvary;
Garden Tomb

HaZanhanim Street

Herod's Gate

Bethesda's Pools
(ancient pools)

Damascus Gate
(known as St. Stephen's
Gate in Crusader Period)

Church of
St. Anne

x 692 m

MOSLEM QUARTER

Notre
Dame

Via Dolorosa

St. Stephen's Gate
(Lion Gate)

New Gate

CHRISTIAN

Golden Gate
(closed since
Mamluke Period)

Jericho Road

Church of the
Holy Sepulchre

Dome of the Rock
(Mosque of Omar)

QUARTER

Church of the Redeemer

Jaffa Rd
Mamilla Road

Hezekiah's Pool
(ancient pool)

HARAM
ESH-SHERIF

Tomb of Absalom
Tomb of Bene Hezir
Tomb of Zechariah

Jaffa Gate
(David's Gate)

David Street

Wailing
Wall

MOUNT OF OLIVES

(section
demolished
in Modern
Period)

Church of
St. James

El-Aksa
Mosque

NEW
JEWISH
QUARTER

Citadel
of David

Dung
Gate

ARMENIAN
QUARTER

Zion Gate

Warren's
Shaft

Sultan's Pool
(ancient pool)

690 m

Gihon Spring

Dormition
Abbey

MOUNT
ZION

David's Tomb

Church of
St. Peter
in Gallicantu

Siloam
Pool

CENTRAL VALLEY

KIDRON VALLEY

MOUNT
OF
OFFENSE

x 713 m

Institute of Holy
Land Studies

743 m x

Hebron Road

HINNOM VALLEY

—— modern walls (built in 16th centur

☐ The Old City

x   spot elevation (meters)

A New Testament

Guide to the Holy Land

John J. Kilgallen, S.J.

 Loyola University Press

Loyola University Press
3441 North Ashland Avenue
Chicago, Illinois 60657

Library of Congress Cataloging-in-Publication Data
Kilgallen, John J.
    A New Testament guide to the Holy Land.

    Includes index.
1. Israel—Description and travel—Guide-books.
2. Christian shrines—Israel. 3. West Bank—
Description and travel—Guide-books. 4. Christian
shrines—West Bank. 5. Bible. N.T. Gospels—Geography.
I. Title. II. Title: Guide to the Holy Land.
DS103.K53   1987   915.694′0454   87-3770
ISBN 0-8294-0543-7

Design / C.L. Tornatore

Contents

table of
Abbreviations

Acts	Acts	*Jer*	Jeremiah
Am	Amos	*Jgs*	Judges
		Jl	Joel
Bar	Baruch	*Jn*	John
		1 Jn	1 John
1 Chr	1 Chronicles	*2 Jn*	2 John
2 Chr	2 Chronicles	*3 Jn*	3 John
Col	Colossians	*Jon*	Jonah
1 Cor	1 Corinthians	*Jos*	Joshua
2 Cor	2 Corinthians	*Jude*	Jude
Dn	Daniel	*1 Kgs*	1 Kings
Dt	Deuteronomy	*2 Kgs*	2 Kings
Eccl	Ecclesiastes	*Lam*	Lamentations
Eph	Ephesians	*Lk*	Luke
Est	Esther	*Lv*	Leviticus
Ex	Exodus		
Ez	Ezekiel	*Mal*	Malachi
Ezr	Ezra	*1 Mc*	1 Maccabees
		2 Mc	2 Maccabees
Gal	Galatians	*Mi*	Micah
Gn	Genesis	*Mk*	Mark
		Mt	Matthew
Hb	Habakkuk		
Heb	Hebrews	*Na*	Nahum
Hg	Haggai	*Neh*	Nehemiah
Hos	Hosea	*Nm*	Numbers
Is	Isaiah	*Ob*	Obadiah
Jas	James	*Phil*	Philippians
Jb	Job	*Phlm*	Philemon
Jdt	Judith	*Prv*	Proverbs

Ps(s)	Psalms	*Tb*	Tobit
1 Pt	1 Peter	*1 Thes*	1 Thessalonians
2 Pt	2 Peter	*2 Thes*	2 Thessalonians
		1 Tm	1 Timothy
Rom	Romans	*2 Tm*	2 Timothy
Ru	Ruth		
Rv	Revelation	*Wis*	Wisdom
Sg	Song of Songs	*Zec*	Zechariah
Sir	Ecclesiasticus (Sirach)	*Zep*	Zephaniah
1 Sm	1 Samuel		
2 Sm	2 Samuel		

Introduction

A pilgrim asked me, "Would you write a guidebook to New Testament holy sites in Israel?"

"What kind of guide? Chatty, in-depth, archeological, theological?"

"A few years ago you were part of a teaching team which visited and taught about the New Testament sites in Israel; what did you contribute to those visits?"

"My job was to relate the New Testament to each holy site. I tried to draw from the New Testament stories associated with each site what the New Testament thought was to be learned from what happened at or is connected with the site. Thus, at Nazareth I tried to indicate what the gospel writers conveyed to their readers about the Annunciation to Mary at Nazareth and about the events in the adult life of Jesus which centered in Nazareth. Further, I hoped that by these presentations a person would learn more about the gospels in their entireties; that is, not only would one see what the New Testament has to say about events tied to a site, but one would also better understand how the gospel writers used these stories to further their overall purposes in writing their Gospels. Thus, one would better understand the meaning of a holy site in Israel and better understand the Gospel which at times spoke of this holy site."

"That's the kind of guidebook you should write!"

And so, I wrote this volume in the first place to emphasize the relationship of the Gospels to New Testament sacred sites and to use the sites as an opportunity to develop for the reader some of the main ideas which preoccupied the evangelists and moved them to write their Gospels.

To be more complete, however, I have added what I thought to be sufficient for a visitor or pilgrim who would want to know the basic geographical and archeological data, as well as biblical meaning, of each site. Such additions may not satisfy all one's questions, and for this inadequacy I apologize.

I hoped this volume wouldn't be too cumbersome and expensive, so I did not include the biblical texts about which I write. I assume that the reader will have a New Testament. I also assume that the visitor will read the appropriate New Testament passages in close association with this book; ultimately, those passages and the holy sites claim our fullest attention and memory.

I presented the holy sites in a certain geographical order: first, Galilee and its environs, and then Jerusalem and its environs. Since visits to Israel don't have to start in Galilee and end in Jerusalem, I also included an index of the sites and themes, as well as ones of persons and biblical texts.

I have assumed that the reader can find on his or her own each of the sites treated in this volume. Thus, I have avoided what is always the most chancy enterprise of guiding a person from an unknown hotel to the door which is now, but not always, used as the entrance to a shrine. Rather, I hope that, when one reaches the holy place, one can read the appropriate New Testament passages and then read the appropriate comments in this volume.

Is this volume meant to be spiritually uplifting? Not directly. But it operates on the assumption that deeper understanding of what God has told us about the events of Jesus' life in Israel can develop our spirituality. The better one comprehends the Word of God, the better, I hope, one will cherish Jesus and his Father. As St. Ignatius of Loyola advises his retreatant, "I ask for what I desire. Here it will be to ask for an intimate knowledge of our Lord."

May the One who made and still makes the sites holy and breathes meaning into the New Testament also live more fully in the lives of those who visit his places in search of him.

city
Herodian fortress
mountain peak
extent of Herod's kingdom

MEDITERRANEAN
SEA

ABILENE
Abila
SYRIA
Sidon
ITUREA
Damascus
Mt. Hermon
Abana R.
PHOENICIA
Litani R.
Pharpar R.
Tyre
Panias
GAULANITIS
TRACHONITIS
Kedesh
Raphana
Hazor
Ptolemais
GALILEE
Bethsaida
BATANEA
Arbela
Sea of
Canatha
Mt. Carmel
Sepphoris
Galilee
Hippos
AURANITIS
Gebae
Nazareth
Gadara
Abila
Edrei
Mt. Hauran
Dor
Scythopolis
DECAPOLIS
Caesarea
[Strato's Tower]
Pella
Dion
SAMARIA
Gerasa
Sebaste
[Samaria]
Mt. Ebal
Amathus
Shechem
Jabbok R.
Antipatris
Mt. Gerizim
[Aphek]
Gadara
Joppa
Alexandrium
Jordan R.
PEREA
Philadelphia
[Amman]
Jericho
Esbus
Emmaus
Cyprus
Jamnia
Jerusalem
JUDEA
Bethlehem
Hyrcania
Medeba
Ashkelon
Herodium
Machaerus
EASTERN
Gaza
Adora
Hebron
Dead
Sea
DESERT
Raphia
IDUMEA
Masada
Arnon R.
Beersheba
Malatha
Zered Brook
Besor Brook
W. el-Arish
Nessana
NABATEA

Petra

0   10   20   30   40 MI.
0 10 20 30 40 50 60 KM.

part 1

Galilee
and
Samaria

GALILEE

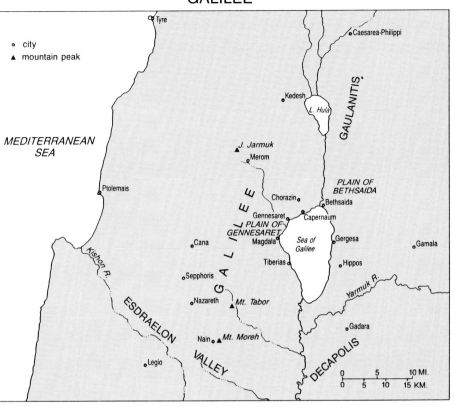

- ○ city
- ▲ mountain peak

Tyre

Caesarea-Philippi

GAULANITIS

Kedesh

L. Hula

MEDITERRANEAN
SEA

J. Jarmuk
Merom

PLAIN OF
BETHSAIDA

G A L I L E E

Chorazin

Bethsaida

Gennesaret
Capernaum

Ptolemais

PLAIN OF
GENNESARET

Cana

Magdala

Sea of
Galilee

Gergesa

Gamala

Tiberias

Hippos

Kishon R.

Sepphoris

Nazareth

Mt. Tabor

ESDRAELON

Yarmuk R.

Nain ▲ Mt. Moreh

Gadara

DECAPOLIS

Legio

VALLEY

0   5   10 MI.
0   5   10   15 KM.

Church of the Annunciation

Nazareth

The modern Basilica of the Annunciation was begun in 1960 A.D. The visitor enters on the ground floor, which serves as the parish church of the local Arab Catholic community. There is a staircase to the lower level.

On the lower level of the basilica, all attention is directed to a simple altar placed under the dome of the basilica, so that we can see the eye of the dome from the altar as our sight passes through the hole of the upper floor to the eye of the dome. The altar is surrounded on three sides by a bank which allows for sitting. On the fourth side are the remains of a natural cave which enclose another grottolike room with a second altar. Within this small enclosure a very old and strong tradition places the visit of the angel Gabriel to Mary; here it is that Mary learned of God's plan for her.

This basilica, begun in 1960 A.D. to honor in a most impressive manner the conception of Jesus, is at least the fourth church or basilica on this site. We know that a man named Conon built a church here in the early 200s; as we face the grottolike structure, but before we enter it through the grille in front of it, we walk to the left and find a mosaic in the floor which speaks of Deacon Conon founding the third century A.D. basilica. Clearly Conon's basilica was built over a site that had been venerated for many decades before; archaeological diggings have uncovered many graffiti written to honor Mary and Jesus by early pilgrims to Palestine in search of the holy places.

Conon's Byzantine basilica was destroyed, but centuries later the Crusaders took it on themselves to build another and larger church to commemorate the sacred events of the Annunciation and Conception of Jesus. Finished about 1100 A.D., the crusader church lasted only about one hundred fifty years. In 1620 A.D. the Franciscans arrived in Nazareth and about 1730 A.D. finally won permission to build a modest church on this site. This small church was destroyed to make way for the striking basilica which we can enjoy today.

Each of these churches, Byzantine, crusader, Franciscan and modern, encloses the sacred grotto of the Annunciation; the newest basilica intentionally encloses remains of the Byzantine and crusader churches—with a guide we can see the remains of each of these earlier churches.

But let us turn our thoughts and imagination to the Nazareth of the ancient times. What can we say about Nazareth in general and its relationship with the New Testament, in particular?

The name *Nazareth* seems to come from a Hebrew word which means both *to blossom* and *to guard.* To some, therefore, Nazareth is the town which guards, from its position in the hills of Galilee, the vast plain of Esdraelon which stretches below it to the south of Nazareth; even today, from the platform surrounding the basilica of the Annunciation, we can catch sight of this plain. But to others, Nazareth, always a small town in the first century A.D., is better understood to symbolize the beauty of the Galilee flowers and, more practically, to be the place which, as archaeology has shown, served for many centuries before Christ as the storage place for grain harvested in Galilee. Even today, in the Church of St. Joseph, about fifty yards from the Basilica of the Annunciation, we can visit ancient caves which served as granaries for Jesus' predecessors in Nazareth.

Imaginatively, we should place ourselves about the area of the Basilica of the Annunciation and face southward; from this perspective we can picture ourselves standing on a hillside with small houses running along the brow of a hill which overlooks the vast plain of Esdraelon below. On this ridge, among these houses, would be found the house in which Mary lived. Tradition would say that adjacent to this house would have been something like a garden; it would be in this area adjacent to the house that the Angel Gabriel spoke to Mary. It is this area which the four churches described earlier have tried to protect, embellish, and honor.

The Old Testament says nothing about Nazareth. It is the New Testament which attributes so much to this small town. Given its unimportance in the Old Testament promises and hopes for salvation sent by God, it is not surprising that Nathanael said to those who spoke of Jesus of Nazareth as the Messiah: "What good can possibly come from Nazareth?" Nathanael's question, reported in John, is echoed in the same Gospel when people in Jerusalem doubted that Jesus was the Messiah. Some believed that the Messiah should come from David's stock, from David's town, Bethlehem; Jesus was excluded from such a qualification. Others believed that the origin of the Messiah would be unknown; Jesus of course admitted that he was from Nazareth, and so disqualified himself for those people as well. Indeed, both Matthew and Luke, for their part, made it clear that Jesus was born in Bethlehem; they thus can show that Jesus, hailing from Nazareth, was born, not in Nazareth, but in Bethlehem.

But for all the unimportance of a small town, Nazareth bursts on the consciousness of millions and millions of people, for it is the site of two precious periods of Jesus' life, that of his conception and childhood and that of his adult, preaching life. Let us look at each of these two moments.

Annunciation to Mary   *Lk 1:26-38*

Luke tells us of the visit of the Angel Gabriel to Mary in Nazareth. *Gabri* means *my strength,* and *el* means *God;* thus, *Gabriel* means *my strength is God.* The function of the angel is to announce a particular phase of the divine plan for the salvation of all mankind. The same Gabriel had, six months earlier, announced another phase of this same plan: the role of a child miraculously conceived by Elizabeth and to be named John. This child was to serve the divine plan in this way: filled with the Holy Spirit from his conception, he would eventually be a prophet like Elijah and would prepare the Israelite people for the coming of their God. Eventually, John would understand that part of his preparing the people for God was a baptism in which the baptized or repentant Israelite would enjoy forgiveness of sins, which should be an experience of salvation.

Now the Angel Gabriel described for Mary the role of the child she would miraculously conceive. Her child should be called *Jesus,* from the Hebrew word meaning *to save;* his role was described as the one who will sit on the throne of David his father, a throne which would endure forever. Thus, this child Jesus would grow into the person who, in Israelite tradition, was the unique intermediary between God and Israel. The king represented the needs and hopes of Israel to God; he was also the one through whom God channeled his blessings: wisdom, power, protection, prosperity. It is this function which Jesus would carry out in the divine plan of salvation.

Mary's question about how the conception would take place—"I have no sexual relations with men"—was instrumental in detailing a crucial insight into Jesus. Through the Holy Spirit's coming on her and the power of the Most High this child would be conceived. From this manner of conception—the terms *come upon* and *overshadow* do not have sexual connotations—we are to draw two inescapable conclusions: Jesus is holy, since he is from the Holy Spirit, and the Son of God, since he is produced by the power of the Most High. Thus, though the precise manner of influence of God on Mary remains mysterious, we can conclude that Mary is the Mother of Jesus and God is, on the analogy of human fatherhood, the Father of Jesus. After the manner of a human father, we can expect qualities of Jesus to reflect the influence of the paternal and maternal sides. In short, whereas many prophets and great men of ancient Israel experienced the influence of the Holy Spirit and whereas John the Baptizer experienced the presence of the Holy Spirit from his very conception, Jesus was, in a mysterious way, produced by the Spirit. In this description Jesus is revealed to owe his very existence and identity to God through Mary; in this Jesus is unique. To explain Jesus' origins this way is to say that no other explanation will suffice to explain what we will see and hear Jesus say and do in the rest of Luke and Acts of the Apostles. In this way Jesus is, among many called *son* or *sons of God,* truly, uniquely Son of God.

One cannot stress too much the emphasis Luke places in these Infancy stories on the reality of the divine plan of salvation; Jesus is certainly to be revealed as the one and only saviour of the world, but even he must be seen as part of a great plan of God which has intermittently been revealed already in the Old Testament and stretches far beyond the public life of Jesus in Palestine—indeed it stretches to the end of time and to the ends of the world. It is with a plan that all the experiences of salvation can be put into a comprehensible order, whether they occur before, during or after the public life of Jesus.

One should not ignore that the first image by which Jesus is described is fully realized only after the public life of Jesus is over; that is, Jesus never becomes king of Israel during his public life, but takes the position of King only after his resurrection and ascension. This means that other images of Jesus will be more appropriate to his life, words and deeds in Galilee and Jerusalem. Ultimately, however, we are to remember that Jesus is destined to be at the right hand of the Father, the position of the beloved King, the intermediary between God and mankind. In being seated at God's right hand, Jesus fulfills the expectation that

David himself longed for; in this the descendant or son of David becomes Lord even of David himself.

Once the angel left Mary in Nazareth, Luke tells of Mary's haste to help her relative Elizabeth who was already six months pregnant. But when Mary arrived at Elizabeth's house, clearly Mary was already with child. Thus, as closely as we can judge, the conception of Jesus took place right after the words of the angel to Mary. At this moment God mysteriously became man; no longer would God send emissaries or representatives to bring God's offer of reconciliation and forgiveness. God now came himself, to offer us forgiveness, to die that the just punishment of sin no longer be ours to pay, to live a human life and thus instruct us by example above all else what is the truly good, holy, happy and noblest life of a human being.

Annunciation to Joseph   *Mt 1:18-25*

The Gospel of Matthew does not tell us where Joseph received his annunciation, his dream in which an angel spoke to him. Tradition assumes that this dream took place in Nazareth at a site very near to the Basilica of the Annunciation, indeed, on the same grounds as the basilica. The angel's words to Joseph were to correct an imminent mistake: Joseph, after noticing that Mary, his intended bride, was pregnant, wished to divorce her. This breaking of the engagement was truly a divorce, for the engagement was a legal bond; Mary would need a document of divorce, for without it, any future marriage would be adulterous and she would be subject to the punishment for adultery: stoning to death.

The angel was meant to stop Joseph from this divorce action. The angel did this by explaining that the child Mary carried had, in some mysterious way, God as his Father, and not some human being. Indeed, this child would be called Jesus, for the name, meaning *God saves through him,* reveals the role the child should play as an adult and thus explains why God intervened to have this child conceived. Matthew himself, true to his way of theologizing, recalled what the prophet Isaiah said: "a virgin will conceive and bear a son; he should be called *God with us,*" (Is 7:14) for surely through this child God is with us. Isaiah did not actually foresee the birth of Jesus; he was speaking about another child, the child of his own time, who would be an instrument of God for the peace and protection of Israel. But

Matthew saw that the words of Isaiah are God's words, and understood them as the prophet Isaiah could not. Matthew lived through the Jesus experience and hence knew how much God is with us through Jesus. It is this he underlined as he emphasized in his own way, as Luke did in his own way, that the degree to which God was with us through Jesus can only be explained by professing God as, in some mysterious fashion, the very Father of Jesus. So strong was Matthew's conviction about this and his desire to profess it that he stated again, before the close of chapter one, that Mary had intercourse with no man before Jesus was born.

Childhood of Jesus   *Lk 2:39-40, 51-42*

Nazareth is the site of still another event in the life of the Child Jesus. Herod the Great tried to have Jesus killed in Bethlehem. An angel warned Joseph to take his family out of Bethlehem to escape the swords of Herod's troops; Joseph chose to go southward, into Egypt, where many Jews had lived since the time of the Babylonian conquest of Jerusalem in 587 B.C. At the death of Herod the Great, Joseph, under the direction of an angel in still another dream, was told he could go home safely. Joseph, it seems, was willing to go back to the Jerusalem area, perhaps to Bethlehem, but the successor of Herod the Great, Herod's son Archelaus, was rumored to be no less cruel than Herod the Great himself, so Joseph went northward into the territory of a more moderate ruler. Thus, Joseph chose to live under another son of Herod the Great, Herod Antipas, who would prove to be the one to condemn John the Baptizer to death and, with Pilate, would try Jesus for a capital crime. Joseph chose the territory of Herod Antipas, that is, he chose Galilee—and within the boundaries of Galilee Joseph settled in Nazareth.

Prophecy of Nazorean   *Mt 1:19-23*

Matthew, however, was not interested in telling of Joseph's settling in Nazareth unless it had significance for the revelation of Jesus' identity. So it is not surprising that, once Joseph was announced as established in Nazareth, Matthew noted that the Old Testament had already said "he shall be called a Nazorean." By joining the Old Testament saying with Joseph's actual choice to make his home in Nazareth, Matthew wanted his reader to

understand again how God's words about Jesus came to
fulfillment through the most simple of humanly motivated
decisions. Indeed, Jesus completed so many of the Old Testament
statements and expectations; it is he of whom they have all
spoken.

But there is a problem with this particular citation of the
Old Testament: these words are not to be found in any version of
the Old Testament available to scholars of any generation. What,
then, did Matthew intend by quoting a sentence which does not
exist? The best we can do with this is to say that Matthew was
aware of the sense of the Old Testament, even if he could not
find one actual sentence which expressed this sense. The sense
of the Old Testament which Matthew reflects here in this
sentence is that the special envoy of God, the messiah, would be
a dedicated person, one vowed to God and to God's causes. The
root of the Hebrew word for *dedicated* is *n-ts-r.* Just pronouncing
these consonants aloud makes us hear the name of the town
Nazareth. And so Matthew found it justified to note that even the
name of the town in which Jesus settled is a reminder of what
the Old Testament looked forward to: one so dedicated to God
and the offer of salvation God makes through him to the entire
world. Thus, to remember that Jesus came from Nazareth was,
for Matthew, to remember the dedication which characterized
the adult life of Jesus.

Adulthood of Jesus: *programmatic episode*
Lk 4:16-30

Nazareth had a significant part to play in the life of the adult
Jesus. Whereas Luke's source, the Gospel of Mark, indicated that
Jesus' preaching career in Galilee was headquartered at
Capernaum, Luke chose to set the tone for the entire public life
of Jesus by narrating a story which is geographically situated in
Nazareth. This story is called by many scholars today the
programmatic episode of Luke. By reviewing its elements we
shall see why the story is "programmatic."

The Gospel of Luke told of Jesus' coming home to Nazareth
very early in his preaching career. As it was the Sabbath, Jesus
went to the synagogue. Near the modern Basilica of the
Annunciation is an ancient synagogue where we can imagine
what Jesus' visit to Nazareth's synagogue must have been like.
The few details of the story Luke tells accurately describe the
way the synagogue service would have been run. Jesus, as a

visitor this day, would be asked to read a section of the Jewish Scriptures and offer a comment on his reading.

Jesus' choice of a scriptural passage is a section from the prophet Isaiah, 61:1–2. Here the prophet described an unnamed person who was anointed by God, which means that he is Messiah; *Messiah* and *Christ* come respectively from the Semitic and Greek terms for *anointed.* Because he was anointed by God, he received God's Holy Spirit. Why was he anointed and filled with the Spirit? So that he might bring good news, proclaim liberty and sight, set free; ultimately, he was anointed and filled with the Spirit so that he could proclaim a time of favor from God. The time of reconciliation and forgiveness was here.

Jesus identified himself as this anointed one. As such, he indicated that the favor of God would be given through him. "This text is being fulfilled today," Jesus says. Jesus dispensed the good news, liberty, sight, freedom. This citation from Isaiah was very important to Luke. Other descriptions of Jesus are true to the person and total mission of Jesus—Lord, Savior, King, Light to the Gentiles. Glory of Israel, Son of God, the Holy One—and Luke depended on them to help the reader grasp the essence of Jesus. but, as far as Jesus' active life in Galilee of preaching, teaching and healing, was concerned, the quotation from Isaiah was the best terminology by which Luke could sum up and introduce the reader to what would happen in Jesus' public life in Galilee. With the rest of Jesus' public life in mind, Luke gave the reader the outlines of the program which Jesus would follow in the succeeding chapters.

It is important to note how much the Isaian quotation stresses the word of the anointed one: announcing good news, proclaiming liberty and sight, proclaiming the year of favor. Jesus would work many miracles, but Luke, like so many other New Testament writers, was anxious to affirm that the blessing given to all Christians is not Jesus' assurance of intervening in our lives to work miracles, but the abiding wisdom of Jesus' mind. Teaching, the early Christians learned, was in the long run more valuable than miracles.

But the program which Luke wanted to anticipate was not fully described, for there is more to the story of Jesus' visit to the synagogue of Nazareth. The initial reaction to Jesus' identification of himself as the anointed of God and to the implication that the year of favor was now here—the initial reaction of the people was favorable.

Within minutes, however, doubts began to rise: the signal of these doubts was the apparently innocent question about Jesus' origins. Apparently innocent, for its true meaning is a suggestion that Jesus' background—born of Mary and Joseph and having grown up here in Nazareth with no eclat—indicated that Jesus should not claim any distinction for himself, that his words might sound pretty, but he surely should not claim a unique relationship to God for himself.

In a very few moments, then, the climate changed. Jesus recognized this and immediately proceeded to condemn his fellow Israelites and Nazarenes. His condemnation revolved around the axiom that a prophet is not honored in his own country. Two examples were drawn from Israel's past to show what Israel can expect when its own prophet is rejected.

In the time of Elijah, the heavens were shut for three years so that no rain fell on Israel; this was a punishment for sin. Yet, God did provide a miracle during that time through Elijah—but it was only for a foreigner, a widow from north of Israel; God did nothing of the kind for Israel, who had turned against the prophet of God.

And in the time of Elisha, who succeeded Elijah as Israel's chief prophet, God cured a leper from Syria, but would not cure any leper of Israel. Such was the reaction of God to the Israelites who rejected his prophet. The lesson was not misunderstood by Jesus' listeners; indeed, Luke intended the meaning of Jesus' words to be applied not only to Jesus' own contemporaries, but also to the Jews of succeeding generations who would not accept the preaching about Jesus and thus would lose the favor of God which would be conferred, strangely enough, on Gentiles.

As scholars see it, Luke here described in miniature the progress of Jesus' popularity and rejection which he would detail now for the reader over several chapters; here then is a further part of the program the reader is given by Luke. In this vein, the next two elements of the story can be seen as programmatic, too. Jesus was taken to a hillside to be killed—and this certainly would be done to him by the end of the Gospel. Jesus, however, escaped from their clutches and avoided death. This scene is a type of the ultimate victory of Jesus, wherein, though he died, he escaped the fate his contemporaries ordered for him by rising from the dead.

This episode from chapter four of Luke is more important than others because it introduces the work of Jesus and the ultimate rejection by Israel of his person and his work. This story in Luke reflects what other Gospels narrate: the reluctance of

Jesus' own relatives and of his fellow Nazarenes to accept him. Perhaps it is too trite to say that "familiarity breeds contempt"; the doubts about Jesus are due to other causes than simple familiarity. Yet clearly we should face the degree of rejection offered Jesus by his own townsmen; it is remarked by all the synoptic gospels. So unresponsive were these Nazarenes that the scarcity of healing Jesus did in Nazareth was put down to their disbelief in him. They probably never even brought their sick to him.

In this reflection on Nazareth, we have talked about the sites which make it famous: the Basilica of the Annunciation, the nearby Church of St. Joseph built in 1914 A.D. on the remains of granaries predating Jesus' time in Nazareth, and the synagogue not far from the basilica, to be found by walking through the marketplace of Nazareth. Two other places of interest are Mary's Fountain and the Church of St. Gabriel, next to one other at the northeast end of the main road running through Nazareth. So popular a place is the town in which Jesus was conceived and reared, however, that there are yet other very interesting places to be discovered in Nazareth. All this interest and development in a village unmentioned till the time of Jesus is its own mute witness to the significance of what happened here—a happening which all the meditation in the world will never fully understand, a happening for which we can be eternally grateful. To make us like him, he became one of us. Strange, wonderful proof of how far love will go.

The First Miracle Church (Cana)

Cana

About four miles north by northeast of Nazareth is the traditional site of the wedding that Jesus, Mary, and Jesus' disciples attended in Cana of Galilee, as John reports. Here, too, according to the same Gospel, Jesus met the court official whose son lay ill in Capernaum; Jesus assured the official that his son would recover; as predicted, the official, on returning to Capernaum, found his son was cured—just at the hour when Jesus gave his assurance. Finally, this village was the original home of Nathanael, one of the Twelve, a Galilean brought to Jesus by Philip (Jn 1:45–50). Nathanael said the famous words, *Can anything good come from Nazareth?* Since each of these three events, all from the Gospel of John only, are of some importance in the development of the Fourth Gospel, let us pause for a moment to consider each of them.

Nathanael   *Jn 1:45-51*

The prologue of John says "In the beginning was the Word, and the Word was with God, and the Word was God.... And the Word became flesh and dwelt among us...." and then tells of the witness John the Baptizer gave at Bethany (See 101, 103) concerning Jesus (Jn 1:35–36). His witness moves two of John's disciples to visit Jesus; their visit convinces them that they have found the Messiah, the one of whom Moses wrote in the law and the prophets spoke. One of these two disciples of John was a man named Andrew, a brother of Simon Peter; the two brothers were originally from Bethsaida, but currently lived in Capernaum. The day after meeting Simon Peter, Jesus met another person from Bethsaida; this was Philip, who, in turn, found Nathanael of Cana (Jn 1:45).

It is hard for interpreters to understand all the ramifications of the encounter between Jesus and Nathanael (Jn 1:47–51). Nathanael certainly moved very quickly from scepticism about this Jesus to confessing him as Son of God and King of Israel.

Granted that Jesus told Nathanael that he had seen Nathanael under a fig tree before Nathanael even knew that Jesus existed, still it seems quite an abrupt psychological change on Nathanael's part that he gave so speedily and surely to Jesus titles which are quite profound in their meaning and usually associated with hard-earned faith. Indeed, these two titles, Son of God and King of Israel (Messiah), are the two titles which the Gospel writer hoped his reader would embrace most avidly after reading the entire report. Nathanael seems to have achieved this goal within three verses—only to be one of those who ran away when Jesus was captured in the Garden of Gethsemani. But rather than bring up further difficult aspects of this story, let us try to offer an interpretation which makes good sense of the entire Johannine report.

First, Nathanael's act of faith or confession of Jesus' identity was a model for later Christians to imitate. Not that we should move as speedily as Nathanael, but ultimately we are to confess Jesus as Son of God and Messiah.

Secondly, Nathanael not only confessed the appropriate titles, but also raised a major objection to acceptance of Jesus as Messiah: the Messiah was either to come from Bethlehem, that is, from the line of David who was associated with Bethlehem, or from a place unknown to any human being. Jesus came from Nazareth, so Nathanael reasoned: why should anyone believe that he was the Messiah?

Thirdly, Jesus, without yet talking to Nathanael, said of Nathanael that he was an Israelite who deserved the name "incapable of deceit." To understand this remark of Jesus, we must remember that Jacob had rested for the night, but was interrupted by a dream in which he struggled with God, called the Angel of God. From this struggle came the name *Israel,* for, for in the popular etymology of Jesus' time, *Isra* means *he contends with, struggles with* and *el* means *God.* Israel, another name for the patriarch Jacob, was a very deceitful man in stories told in the Old Testament. And Israel was a founder of the holy people of God, for from him came the twelve sons who gave their names to the twelve tribes of Israel. Therefore, when Nathanael approached him, Jesus looked on him as a founder of the new people of God, but one who was incapable of deceit and thus morally the opposite of the ancient Jacob, founder of the ancient People of God. Jesus' calling Nathanael "incapable of deceit" also confirmed that Nathanael's confession of Jesus was true and not misleading. Thus, the first witnesses, the Twelve, were already recognized as reliable and trustworthy in their perceptions. The Gospel of John was interested not only in the story of Jesus, but in asserting that the witness about Jesus was true.

Fourthly, the confession of Jesus as King and Son of God rested on Jesus' superior knowledge of Nathanael and his habits before Jesus and Nathanael ever met. Here, too, the figure of Nathanael is symbolic. Nathanael was correct in concluding from a miracle that Jesus was King and Son of God; that we should conclude this from the signs Jesus worked is a major argument of the Gospel as a whole and so was very appropriately introduced here. Again, John was not interested in showing how one moves psychologically from a work of Jesus to belief in him; he only wanted to state, in an abbreviated story form, that the signs Jesus worked should lead to confession of him as Son of God and King of Israel.

Finally, the sign which led Nathanael to belief in Jesus would be surpassed in importance and greatness; one example of a "greater and more important sign" was the raising of Lazarus from the dead. (See 133–135.) But this mentioning of *greater* things than Jesus' knowledge about Nathanael leads to the mention of something *greater* than even the raising of Lazarus from the dead: the reader was to think of Jesus as the very Temple of God. Why was this?

Jesus says that Nathanael would see angels ascending from and descending on the Son of Man. This must be a reference to a story the book of Genesis told about Jacob's dream of angels descending to and ascending from a special place; the dream included what became known as Jacob's Ladder—by this ladder the angels ascended and descended. (Gn 28:10–19.) When Jacob awoke from his dream, he identified this holy site of the angels as a site very close to him. He also thought of this site as the dwelling place of God since angels hovered about it. God has, in other words, a residence on earth as well as a dwelling place in the heavens. Jacob gave this holy place a name: Bethel or House of God. *Beth* means *house of* and *el* means *God.* Here, then, was the beginning of the holy shrine of Israel, the place where God was believed to have dwelt before he took up his residence in the House or Temple of Jerusalem.

To this scene concerning Jacob and Bethel Jesus now referred. Jesus identified himself as the new shrine, the new residence, the new House of God. Later, Jesus would tell the Samaritan woman at the well dug by Jacob that there would come a time when people would worship neither on the

Samaritan mountain of worship, Gerizim, nor on the Israelite mountain of worship, Zion or Jerusalem (See 87, 187–205). Jesus alone would be the Temple of God, the Presence of God, and the key to true worship of God would be acceptance of Jesus as the one in whom mysteriously dwells God himself.

The story of Nathanael capsulized several important points John would make here and throughout the Gospel. That Nathanael, as a human and individual person, weakened in his faith was immaterial to John; he was interested in showing in brief the truth Jesus' signs should lead us to confess, what faith founds the new people of God and should be accepted as reliable from witnesses about Jesus, and the deepest identity of Jesus: the very Presence of God. The story about Nathanael, then, was really a thinly disguised argument, in story form, to encourage the reader to confess Jesus, King and Son of God, as the Presence of God himself; signs show this, as does the witness of Jesus' earliest and constant companions.

Wedding at Cana   *Jn 2:1-12*

The episode in John which follows immediately on Jesus' meeting with Nathanael describes the marriage feast of Cana. In a sense this story is easy to understand. Jesus anticipated the needs of a couple who would be embarrassed when the wine ran out; the miracle did not involve healing, but helped people in a certain need. But other considerations qualify this essential core of the story, circumstances which prod the interpreter to look more deeply for the meaning of this story.

Mary brought the need of the wedding couple to Jesus' attention. Jesus' response to Mary's hint in her words, "They have no wine," is startling, if not disconcerting: "Woman, what is this to you and to me? My hour has not yet come." What possibly could this mean and what bearing does it have on a story in which Jesus proceeded to do anyway what he thought objectionable?

Once again we are in a particularly Johannine situation; John loved to take an ordinary story and draw from it a deeper significance, even if it were somewhat at odds with the thrust of the story from which it was drawn. Here Jesus was trying to signal a very important fact: the happiness, symbolized by the plentitude of wine that he can miraculously produce, would be fully realized for those who believe in him only after his "hour," that is, after his death and Resurrection. That is to say, Mary's request for wine was received at a deeper level than that of mere wine for a wedding feast; it was interpreted as a request for the happiness, the fullness which the Messiah was to bring. But these would be available to those who believe in Jesus only with the outpouring of God's Holy Spirit, the Spirit given, as John later said, only after Jesus' departure from this world, a departure which followed Jesus' death, his "hour." Right from the start of the miracle working, therefore, John wanted it made clear that miracles sign or signal something more than just a manifestation of power. Signs worked by Jesus reveal, Jesus insisted, that he came from God, but they also reveal other profound truths about him. For instance, in the raising of Lazarus to life, Jesus showed great power—power, he argued, which came from God and showed his intimate union with his Father. It also showed that it was Jesus who would bring the dead to the fullness of life which we call heaven, to a life with God forever—and this life Lazarus did not receive in Jesus' miracle on his behalf. (See 133–35.) The turning of water into wine was a great manifestation of power, it was true; but the miracle also revealed Jesus as the one who brings about the messianic Kingdom in which the fullness of life was to be found. Thus it was a sign which should lead to belief, because of the divine power manifested right before one's eyes; at the same time, the sign introduced the reader to a profound truth about this Jesus who wielded the power of God.

The Gospel of John also tells the reader that through this sign Jesus revealed his glory to his disciples. The glory of Jesus was a quality usually reserved for the resurrection when the relationship between Jesus and his Father was most visible and nothing could obscure it; Jesus then most fully shared in the glory of God. But the cause for glory was expressed throughout the life of Jesus; it involved the use of divine power by which are overcome elements from which human beings cannot save themselves. When that power was used, we saw the reason for glorifying the one who uses that power. The cause for glorifying Jesus, however, was also that profound meaning about him which a sign or miracle revealed. Thus Jesus was glorified for his power to work this or that miracle, but he was also glorified as one who gives life in the deepest sense, as one who gives sight in the deepest sense, as one who gives the water and bread of life in the deepest sense, and as the one who would provide the wine of the messianic banquet—another metaphor for that deepest happiness that God can give a human being.

Finally, John noted that Jesus' disciples believed in him. By this John meant that Jesus' disciples were convinced that Jesus was from God and that on the basis of this conviction they would leave all to follow him. That they have a faith which would stand up to trials was not said; John was more interested in showing that the disciples gave the response which logically should follow from a miracle, a sign, a revelation of Jesus' glory.

At Cana, then, Jesus did not simply work a miracle. As far as John was concerned, to report this miracle was to link Jesus inextricably with his Father and to reveal him as Son of God; to open the meaning and identity of Jesus was to touch on the essence of his glory. Jesus was the Son of God destined to bring about that time when the Spirit of God could be poured on the world of believers.

Cure of a Court Official's Son   *Jn 4:46-54*

Two chapters later John told the story of a cure Jesus worked in Cana for a young man who lay helpless in Capernaum. Like miracle story reports in general, this account told of a sick person, Jesus' response, and a cure, and rounded off with a reaction of the audience. The details of the miracle story formula are brief and terse, to highlight the wonder Jesus has worked; compared with that, all else was secondary.

But, like many another miracle story, it enveloped a saying of Jesus, which was all the more important precisely because it seemed out of place. In this story Jesus, on hearing of the plight of the young man, exclaimed, *If you [plural] do not see signs and wonders, you [plural] would not believe!* Given that the boy's father, possibly a Gentile, did seek out Jesus, we wonder why Jesus was so harsh to him. But there was something behind this cry of Jesus which was a strong reprimand because it went far beyond the boy's father. The plural *you* very clearly indicated that Jesus had many people of Galilee on his mind when he gave his criticism.

What is the point of Jesus' criticism? Were not signs and miracles part of his ministry and a way to lead people to believe in him? At least, such seems to be a part of the message of the Gospel of John. There is a certain truth to these objections, yet there is something else here of greater meaning. From what we can tell from the entire gospel tradition, and thus not simply from the Fourth Gospel, the central ministry of Jesus was his call of Israelites to return to the Lord God, to repent. This call to repentance in turn inevitably raised the question of Jesus' authority to speak for God. It was at this point that the miracles of Jesus are important, for they substantiate his claim that people must listen to him, that he does represent God; these signs are meant to lead people to God through listening and obeying what God says through Jesus. But the people ought to repent, whether miracles were given to them or not. In this framework, Jesus wanted to know why people did not respond to his message of repentance, why they must have signs and miracles before they repent, before they accept him.

From what we can tell, Jesus never refused a request for a miracle, and many times he worked a miracle without being asked. For all that, he felt that such miracles, such justifications for his call to repentance, were unnecessary: the message, the call, was just in itself. Those who truly loved and sought out God knew the truth of what Jesus was asking; these needed no miracles.

Yes, Jesus worked the miracle for this dying young man; he worked the miracle gladly, and it led the father to accept Jesus' claim that he was from God. Cana, tiny Cana asks us, too, to see the wisdom of Jesus' call to return wholeheartedly to the Father of us all. Let us accept Jesus wholeheartedly, for his word was true wisdom and to live in union with him was to enter that life which he gives through the gift he gives: the Spirit of God himself.

The Sea of Galilee

The Sea of Galilee

The Sea of Galilee is a harp shaped body of water, about eleven miles long at its longest and about seven miles wide at its widest. It is called *Sea of Galilee* because it is adjacent to the territory of Galilee. This body of water is also called the *Sea* or *Lake of Gennesaret* or the *Sea of Chinnereth,* from a Hebrew word for a harplike instrument. It was also known in the New Testament times as the *Sea of Tiberias,* named after the new town of Tiberias on its western shore.

This town was built by Herod Antipas, son of Herod the Great and stepfather of Salome who won the head of John the Baptizer by her dancing. Herod Antipas named the town, which he wished to be the capital of Galilee, after the Roman emperor, Tiberius Caesar, who was emperor during Jesus' public life. Because the town was built over a cemetery, pious Jews refused to have anything to do with it, although it became the premier town of the region for trading and fishing. As far as we know, Jesus never entered Tiberias.

Calling of Apostles   *Mt 4:18-22; Mk 1:16-20; Lk 5:1-11*

This sea, which is about thirty-two miles in circumference, provided a good living for fishermen like Peter and his brother Andrew, for the brothers James and John. It also provided the setting, at least in part, for three types of New Testament events.

Along the shores of the Sea of Galilee Jesus called Peter and Andrew, James and John to follow him; they left all and followed him. The Marcan and Matthean stories of this call are brief so that the reader sees the logical response to the preemptory call of the Master: when Jesus said "Come," the disciple who realized who was calling left all to follow immediately. Life cannot always be lived so logically, but the logic itself was worth underlining, for it showed how different was Jesus from all others who called for one's attention and company. In Luke's version, Peter responded to Jesus once he saw a miraculous catch of fish and it dawned on him who this Jesus might be and how awesome was the calling.

Calming the Waves   *Mt 8:23-27; Mk 4:34-51; Lk 8:22-25*

Another type of event occurring on the sea was made up of two happenings. First, Jesus calmed the waves. Another, later time Jesus walked on the waters. The calming of the waves was another wonderful sign of the dominance the Master had over all elements of the world: spiritual powers, disease and death, and nature itself. The story of the calming of the waves was told, however, to emphasize the trust the disciples should have in Jesus. Their cry to him, "We are lost," did not reveal a true appreciation of the power or love of Jesus for his disciples. The story was told, then, not only to show Jesus' power over nature, but to encourage the reader never to lose heart in the rough waves of life; the power and love of Jesus have been promised to the disciple, and Jesus would not fail.

Walking on the Waters   *Mt 14:22-33; Mk 6:45-52; Jn 6:16-21*

The second story about the Sea of Galilee described Jesus as walking on the waters, as if to go ahead of his disciples to prepare their way. Again, we have a miracle which the gospel writers used to show how the Christian community, often left to row against the tides which threaten it, has a Master of such power and dominance that he can protect and smooth the community's journey, no matter how difficult the trials. In this walk on the water, the mystery of Jesus' identity was placed before the reader; we are expected to ask, *Who was he that can do this?* The hope is that we would find it reasonable to call Jesus divine.

Curing the Demoniac   *Mt 8:28-34; Mk 5:1-20; Lk 8:26-39*

Another story associated with the Sea of Galilee is a bizarre account of a man freed from possession by evil spirits. Since these evil spirits were content to live in the depths of the deepest waters, always a fearsome place in the history of Israel, they asked Jesus, who was about to send them away from the poor man, to send them back into the waters. Jesus sent them into pigs, animals unpleasant to Jews who were forbidden to eat such an unclean animal. The pigs rushed over the eastern hills into the Sea of Galilee. The story was meant to impress the reader with the power of Jesus, even to the disposition of those powers which no man can dominate.

The Sea of Galilee holds its own charm, its own mystery, for it is a silent, yet living, body of nature which in its own way communicates to anyone who touches it the joy of having carried, if only briefly, the Lord of the Universe. The sea invites contemplation about turbulence and peace, about power exercised out of love and calling for trust. Like so many other voices of Israel, the sea calls for faith in the one whom it carried to his people in distress. It obeyed his voice and hopes that many others would do as well—for the ultimate happiness of the entire universe God made.

St. Peter's House (Capernaum)

Capernaum

Capernaum, which means *town of Nahum,* rests on the northern shore of the Sea of Galilee, about two and a half miles west of the upper Jordan River which pours into the Sea of Galilee from the Lebanese mountains—the ancient Mount Hermon—to the north. In the time of Jesus, Capernaum was a small town by our standards, but it was a tax post and money exchange for those coming from the east into Israel on the Way of the Sea—the road that passed the north end of the Sea of Galilee and headed over to the Mediterranean shoreline.

Capernaum today offers some very interesting ruins. Probably the most eye-catching are the remains of a fifth century A.D. synagogue which, many agree, stands on a basalt synagogue which goes back to the first century A.D. and was probably the very synagogue that Jesus and his friends attended, where Jesus revealed himself as the bread of life. To the south of the limestone fifth century A.D. synagogue are the ruins of a basalt octagon. This octagon, really three octagons together, shows the base of an octagonal church built here in the fifth century A.D. This church replaced a fourth-century A.D. church on this exact spot. Archaeological diggings have discovered beneath these two churches graffiti from very early Christian times which identify the area enclosed by these two churches as the house of Peter, who spent his adult life with his family in Capernaum.

Looking beyond the octagonal forms, we see the traces of many square rooms, some of them separated by narrow lanes. This is considered the outline of the city of Capernaum. Its buildings were not very fancy; the roofs were a combination of tree limbs and a kind of plaster made out of mud, twigs, leaves, and the like, and there was not much room or light in them. But this was the town Jesus used as his center of activity, when he chose to have a home at all. Unfortunately, Jesus' home town had deep reservations about his relationship with God and ultimately rejected him; Capernaum, after a longer time, followed the attitude of Nazareth—and Jesus cursed Capernaum because it refused to repent (Mt 12:23; Lk10:15).

Call of Matthew   *Mt 9:9; Mk 2:13-14; Lk 5:27-28*

From his post came the tax collector Matthew, to whom Jesus spoke the words, "Come, follow me." Are these words too simple to serve as the only means Jesus used to draw Matthew's attention? Yet they are the words which the Lord spoke, and the reader who loves the Lord was the one they are meant to inspire. Jesus was highly criticized for dealing with Matthew and his kind of people; tax collectors drew their salary out of the taxes levied on people. One need only a moment to imagine the injustice these tax collectors were rightly accused of. Jesus once again showed his willingness to distinguish between the sinner and the sin, in the hope that he could save the lost of Israel. His contemporaries followed another model: reject the sinner in the hope that avoidance would lead to repentance and as a means to avoid falling into the sins of the sinner. They could not understand Jesus' approach.

Capernaum, called by Matthew 'Jesus' own town,' was the setting for some very important sayings and cures by Jesus. Throughout the Gospel accounts the reader finds that miracle stories often go beyond the telling of wondrous actions to stress controversial and significant statements of Jesus. In Capernaum Jesus cures a man of an unclean spirit. The miracle was marvelous, but Jesus' command to the spirit not to continue its publicly acknowledgment that Jesus was the Holy One of God is mysterious—until we realize from the rest of Mark that Jesus was consistently worried that people would identify him only as a miracle worker. Jesus understood his mission to be something quite different from solving the world's hunger for happiness through miracle working; he came to call sinners to repentance and holiness. His was a mission essentially to the will of human beings, to help them know and return to the one and only God.

Cure of Paralyzed Man   *Mt 9:2-8; Mk 2:3-12; Lk 5:18-26*

Jesus later cured a man who had for a very long time been paralyzed. When this man had been lowered through a roof made from various bits of shrubbery and wood, as mentioned above (See 29), Jesus praised the faith of those involved in the man's

entrance—and forgave him his sins! Accustomed as later
Christians may be to the truth that Jesus forgives sins, we still
appreciate the people's bewilderment at Jesus' words of
forgiveness. Putting it bluntly, the man hoped for a cure of his
paralysis, not forgiveness of sins. Certain religious figures nearby
took offense because Jesus had taken to himself a power which
belonged to God alone. By the end of the story, the paralyzed
man was cured and Jesus argued aggressively that he indeed had
the power reserved to God.

This conclusion of the story is powerful; the miracle
convinces the reader that Jesus not only cures, as God does, but
also forgives sins, as only God does. The cure helps reveal the
deepest identity of Jesus and warns the reader that the meaning
of Jesus far surpasses the very visible powers of physical and
mental curing which initially capture the attention of his
contemporaries.

Cure on the Sabbath   *Mt 12:9-14; Mk 3:1-6; Lk 6:6-11*

A third miracle happened in the synagogue of Capernaum. Here
Jesus cured the withered hand of an Israelite—and he did it on
the Sabbath. Israelite tradition had interpreted the law of Moses
against work on the Sabbath to include miracle working as a
work to be avoided then. The Gospels offer more than one
argument against the unreasonableness of thinking that God's
law prohibits curing the sick on the Sabbath; but the
understanding at the time of the Sabbath. At an earlier moment
Jesus had, in Capernaum, claimed that he was Master of the
Sabbath, that his way of understanding the sanctity of the
Sabbath was the right, godlike way to understand it Now, in the
synagogue he continued to defy the common understanding,
only to have the authorities begin the search for ways to do away
with him.

In Capernaum, then, Jesus claimed a power to forgive sins,
an understanding of God which went against tradition, a mission
which essentially called for repentance rather than sought to
work miracles. In Capernaum Jesus also ate with sinners, in the
hope that, as with Matthew, he could separate the sinners from
their sins. This new entity called *Jesus* was entirely foreign to the
Pharisaic way of living the will of God; as a result, Jesus was
marked for extermination. Truly, the crunch of the antagonism
Jesus raised to a point that it killed him was his insistence that
he was the true representative of God. Indeed, everything in

Israel's past was to be reevaluated by him. This claim was what put him on the road to death.

Meaning of Miracles

A word is in order about the miracles of Jesus at Capernaum. Jesus cured both the paralyzed and the possessed. These cures represent the spectrum of immense power Jesus enjoyed over all that dominates human beings. Whether it be a question of physical or mental bondage, a word from Jesus set free—just a word. His domination over what man cannot free himself from was so complete and so ever-present that Jesus, in any world of miracle working, stood out as supreme in power over inimical and crippling dominance. Whereas to other miracle workers power was given in measure, Jesus' power seems limitless. It was only with the realization that his mission was aimed at something other than physical and mental cures that we begin to understand why he did not simply change for the good all that crushes human beings physically and mentally.

The miracle working of Jesus was not, then, his main work. But it is all the more striking that he cured and healed so often. It was as though, while he aimed at winning over human beings to love and obey him, he could not restrain himself, asked or not, from intervening in the grief of others to bring them some measure of peace and health, though they would remain subject to the further trials inherent in living in this world. His miracles were, then, a sign of the total concern which defined the love of Jesus for every human being suffering under the domination of forces unleashed in the world, not by God's choosing, but by man's sinning.

Through Adam sin and death entered this world and control it. Adam had separated himself from Love and the effects of Love, one of which was Life; human beings share in that separation, so that *this age* was lived under the warring powers of divine Love and Satanic Death and corruption. To separate oneself from God was to separate oneself from the health and life originally intended by God to last forever. Jesus' entry into *this age* changed little of the continued dominance of the powers unleashed on us by sinning against God. The final solution to removal of these evil powers was conversion away from sin, joined to union with Jesus so that, after death, we can rise to new life. This *new life,* this *entry into the new age* occurs only after death. Though the New Testament argues very well that certain effects of the "age to come" already exist in "this present wicked age," such as God's forgiveness of sins now and his dwelling in us, by and large the structure of the world was still under the dominance of the powers unleashed by sin. The greatest of these powers was death.

Jesus entered a world dominated by Satan—indeed, Satan was so powerful that he tempted Jesus by promising Jesus all the kingdoms of the earth if Jesus would worship Satan. Jesus' miracles did not completely reverse the decline and corruption of our world and of our bodies and minds, but they are signs of what the irrepressible love of God would eventually achieve. What Jesus hinted at in miracle working was a time when, after sin was repaired, God would change all and make all new again—then there would be no more suffering, for the total person, now a willing and loving friend of God, would enjoy the full effect of God's love. This effect we call *total perfection.* Paul rejoiced in the first step towards perfect happiness when he said we are no longer slaves, but actually children of God. John the Evangelist tried to go even further; he said that now we are children of God, but we cannot even guess what we would be when we finally emerge from this wicked and corrupting age to be face to face in friendship and intimacy with Goodness and Life itself.

Capernaum never perceived who this Jesus was who worked miracles in it. We must do better than they, for the miracles of Jesus worked at Capernaum suggest the fulfillment of the deepest hopes for happiness that we know. The right appreciation of the Wonder-Worker will help us achieve what he ardently hopes we will freely choose. He will in time reverse all the evil forces, especially the evil spirits, allowed into his world by man's free choice to live without God; but then he was concerned to win back that free will, so that all the benefits of friendship with God—health, peace, wholeness, unending life, happiness—can follow.

The Greatest Wonder

In the synagogue, Jesus gave his great discourse about himself as the food of life. (See 38–9.) He had fed the multitude in a lonely place, but taught them when they were not prisoners of physical hunger. But he would lead them to realize that the deeper, never-ending hunger for life itself is satisfied by the only one designated by God to calm that hunger: Jesus, the food of life. In this town we can hear again those words of such great promise: he who eats my flesh and drinks my blood will live—forever.

Multiplication of the Loaves and Fish Church

Multiplication of Loaves and Fish

The fields along the slopes about two miles to the west of Capernaum are traditionally considered to be the area where Jesus multiplied the loaves and the fish for the crowds following him. In the fourth century A.D. the Christians took advantage of the peace the Emperor Constantine allowed them. They built a chapel to commemorate the multiplication of the loaves and fish, the only miracle recorded in all four Gospels, with two other chapels, one in honor of the Sermon on the Mount and the other in honor of the appearance of Jesus to his disciples. In the fifth century A.D., a larger chapel was built to replace the century-old smaller chapel of the loaves and fish; but then this larger chapel was itself destroyed through the Persian (614 A.D.) and Moslem (637 A.D.) invasions and never rebuilt. Though the Church of the Multiplication was destroyed in the seventh century A.D., there are remains, including impressive mosaic remains, of the fourth century A.D. chapel. The Benedictines rebuilt a church here.

Here, then, near Capernaum and the northwest shore of the Sea of Galilee, tradition tells us that the famous multiplication of loaves and fish occurred. Let us consider this miracle for a moment, especially how the miracle was reported in the Gospel stories.

In Mark and Matthew Jesus performed this miraculous multiplication on two different occasions; in Luke and John we have reports of only one multiplication of loaves and fish. Let us consider each of these miracles in turn, beginning with Mark, the source for much of what Luke and Matthew have given us.

Mark's Account   *Mk 6:34-44; Mk 8:1-9*

Mark's first story of the loaves and fish has four circumstances. First, the multiplication of loaves followed Jesus' teaching the crowds, teaching that was itself a response to the appearance of the crowd as "sheep without a shepherd." Secondly, before working this miracle Jesus asked his disciples to provide bread for the crowd; they could not even imagine doing this. Certainly their admission of impotence here emphasized the miracle which was not beyond Jesus' own powers, but we wonder if Mark refers to the Apostles' inability to provide food for some further purpose of his own. Thirdly, twelve basketfuls of leftover bread and fish were collected—for what purpose? Finally, those who ate the bread are numbered at five thousand people; was this number significant, beyond simply showing how powerful a miracle Jesus worked?

These four elements frame the wondrous multiplication of loaves and suggest a direction to which Mark wanted us to attend. Since the Eucharist of bread and wine was celebrated at least every Sunday from the earliest times of Christianity to the period when Mark wrote, about 65 A.D., it would not be surprising to find a miracle of Jesus written up to support this eucharistic practice without distorting the basic intention of Jesus to feed the hungry. Many scholars suggest that Mark described this miracle of the bread not only to underline the wonder Jesus worked, but also to link it with the Eucharist by which hungry Christians of every time can share in the food provided by Christ. Let us look at this more closely.

Since the feeding of the crowd followed immediately on the teaching of those whom Jesus pitied, we are reminded of the deepest structure of the eucharistic celebration: the teaching of Jesus, read and explained, precedes the gift of the bread of life. And then the disciples would have to hand on the teaching and provide the eucharistic food; now, they do know how to provide food for so many. And the gathering of the basketfuls, one for each disciple, reminds us that each of the Twelve would have the task of feeding those who are like sheep without a shepherd. Finally, the number five thousand symbolizes the people of Israel, and suggests that the spiritual feeding of Christians began with the Christians who are part of Israel and faithful to Jesus. Thus, the wonderful feeding of the crowd at the Sea of Galilee became a symbol of that new feeding of the Christian people, as details of the storytelling lead us to understand.

The second multiplication of loaves took place before four thousand people and ended with a collection of seven baskets of fragments. The number seven may symbolize the Gentiles, as the number five may symbolize the people of Israel. Thus this second multiplication appeared to complement the first multiplication, just as the Gentiles complemented the people of Israel in the Christian community. Once again, the movement to feed the needy crowd came from Jesus, who was sensitive enough to realize the hunger of the crowd. His disciples accentuated the wonder of what Jesus would do when they expressed their bewilderment at trying to find a way of feeding all these hungry people.

Matthew's Accounts   *Mt 14:13-21; Mt 15:32-39*

The first miracle of the loaves and fish in Matthew has an orientation similar to the corresponding story in Mark; this is no surprise since Matthew drew heavily on Mark as a source. Matthew reduced the story's length by reducing the exchange of words between Jesus and his disciples as they moved towards the miracle. In his story the disciples brought the hunger of the people to Jesus' attention; as in Mark, Jesus suggested that the disciples feed these people—indeed, in Matthew, Jesus strongly implied that the disciples actually had the wherewithal to feed these people.

Matthew's story of a second multiplication of loaves and fish again paralleled what Mark gave as Jesus' second miracle of the bread. One should note, here and in the previous three stories we have considered, that Jesus "takes the bread, gives thanks [which is the meaning of *eucharist*], breaks the bread and gives it ..." This sequence of actions is reminiscent of a eucharistic celebration to anyone who has attended the sacred meal.

Luke's Account   *Lk 9:10-17*

Luke recounted only one miracle of loaves and fish. But then Luke never shows Jesus going through Gentile, non-Israelite, territory. It was precisely at the end of a journey through pagan country that Jesus, in Matthew and Mark, worked a second bread miracle for four thousand people, with seven baskets left over.

Luke's story has essentially the same elements as the Marcan stories, which served as his source material. As did Matthew and Mark, Luke emphasized the suggestion of Jesus that the disciples care for the hungry crowd; when they confessed their impotence, Jesus provided the food, but in such a way that the disciples actually administered it. It is interesting that Luke took into consideration the effect on the crowd, that "each one had as much as he wanted." Each one was satisfied. The multiplication of the loaves, in Luke's outline, came just before Jesus' question to his disciples: "Who do people say that I am?" "Who do you say that I am?" By virtue of this juxtaposition of stories, Luke seems to suggest that Jesus was looking for an answer which would be influenced in a significant way by the multiplication of the loaves and fish. Since both Elijah and his disciple, Elisha, were involved in miracles of providing food miraculously for people, it is not surprising that Elijah was one of the answers people gave when trying to come up with the identity of Jesus. For the Twelve, however, the multiplication of loaves supported their conviction that Jesus was nothing less than the Messiah, the Christ, of God. In Luke, then, the wondrous bread serves both as symbol of the Eucharist and as help in discovering the identity of Jesus.

John's Account   *Jn 6:1-5*

John has left an indelible story in the minds of its readers concerning the miraculous bread. Not only did John tell the story of the multiplication, but he followed it with a major speech of Jesus the next day in Capernaum (See 33); considering that Jesus did not speak in John about the meaning of bread and wine at the Last Supper, we can consider what Jesus says at the multiplication of loaves as the Johannine contribution to the eucharistic practice of the Church.

The story of the loaves and fish, as told in the Gospel of John, has the eucharistic overtones we have seen in the Matthean, Marcan and Lucan stories. Added to these elements are two points typical of Johannine story telling. Jesus, though he asked the disciples where enough food may be found for all these people, "knew exactly what he would do." Here, as everywhere in John, Jesus was in command of the situation and was not at a loss for word or action—as was befitting his divinity. Secondly, the people responded to this miracle by attempting to make Jesus king. This too was a temptation elsewhere in the Gospel, but such interpretations of Jesus as this one are given in John with the clear intention to show how far short they fall in their perception of Jesus' deepest identity.

The people who received this wondrous bread were not satisfied; they wanted the power to do what Jesus did and thus not be dependent on Jesus. They wanted to do the works of God, miracles. Jesus turned their phrase, "works of God," to his own phrase "work of God." By this he indicated that the only work for them was faith in him; faith in him was the only way they would have the food which they seek to create. In short, they would depend on him, not on themselves, for the life which comes from eating the food of God.

The food of God, however, needed explanation, and so Jesus began his lengthy discussion of the food of heaven. The discourse Jesus gave concerns four points. First, Jesus was the food, for it was only by living off him that one can have life. Secondly, living off him does not mean simply obeying his words; it includes actually eating his body and drinking his blood. In this way, God draws so close to us that we live by virtue of his intimacy and love, as though he were the very food by which we live forever.

There was a very profound belief here: our life has a new source, different from that rooted in our parents, a source which can alone make us live, for it was only good and from good can only come life. Thirdly, this food by which we live really gives a life which never ends; in this it was different from that manna in the desert, which, no matter how miraculous we esteem it, could give life for only a short time. Jesus is the food that truly is from heaven, where only life was to be found, and no death.

Finally, Jesus carefully taught that to accept him as food of life we must have the calling and grace of God. Further, we must be open to belief that he really can save, that he really wants to be our food, that he really can keep us alive and wants to do it through the Eucharist. Unfortunately, this element must be a regular part of Jesus' discourses to his contemporaries, for they by and large did not have the predispositions, the openness, the readiness to take him at his word. Jesus always noted that he did his best to reach everyone; if he failed, it was not his fault, but the failure should be traced to the hearer.

Primacy of St. Peter Church

T abgha

About two miles west of Capernaum is an area which was named in Greek after its seven springs of water; the Greek name was *heptapegon,* a word which was corrupted into Arabic *ettabgha.* The area is called *et-Tabgha* or *Tabgha* today. Associated with this area is the wonderful apparition of Jesus to his disciples, related in Jn 21, as these disciples were fishing in the Sea of Galilee. A lovely chapel was built in 1934 A.D. on the shore of the Sea of Galilee to commemorate Jesus' words to Peter at the time of this apparition, "Feed my lambs, feed my sheep." Recent though this church is, the site has had, often for centuries at a time, a shrine here since about 315 A.D., to remind visitors of Jesus' time spent on the shore this day with his disciples.

Jesus after the Resurrection   *Jn 21:1-14*

John 21 underlines three elements of interest. First, the disciples had scattered to their homes after the death and resurrection of Jesus. Peter and others were from Capernaum and so they returned there and, for want of knowing what to do next, resumed their old trade of fishing. While these men were fishing, Jesus appeared and revealed himself by his wondrous knowledge that, if they would only drop their nets where he suggested, they would find fish for which they had been searching all night long. On recognizing Jesus on the shore, the disciples hurried to him and found him preparing a breakfast. Now came the important moment: Jesus ate the fish served for breakfast. Thus he proved that he was the entire, complete, full Jesus who had risen from the dead.

To say that the complete Jesus rose from the dead may seem confusing or of little significance. Yet, as was clear from the New Testament efforts to affirm it, the resurrection of Jesus, which included the notion of bodily resurrection, had to be struggled for in the first century A.D. Luke 24 emphasizes Jesus' eating with his disciples and thus explicitly states that Jesus could not be simply a phantom or ghost. John 20 tells that Jesus invited Thomas to touch his scarred hands, feet and side. In its own way this story also suggests that Jesus was risen with his crucified body. One notices that in Matthew 28, as Jesus met his disciples in Galilee and was about to depart from them, some still doubted; this doubt seems centered about the reality of the resurrection of the body of Jesus. In short, it was possible for some people in the first century A.D. and afterwards to make a distinction that satisfied them: Jesus may have risen from the dead in some spiritual sense, and that would account for his being seen in vision, but he surely did not rise body and soul from the tomb outside Jerusalem.

In various ways Christians refused to settle for this spiritual understanding of the Resurrection. Their initial argument centered about the fact, visible to anybody who wanted to look, that the tomb in which Jesus was buried was empty. The empty tomb did not prove that Jesus rose, but it did support the resurrection, once Jesus showed that he had risen, body and soul. Another argument involved the teaching of the Old Testament, which indicated that a descendant of David would die, but not stay dead, and that this escape from death involved the body of this person as well as the soul. The third argument Christians used was that, as the story of John 21 affirms, Jesus at various times deliberately showed that he had risen physically as well as spiritually.

There was a very important aspect to the persistent determination of Christians to present Jesus as bodily risen from the dead. In presenting him this way, they first underlined the reality that the Jesus who rose was none other than the Jesus who lived and died before their very eyes. Thus, not only does the entire Christ rise, but the identity of the risen one was affirmed to be that of Jesus of Nazareth. Secondly, contrary to the Greek philosophical way of thinking that happiness was to be achieved by getting rid of one's mortal, changing body, Judaism knew the entire human being to be good, for God called Adam, body and soul, *good.* God made no distinction between body and soul in his calling Adam good, and so we can expect that the totality of Adam would be saved from death and all other evil when God intervenes. Thus it really makes no sense to say that Jesus was saved by his Father, if the Father only saved the soul of Jesus and not his body. Thirdly, the Christians saw the union between Jesus and his followers to be so intimate that the fate of

Jesus would be the fate of the believer. The belief that Jesus rose from the dead physically, then, grounds the belief that Christians rise bodily from death. True, Jesus rose so soon after his death that corruption did not enter his body, whereas for others corruption was a very real condition of the deceased body. For all that, people like St. Paul would argue tenaciously that the resurrection of the Christian includes physical resurrection; somehow God would provide a body for the risen Christian, a body which the Christian would know as his own. Paul's analogy here was very apt. Take a seed: in vain would you look for the leaves and stem and blossoms that would come from that seed; indeed, we would be inclined to swear that nothing would come from the seed. Yet, once it goes into the ground and dies or corrupts, there arises stem, leaves, blossom and petals—a body undoubtedly drawn from the corrupted seed, and not the body of the seed, which in its seed stage has only a husk for a body, but the body of the flower (1 Cor 15:35–44).

Commission of Peter   *Jn 21:15-17*

The second important element of Jesus' appearance to his disciples at the seashore centers on Jesus' words to Peter. Peter had denied Jesus three times in Jerusalem when Jesus was tried before his crucifixion. Now Jesus asked Peter three times whether or not he loves him. Peter affirmed three times that he indeed loved Jesus. The important element of this interchange between Jesus and Peter lies in the command of Jesus which follows each of these three protestations of love. Jesus said, "Feed my lambs," then "Tend my sheep," finally "Feed my sheep." What is the meaning of this triple command?

A centuries' old image of Israel is that of God's flock or sheep. At one point the prophet Ezechiel, under divine inspiration, strongly criticized the shepherds of Israel, crowning his criticism by stating that Yahweh would rid himself and Israel of these shepherds and become Israel's sole, responsive and responsible Shepherd. Not unlikely, then, was the account in Jn 10 wherein Jesus distinguished the true, good shepherd of the flock of Israel from thieves and brigands. Before Jesus, the Good Shepherd, left earth definitively, however, he took the opportunity to give Peter the responsibility to tend Jesus' flock, the flock of the new people of God. This responsibility was built on the fact that Peter truly loved the Shepherd and thus could be entrusted with the care of Jesus' own flock.

That it was to Peter and to no others that this responsibility was given here at the shore of the Sea of Galilee accounts for the naming of the little chapel here the Chapel of the Primacy. In other words, Jesus here conferred on Peter a responsibility that made Peter primary in caring for Jesus' flock; hence, we have the term *primacy* to sum up this event.

Peter was to tend and feed. Though these two terms might be simply elements belonging to the metaphor of shepherd used here, many scholars think that they pertain to two distinct and essential elements of Christianity: teaching the will of God and the eucharistic food. Thus Peter was asked to care for feeding the flock with the body and blood of Christ and for tending the flock with truths drawn from the mind and will of God. This task of Peter puts him in sharp contrast to the errant scribes and Pharisees of Jesus' time with whom Jesus had quarreled so often precisely about things which involved the good of God's flock. It is, finally, from this story that the popes, patriarchs, and and other bishops have traditionally drawn their symbols: the staffs by which they show they are pastors, shepherds of their flock, responsible for their feeding and tending.

Prediction of Peter's Death   *Jn 21:18-23*

The third element of Jesus' appearance at the shore of the Sea of Galilee is his prediction of the kind of death Peter would suffer; it also tries to clear up a misunderstanding among certain Christians who thought that John, the gospel writer, would never die. Jesus had told Peter, after Peter had heard about his own dire end and had asked about the future of John, that what happens to John was no business of Peter—indeed, Jesus went on to say, "what does it matter to you, even if I want him to stay until I return?" It seems that some Christians understood Jesus' question to imply that John was actually not going to die, but would live till Jesus' return. John went out of its way, in this appearance story, to say that Jesus' question was merely a question with no implication that John would not die. Peter was to concentrate on his own fate, that in Rome he too would be crucified.

Church of the Beatitudes

Mount of the Beatitudes

On a hilltop less than two miles west of Capernaum is the lovely chapel dedicated to the most famous sermon given by Jesus in the Scriptures, the Sermon on the Mount. The chapel is modern, but in this area was built in the fourth century A.D. and again in the fifth century A.D. a shrine—each later destroyed—in honor of the discourse which has been called a blueprint for Christian holiness. The gardens of the present church or chapel are very inviting and the view offered from the south porch of the chapel overlooking the Sea of Galilee rewards the pilgrim and evokes the many events of Jesus's life in this area.

The chapel is dedicated explicitly to the Beatitudes with which the Sermon on the Mount begins. But the chapel should serve to recall all that Jesus then said, for practically every sentence of his discourse has had its influence on the cultures which have accepted Christianity. This Sermon on the Mount has done much to make Matthew the primary gospel for Christian teaching from the earliest times; this sermon, in its full length of three chapters is only in Matthew. A closer look at this sermon shows what Matthew had in mind in giving it to his readers as Jesus's first major teaching in his Gospel.

Many scholars suggest that the Sermon on the Mount was actually not one, uninterrupted sermon given by Jesus on one occasion but that Matthew added to a core of sayings at one time by Jesus to his disciples things Jesus said on different occasions and in different places. Looking at the Sermon in this way best explains three things: first, why no other Gospel has a sermon of the size and importance of what we have in three chapters of Matthew; secondly, why some sayings of Matthew's Sermon on the Mount are found scattered over Jesus's public life described by Mark and Luke; thirdly, why, for all the differences,

Matthew and Luke essentially agree on a core of a sermon that Jesus gave his disciples.

Indeed, Luke has a sermon given by Jesus which in two aspects closely parallels what we read in the Sermon on the Mount in Matthew, although in Luke the sermon takes place at the foot of the mount and was reduced from Matthew's three chapters to just thirty verses of Luke's chapter six. Concretely, the material which was so much alike in Matthew and Luke was made up of Beatitudes and the love and integrity which should characterize the actions and thinking of a follower of Jesus. The sermon as given in Matthew will be analyzed here, with attention given to some of the differences in Luke, where the sermon in Luke transects that given in Matthew. Let us, then, look to this magnificent discourse of Jesus, given to his disciples, as Matthew reports it, on "the mountain top."

The Sermon in Matthew   *Mt 5-7*

In a sermon of three chapters' length it may not be easy to recognize at first reading the topic sentence or essential theme which holds it together. But here most scholars agree that the topic sentence, the idea around which the entire Sermon on the Mount revolves, is this: "For I tell you, if your virtue goes no deeper than that of the scribes and Pharisees, you would never get into the kingdom of heaven" (Mt 5:20). A more positive way of putting this, though we lose the sense of "doing better than the Jewish religious leaders," is the later statement, "You must be perfect as your heavenly Father is perfect" (Mt 5:48). In the concrete circumstances of Jesus's audience this meant that "the person who keeps the least of the commandments from the Mosaic Law and from the Prophets and teaches them would be considered great in the Kingdom of Heaven" (Mt 5:19). These three elements, then, characterize the follower of Jesus: perfect as the Father is perfect, which is to say that one has to do better than the scribes and Pharisees, that one keeps the law of Israel's tradition as that law is reinterpreted by Jesus. Let us see, then, just what that perfection was for Jesus's audience.

The Meaning of *Beatitude*

The first section of the Sermon on the Mount is dedicated to beatitudes. *Beatitude* is a Latin word *beatitudo* made into an

English word; it means *blessedness* or *happiness,* and a person who has this quality of blessedness is called *blessed, happy— beatus.* A beatitude is a particular form of expression; the Scriptures have over two hundred fifty beatitudes; eight are in the Sermon on the Mount as given in Matthew; in Luke's sermon there are only four beatitudes. A beatitude is simply characterized: it is a saying which starts with the word *blessed,* then usually identifies the person who is blessed and the reason for this person's being considered blessed. Since Jesus taught orally rather than by writing, he constantly sought out forms of speech which were simple and could help people remember, even memorize, what he taught. Thus this kind of saying is a good form to help people recall the essence of what Jesus thought important; indeed, the Sermon on the Mount is filled with many formulaic ways of conveying teaching. The strengths of such teaching are obvious: clarity, simplicity, memorability. But such teaching may lack reasoning about morality and be difficult to apply as a general moral principle in some situations.

By comparing the beatitudes given by Matthew with those given by Luke for the very same sermon, we conclude that Jesus probably addressed the beatitudes directly to his immediate audience, hence, "blessed are *you.* . . ." This means that Matthew changed the beatitudes slightly to read, "blessed are they who . . ."; by doing this, he extended Jesus's teaching to all those who would read his Gospel. Various qualities are emphasized by Jesus and stressed in the Gospels of Matthew and Luke. In general, Luke recorded Jesus's effort to bring, by way of beatitudes, consolation and encouragement to the poor faithful of Israel, to those who are hungry and weeping and must suffer for their allegiance to Jesus; Matthew also wanted to assure such people of God's care for them and of his promises of love and eternal happiness. But Matthew also wove into these beatitudes encouragement for those who, whether rich or poor, emphasize the spiritual life and treat material life, the "life of this world," as secondary to the demands of the "world to come." For instance, those "blessed poor in spirit" are no longer simply "you here in front of Jesus who are physically poor, but faithful"; they are all those who, even though wealthy, remain detached from the things of this world to be rich in the things of heaven. They are the "poor in spirit," the spiritually poor or detached from this world.

The Christian Life

Having described qualities of his followers by beatitudes, Jesus told them that they are the salt of the earth and the light of the world. To be the salt of the earth seems to mean that Christianity is what gives taste to an otherwise insipid or tasteless life. The term *light of the world* echoed Isaiah who once called Israel the light of the world in the sense that it would be through Israel that God would attract the Gentiles to himself. Jesus, in the Gospel of John, identified himself as the "light of the world," thus indicating that those who sat in darkness and under the shadow of death would find light and life through him. Here in the Gospel of Matthew, Jesus' followers were to be the way by which the rest of the world would escape its darkness to find the true and only God. Being the light of the world suggested that one live one's Christian life without excuse; to be what one is called to be needs no explanation, nor should one hide what one knows to be true living.

At this point in the sermon Jesus made explicit what he had implied. Jesus, a man of his times, was concerned for the welfare of his own contemporaries. He was eager to give what he considered a true understanding of God's will, an understanding different in many respects from what the religious leaders of Israel were teaching. To understand what God wanted—and to do it—are two immensely important concerns of the Israel of Jesus's time, for all the past history of Israel had been interpreted as events influenced by Israel's obedience or disobedience to God. Happiness, in short, depended essentially on fulfilling God's will. Thus, it is of immense importance to know what God asks and not to teach falsely about it, or worse, not to obey it. Jesus defined his work, then, as teaching his contemporaries what was the true will of God.

Christianity and Judaism

To look at Judaism in its strict interpretation today and to compare it with Christianity is a good way to understand how differently Christianity developed out of Judaism. The key to this difference is the mind of Jesus: what he said, however like or unlike it might be to Israel's Law and Prophets, was now the starting point and criterion for all obligation on Christians. Often in the first century A.D. it seemed that Jesus's understanding of God's would make him deny all that the Law and the Prophets of

Israel had said, but this is not true. It is truer to say that Jesus rethought the Old Law and Prophets, then kept what was still valid, eliminated what was not necessary for holiness, and readjusted still other elements of Israel's inheritance.

The criteria Jesus used to evaluate the old system were the fundamental laws of Israel: "Love God with all your heart and soul and strength," and "Love your neighbor as yourself." Each individual law or saying of Israel's tradition should be judged by these two laws; each individual law was kept, dropped or adjusted insofar as it promoted or did not promote love of God and love of neighbor. Thus, Jesus never denied the laws forbidding idolatry, murder, stealing, and uncharitable speech and action. But Jesus did away with the laws of worship and special foods, for they did not really touch on the essence of proper worship or personal holiness. Thus, Jesus adjusted the law about divorce, making clear that for his contemporaries there should be no divorce, though Israel had grown to understand that God would not consider divorce a cause of unholiness.

Jesus, then, saw his role as that of making Israel's law more perfect; Jesus became, in effect, the new and surest way of knowing what God asks of human beings in order that they might stand worthily in his presence. This new way of understanding the mind of God has repercussions throughout the rest of the Sermon on the Mount. Let us look briefly at some of these effects, remembering always that Jesus was laboring here to show how his understanding of what God wants differed from the other contemporary teachings of Israel and how his teaching leads to the truest, fullest holiness.

Six Differences between Jesus and the Tradition

Jesus gave six examples of how he understood Israel's laws differently from the authorities of his time. In none of these examples did Jesus give the philosophical or more broadly intellectual justification for his teaching; he simply supplanted the old laws by his new laws.

The first distinction Jesus drew is between killing, which Israelite law explicitly forbade, and bitter unkindnesses which are not directly forbidden by any Israelite law, but which, according to Jesus, were just as destructive as killing, and thus deserved the punishments assigned to killing.

The second distinction Jesus drew has to do with adultery. Though the Jewish law never approved of divorce *per se*, Jewish authority was long accustomed to divorce and was concerned only that the woman, who could never ask for divorce or refuse to be divorced, be treated at least with minimal justice when divorce occurred. Jesus looked at divorce quite differently. He understood divorce to be adulterous; thus, not only was divorce wrong in itself—Mt 19:1–9 argued this point most clearly—it also was wrong because it made the woman an adulteress. Moreover, the ancient law against adultery should be extended to include adultery in one's heart, even though one only lusts after a woman while never touching her physically. In this way, Jesus not only accepted the traditional understanding of what was prohibited as adulterous action, but included under this law lusting after a woman and divorce.

The third distinction Jesus drew has to do with an aspect of the law of fulfilling oaths; Jesus does not oppose taking an oath, but he finds all too common that element of oath taking which involves swearing by God's name. Too often holy people were calling on God to confirm their own opinions. Jesus would prefer to keep the name of God holy and out of constant, petty usage to bolster an opinion; if we want to affirm his opinion about something, we should find another form than calling on God to affirm it.

A fourth distinction Jesus drew concerning the ancient law has to do with the Mosaic command: an eye for an eye, a tooth for a tooth. Originally, the intent of this Mosaic law was very good; it limited punishment to what actually fitted a crime and thus forbade excessive punishment—"as many eyes as I can get for the one eye taken from me"—or the wrong quality of punishment—"I'll take a tongue for an eye." However, by Jesus's time this Mosaic legislation had created an attitude which Jesus found very odious. To live by the law of retaliation created an attitude towards one's neighbor which made the supreme law, love of one's neighbor and its tendency to forgive, almost impossible to embrace practically. Jesus gave several examples at the core of each of which was an attitude or way of sizing up one's neighbor which prohibits the instinct to love and forgive which characterizes Jesus's teaching. The alternative to this way of approaching one's neighbor was given in the next and final distinction, that concerning love of neighbor and hatred for one's enemy.

Jesus noted the Israelite traditional law: you shall love your neighbor; he added to this what had become the law in practice, though it appears nowhere in the Old Testament: you shall hate your enemy. The notion of "hating one's enemy" is a very limited one: it has to do with hating those who hate God. Thus, a sign of religious people was understood to be hatred for those who disobeyed God, who flaunted idols before him, who treated God's loved ones brutally and harshly. In a sense this matter has nothing personal; indeed, one's hatred grew or diminished to the degree that offense against God grew or diminished.

To Jesus, the distinction must be maintained that separates the sin from the sinner. True, the Old Testament way of story telling often depicted God as angry and punishing those who offended him. Yet here by word and later by example, Jesus taught that the love God has for a person, sinning or not, is to be the true and constant approach each human being should have towards every other human being. True, God punishes, but then again God gives rain and sun to those who dishonor him.

Thus, whatever the circumstances which put one human being into contact with another, love of neighbor in imitation of God's love for that neighbor is to rule all actions done to that neighbor. In this regard, such things as self-defense, war, capital punishment, are ultimately governed by love which imitates God's love for the just and the unjust. No other principle replaces love as the criterion for action or esteem.

Before moving to the next part of the Sermon on the Mount, we should consider Jesus's words concerning "cutting off one's hand, plucking out one's eye." In saying these things, Jesus did not advocate actually cutting off one's hand or plucking out one's eye; he was stressing very graphically how much we are to discipline ourselves out of the realization of what was at stake in lust. In somewhat the same way, Jesus did not earlier command that one leave one's gift at the altar and first be reconciled with one's brother, then go back and offer the gift; Jesus stressed the tawdriness of a gift offered by a person who thought his brother to be a fool and unworthy of God's love.

Later Developments of Jesus' Teaching on Marriage

In all these distinctions which Jesus made, he tried to show how his way to pleasing God differed from and more accurately reflected God's will than the way his contemporaries—

Sadducees, Pharisees, chief priests, Essenes, and others—taught and lived. Rooted as his sayings were in the circumstances of his moment in Israel, it is not surprising that his followers in later decades had to adjust to some degree what he had said, to cope with circumstances which Jesus never had to face. Thus, whereas Jesus never approved of divorce—compare, for example, the teaching in Mark and Luke. Matthew and Paul, in his First Letter to the Corinthians, face situations which are solved only by a very restricted approval of divorce.

For Paul, a converted spouse begins to suffer from his or her pagan spouse precisely because of the newly found Christianity. Paul was faced with this dilemma: let the pagan spouse so pressure the newly converted so that the newly converted collapses and gives up the faith, or allow the two to divorce. Paul counseled the latter, provided it be the pagan partner who asks for the divorce.

In the Matthean Gospel it is not altogether clear what constituted reason for divorce, though it did have to do with some meaning of the word which has to do with sexual sin. Some scholars, for example, think that the exception to the law against divorce arose out of a situation in which people had been married as pagans within relationships which forbid marriage in the Old Testament: for instance, someone marries a first cousin, or an uncle marries a niece. Perhaps, for the pagans this would be tolerable, but, on becoming Christians, they contradict what God had stated as forbidden in the Old Testament. Thus, though Jesus is not on record as permitting divorce, the Matthean community thinks that he would have allowed for divorce, if he had been confronted with this circumstance—and so the Matthean community allows for divorce in these special circumstances. Indeed, it falls to the Church to fit the teaching of Jesus to circumstances, all the while remaining faithful to the mind of Christ.

Three Practices

The Sermon on the Mount next took up three practices which in Jesus's time were considered to characterize a person who was serious in seeking to stand worthily in God's presence: almsgiving, prayer and fasting. Jesus did not create these three practices, nor did he forbid them in the Sermon; rather, he corrected wrong motives which seem to have inspired many people of his time to fast, pray and give alms. In this part of the Sermon it is not a question of what a person does, but the why which moves him to act.

Prayer

Within the discussion of prayer, Jesus offered a type of prayer which was most satisfying to God without being the type of interminable prayer other authorities thought pleasing to God. (See 142.) It was a simple prayer, divided into two parts and very faithful to the traditional prayer of Israel. First, one praises God and asks that God's kingdom come, that earth reflect the perfect harmony of heaven where God's will is the cause of perfect peace. Then, one asks for one's most fundamental needs: food, forgiveness, freedom from the trials which would test to the breaking point one's fidelity to God. To these petitions is added the reminder that one can hardly expect forgiveness from God if one was unwilling to forgive others; there was little logic in such an expectation. With all his persuasiveness Jesus was trying to bring to birth in his followers a willingness to forgive others; to him, it was this willingness which would prevent most of the actions done to harm one's neighbor. Thus his teaching was the one which brings peace.

Jesus had given several statements in the Sermon on the Mount which outline the characteristics of those who want to be his followers. In many ways they are encouraged to be holy, as the Jewish traditions had encouraged them: prayerful, fasting, giving alms, loving of neighbor, and all those things described by the beatitudes; in other ways, too, he has described to his followers, ways in which they should think differently from their contemporaries and act differently from them. Now Jesus turns to another major concern: riches.

Concern for Riches

Jesus had three principal thoughts about riches to give those who wish to follow him. First, treasures are valuable if they are indestructible. It follows that we seek those treasures which would not fade or be taken away. This, of course, can happen only in heaven, and so Jesus exhorts His followers not to commit themselves to things which would break their hearts when they lose them; wisdom says that one's heart would be happy if it has invested in treasures that would endure forever.

Secondly, human experience has taught that possessions and money can become effectively a god in one's life. A person does not readily recognize this fact always; yet, when we realize how money dictates his actions and how much we would sacrifice to have and preserve it and how much affection we have for it, then we begin to realize just what a god money has already become in a person's life. Jesus' insight was simply built on this experience: we cannot serve two gods at once. Jesus' encouragement was to choose the true, the only God. True, service of this God may at times require that we lay aside the demand and service of money, but there is only one God and him we must serve ahead of all else.

Given the revelation of God as Father to us, we can only draw the conclusion that God would care of us as a father would. Thus it follows that the kind of worry about life is to be abandoned which assumes that God does not care about us. Jesus was not saying that worry and concern and effort and labor to wipe away worry are bad; he was concerned about the conclusion people draw at times from life, namely that God does not care about us, that he cannot be trusted and that I should go elsewhere to find my happiness. Amidst all life's trials, as in the midst of his own, Jesus never doubted that God is a loving Father. If God does not answer my needs, the reason may not be apparent; but, for all that unclarity, we should not conclude that God does not care; we must solve our problems within the conviction that God is Father to me. That is the reality.

Judging One's Neighbor

The Sermon on the Mount concludes with further exhortation to love one's neighbor by not being harsh in judging one's neighbor. People have the tendency to ignore their own evil ways and to concentrate on the evils, often less than their own, of others. Fairness is a prized virtue in these kinds of circumstances. Indeed, should we not be fair, if we expect to be treated fairly?

Jesus again called for trust in God as Father; this time he was thinking specifically of prayer wherein we ask favors from God. We must truly ask, truly seek, truly knock, before we can say that God does not answer prayers. But, even then, should not God be trusted as Father, even though we cannot be sure why he sometimes does not answer? Indeed, if we use the fatherhood of a person to explain why a child would surely be treated well, how can we doubt that God's child would be treated well? Surely, God is the best of fathers!

Disciples must be wary of false teachers, those who teach differently from Jesus, and those who teach differently about Jesus than does his Church. Above all, Jesus' teaching provided grounding of a life which leads to fullest happiness; to take another's teaching was to entrust one's life to another—and this was like building on sand. Jesus' way, though narrow and often difficult because it calls us to love God and neighbor so thoroughly, is the only way to full happiness. It is this happy ending which makes the Sermon on the Mount so admirable.

The Sermon in Luke   *Lk 6:20-49*

Luke's rendition of the sermon—for Luke it is more properly called the "Sermon on the Plain"—concentrates on two facets of what we have seen in Matthew's longer sermon. First, Luke contrasts beatitudes with curses. In doing this, Luke contrasts those poor, sad, and hungry with those who go their own way with wealth, joy and plenty and ignore those who are in need. Concretely, this situation was unbearable for Jesus; it contradicted the very meaning of God's great commandment to love one's neighbor. Jesus' disciples could not live this contradictory kind of life. Secondly, Jesus went on to work out further the implications of love of neighbor, specifically, how this command relates to one's enemies. In brief, Luke looks for the same love and fairness and generosity which characterizes the Sermon on the Mount in Matthew. Truly, the foundation of relationships is only love, as far as Jesus was concerned. What a difference in the way human life might be lived if his sermon were really accepted and lived! It is a simple sermon but a narrow way. Yet it is the way to life, as many know by experience and not simply by taking it on faith alone.

The shrine to honor the Beatitudes is a holy place to remind us that Jesus' way of understanding what the Father asks of us gives us joy and peace. He died because of his teaching, because he claimed to represent God better than all the traditions and contemporary interpretations of those traditions. But he would not back off from his teaching, for he knew that he had to tell others, even at the risk of his life, what was for their deepest happiness.

Caesarea Philippi

Caesarea Philippi

At Caesarea Philippi there are a series of pools and a lovely grove which lie at the foot of a mountain, where a guide may point out Greek words inscribed in honor of the ancient Greek and Roman god of woodlands and pastures, Pan. Though his name originally came from a Greek word for *pastures,* a ancient pun linked it up with the Greek word for *everything,* and he became a god of nature as a whole. Caesar Augustus Octavian gave the ancient shrine and its surrounding city to Herod the Great. Herod's son Philip inherited the town and, to honor Octavian, who in 6 A.D. had made Philip tetrarch of this entire northern territory bounding Palestine, rebuilt the town into a more glorious one and named it after Augustus. Joining his own name to that of Caesar, Philip called the place Caesarea Philippi. *Philippi* serves to distinguish this town from another Caesarea on the Mediterranean coast. (See 77–83.)

Who is Jesus?   *Mk 8:27-30; Lk 9:18-22*

In or near Caesarea Philippi, Jesus asked his disciples who had been following him for several months, "Who do people say that I am?" The question was meant as one of curiosity: after seeing all that Jesus had done and heard all that he said, what conclusions are people whom the disciples encounter drawing? The answer given in Matthew, Mark and Luke are quite similar; John does not have this episode. Some thought that Jesus was the prophet—by this they meant that Jesus was the one promised in Deuteronomy 18:15, 18: "Yahweh your God will raise up for you a prophet like me [Moses] from among your brothers." Some thought Jesus was John the Baptizer, in the sense at least that the spirit of John, who had died at the command of Herod Antipas, was in Jesus. Others thought of Jesus as the Elijah figure whom the prophet Malachi had promised would return to prepare the people for the great and

terrible day of the Lord (Mal 3:1). Others yet thought Jesus to be
Jeremiah or one of the other prophets, for Jesus constantly
exhorted the people to return to their God, even when
authorities opposed him.

Jesus never denied the aptness of these categories by which
people tried to express their perception of who he was and what
he attempted to do. Rather, he changed the question to "Who do
you say that I am?" Peter answered this question for all the
disciples, "You are the Messiah [which is equal to the Son of
God]." In Mark and Luke, Jesus neither accepted nor rejected this
title; in Matthew he implicitly accepted it. Let us consider Jesus'
attitude towards the title of Messiah more closely, and especially
look at what he said to Peter in Matthew, after Peter confessed
Jesus to be "the Messiah, the son of the living God."

The Messianic Secret

As mentioned above, when Jesus heard Peter identify him as
"Messiah," Jesus neither denied nor approved of the title. But he
warned Peter and the others not to speak of this title to anyone.
In this scheme Luke followed Mark; secrecy about Jesus as
Messiah is a fundamental theme of Mark. The point of the
"Messianic secret" is that for Mark, the disciples were simply too
inexperienced to know what they were saying when they said
Jesus was "Messiah." Oh yes, they had seen him work miracles
which suggested that he was the Messiah. But they had not lived
through the complete Jesus experience, which involved both
ignominious and powerless death and astounding resurrection.
Mark was most precisely concerned with what the disciples
would call Jesus when they see him—if they had not run too far
away to see him—hanging in pain and humiliation on a cross till
his life oozes out of him. This Jesus was not so easily identified
as Messiah, the one anointed by God to bring about the holiness
of the people of God. First, where was God in all this? Secondly,
how could Jesus be the beloved of God and still die like this?
Thirdly, how would the Messiah accomplish the task for which he
was sent, if his career was so abruptly and easily ended by
people who are proving themselves more powerful than God?
Until we have the answers to these questions, which lie at the
heart of any attempt to make sense of Jesus, we should not speak
too readily of him as Messiah.

In other words, Jesus did not want to be known as Messiah

only because he worked miracles. Most essentially, he wanted to be known as Messiah precisely because of his death; it was his death, more than his miracles, which revealed the true task and identity and fidelity of Jesus. Mark wrote his Gospel to protect this meaning of Jesus and to make sure that we do not accept a Jesus who does not die or a life in which we are unwilling to carry our own crosses as a price for belief in Jesus. Luke was very willing to follow Mark's lead in stressing the "full" Jesus, who dies as well as works wonders and teaches attractive truths.

In short, Christianity had to come up with a satisfactory explanation of the death of Jesus in order to show that Jesus qualified to be called *Messiah.* For Mark, Jesus' death was a death for others, a death by which the sins of others were wiped away. For Luke, Jesus' death was part of the divine plan: God knew what people would do to Jesus and thwarted it by raising Jesus from the dead. Thus in neither Gospel was the death of Jesus a proof that God was not Jesus' Father; rather, the death itself was understood in such a way as to heighten the relationship between Father and Son. But only after we have lived through the entire Jesus experience, and not just that part of it which had been shared in up to Jesus' questions at Caesarea Philippi, can we truly call Jesus "Messiah" with any real understanding.

Peter's Confession in Matthew   *Mt 16:13-20*

Matthew affirmed all that Mark taught about the Messiah, but for Matthew, the episode at Caesarea Philippi meant something more. First was an item in Matthew only, not in Mark or Luke: when Jesus answered that revelation from the Father, Jesus implicitly accepted the title as a just one. Matthew was intent here, however, to stress something else. He saw this profession of Peter as an act of faith caused by the Father. Jesus recognized that what Peter was saying was inspired by the Father. Recognition of this inspiration moved Jesus to identify Peter as "Rock,"for *petros,* in Greek, means *rock.* The significance of this new name for Peter was twofold. First, the truth that Jesus was the Messiah, the Son of the living God, was the foundation of the Christian people of God, the Church. Thus, whatever else may be considered important or essential to the makeup of the Church, the foundation of the Church depends upon the Church's continuous profession of Jesus as Messiah, Son of the Living God.

To give this up was to take away from the Church the solidity of
its very foundation. Secondly, though Peter spoke for the other
eleven, it was to him alone that Jesus addressed his words and it
was to Simon alone that the new name, Peter, was given. Thus,
this one man was the Rock of the Church. The Church, then, was
founded on two elements: the *man* Peter and his *profession* of
Jesus as Messiah, Son of the Living God. Should either be
removed from the Church, the Church loses the rock foundation
on which it stands.

What is the Church?

One must be careful to understand what is meant by *Church*
here. Scholars agree that this term, so sparsely used in the
Gospels, is to be understood in the light of its Old Testament
usage. And what is this usage? Perhaps the best way of
explaining it was to recall the meaning of the word; basically, the
word has the meaning of *those called out.* This meaning was
particularly significant for explaining the nature of the group of
Israelites who are called out of their tents to wait at the foot of
Mount Sinai, to wait to hear the word of God and to worship him.
When the Israelites are in this type of gathering, we read that
they are a "church," (Hebrew: *qahal*; Greek: *ekklesia*; Latin:
ecclesia; French: *eglise*; Spanish: *iglesia*; Italian: *chiesa*) a
liturgical gathering ready to listen to God and to worship him.
Now, the important point to note is that the grounding, the
foundation of this listening and worshipping is the confession of
Peter that Jesus is the Messiah, the Son of the Living God. It is
only with this foundation that the worshipping people would
truly be the people of God.

This profession of Jesus as Messiah, Son of the living God, is
the strength of the Church. As long as belief in Jesus is strong, no
power can overcome the Church; the destruction of the Church
will come about only with the abandonment of its "Rock."
Indeed, acting out its profession that Jesus was Messiah, the
Church will overpower all evil.

The Keys of the Kingdom

The notion of *Rock* involves not only profession of Jesus as
Messiah, but the person mysteriously chosen by God to give this
profession. To this person are given the keys to the kingdom of

heaven. Obviously, this imagery indicates that it is Peter who opens and shuts the doors to heaven. It seems that he is to do this opening for those who profess with him the belief that Jesus is the Messiah, the Son of the Living God.

It is, however, clear enough that the profession of Jesus as Messiah carried with it implications for the living of human life. In Mt 23:13 Jesus would excoriate the scribes and Pharisees because they "shut up the kingdom of heaven in men's faces, neither going in yourselves nor allowing others to go in who want to." This power to "open and close" is the power by which authorities taught the will of God. Thus, these teachers of Israel failed miserably, for they not only misinterpreted the will of God for themselves, but for all those who depended upon them. Now, Jesus transfered this power to "open and close" to Peter, using now the terms "binding and loosening." The implication, again, is that to interpret the will of God for human happiness, to "bind and loose," is a power which grounded on the belief that Jesus is the Messiah. Without this foundation there is no right understanding of God's will, and God would not recognize in heaven the decisions that are made by Peter on earth.

Such, then, was Jesus' immense gift to Peter upon his divinely inspired acknowledgment that Jesus was the Messiah, the Son of God. On this profession and on this man the worshipping people of God rests; on these two depends the Church for the true teaching of what was God's will for man's complete happiness. No power will ever defeat those who seek God through belief that Jesus was their Messiah. In this lovely, peaceful spot called Caesarea Philippi, on the northern border of Galilee Jesus pronounced these very important words. These words were one more way of Jesus' extending to us means by which he could lead us to happiness—which, after all, was indeed his task as Messiah.

Greek Orthodox Church of Elias (Mount Tabor)

Naim

About eight miles southeast of Nazareth and five miles southwest of Mount Tabor, the Mount of the Transfiguration, lies the village of Naim. It is a Muslim village today and overlooks the mighty and fertile Plain of Esdraelon which stretches east-west across northern Palestine. Naim has no Christian archeological remains, but a chapel, built by the Franciscans in 1880 A.D. over the remains of a medieval Christian church, commemorates the astounding miracle worked by Jesus for the poor widow of Naim and her only son.

Luke's story says that Jesus met a funeral cortege near "the gate of the city"; no one has found remains of a gate or its wall; many conjecture that Luke had in mind a formal wooden or stone marker through which the road passed just before the outlying houses of the town.

Raising of Widow's Son   *Lk 7:11-17*

The story of what happened in this village has much to offer Luke's reader. Note that this miracle happened not because anyone requested it, but simply because Jesus could not help responding to the pitiableness of the situation. In a sense, he was like the Good Samaritan he himself would later describe; he was moved by the sorrow and pain of another human being. One has to keep reminding oneself that Jesus did not enter this phase of his life to work miracles. Total relief from pain and sorrow was part of the kingdom of God, and to be in the presence and love of God was to be assured of complete happiness; yet, before that happens, before this age—according to the moment the Father chooses—passes away and the next age begins, God through Jesus seeks the cure of the heart, repentance, return to God. This reunion with God creates the love which shares all things: good health, freedom from death and dangers, peace, total happiness. It was possible to hope that God would give me all things and to accept them without my ever loving God. Jesus's life, however, was based on another premise: to be with God was to have loved him, not remain alien to him. Surely, God must give me not only the gifts of a lover, but the very grace to love him, to change my heart about him. But that grace would never deny my right to freely choose him; and it was to this freedom, encouraged by his call for love and his grace, that Jesus speaks. This change of heart was the miracle of miracles, the miracle which logically precedes all others. What we witness at Naim, then, is not the response Jesus dedicated himself to seek, but the effect of God's constant longing to provide all things—even if his action upsets for the moment the rules of the game he defines by the goals he sets for Jesus.

The Naim miracle is particularly poignant when we consider the social situation to which the miracle responded. Wonderful as was the raising of a person from death, this particular miraculous word of Jesus restored to a widow her only son, still but a young man. Without this male support, who knows what would have been the life of this woman, already poor? She certainly was not allowed free access to the "market place," as though she could apply for many types of jobs. Women were very dependent on husbands and male children for income; the raising of a family and performance of household chores earned no income.

Throughout many centuries, Jewish religion had developed a system of charity for widows. Acts 6:1–2 shows how the Jews who had become Christians kept this system alive for their widows. But such financial support was hardly an adequate replacement for what family members provide one another.

It was this situation, very precarious for the widow, which Jesus entered with his restoring word. Luke is very clear about what caused Jesus' rush of sympathy: "He was the only son of his mother, and she was a widow . . . and seeing her the Lord felt great pity and sympathy for her." Jesus could not abide the effects of death; he instinctively wanted to give life. To appreciate more deeply the gift of life here, however, means that we keep in mind the full effects this restoration of life; by keeping the situation of the widow in mind, we can understand a precious part of Jesus' own sympathetic person.

Jesus and Disciples of John   *Lk 7:18-28*

Though Luke emphasized the benefit the widow of Naim enjoyed from this resurrection to life and though such a miracle as this

young man experienced was not the stated goal of Jesus'
ministry, resurrection from the dead has its own particular
significance in Luke's story. I refer specifically to the meeting
which took place between Jesus and the disciples of John the
Baptizer, who was in prison east of the northern part of the Dead
Sea. This meeting occurred immediately after the wonder at
Naim and served as a way of interpreting all that Jesus had done
for people up to this point in Luke's story.

John, imprisoned according to Luke's presentation since Lk
3:20, sought to learn now if Jesus was really the one John knew
himself to be preparing for (See 104). Jesus answered in terms of
the Scriptures known to Jesus, John, and all Jews. He
summarized the deeds he has done, as Luke has narrated them
for us, but he did this in such a way as to remind John of what
Isaiah had said God's servant would do: blind see; those who
cannot walk walk; unclean are cleaned; deaf hear; dead live;
those who know no good news are given good news (Is 61:1–2).
From these mighty reversals of human pain, of those things
which characterize this age and from which man cannot free
himself—from all this, rather than from titles drawn from the
Jewish Scriptures, John was to grasp the identity of Jesus.

That Jesus had such power, even to raise a young man from
the dead, and had it to such an extent, meant that what was
expected to happen in the next age was happening where Jesus
was present, something reserved for the kingdom of God was
poured out where Jesus was. Who, then, was Jesus, and what, in
particular, does his raising of the young man of Naim say about
his identity?

Luke had already introduced his readers to the possible
significance of Jesus. At the beginning of Jesus' public life (Lk
4:18), Jesus had used Isaiah's words to indicate what his life
would be from then on (See 11–14). All that Isaiah foretold is
realized in the stories Luke tells, finishing with the raising of the
young man at Naim, up to the visit of John's messengers to
Jesus.

Through these Isaian words, set in chapters four and seven
of Luke's story, we are asked to grasp the identity of Jesus and
the sense of his proclamation that "the kingdom of God was
among you." There were still more words and deeds of Jesus to
come which would justify the estimate of Peter that Jesus was
the very Messiah of God (Lk 9:20). What Luke ultimately hoped,
however, is that his reader would conclude from all Jesus' deeds
and words that Jesus was what Luke described him to be in his

first chapter; "what is born will be called holy, Son of God" (Lk 1:35). It is to this title in all its profundity that Luke thinks all of Jesus's life, words and deeds—including the raising of the young man of Naim from the dead—lead us.

Jesus and Elijah

Finally, Luke described the miracle of Naim so as to make one automatically think of the prophet Elijah, if one knows the Old Testament as well as did Luke's original audience. At one point in Elijah's preaching life, after being responsible for providing for a widow from practically nothing enough bread to see her through a prolonged drought and famine, Elijah was held responsible for the death of her son. Elijah prayed that the son be given back his life, and so it happened. The story ends: "the breath of life returned to the boy's body and he lived. Taking the child, Elijah . . . gave him to his mother. . . . 'Now I know that you are a man of God,' the woman replied, 'the word of the Lord comes truly from your mouth.'" (1 Kgs 17:7–24.)

Many interpreters think that there was enough indication in the Lucan way of telling the Naim miracle to say that Luke wants us to see the image of Elijah hovering behind that of Jesus and helping, in its own way, to make the identity of Jesus ever clearer. The people of Naim, like the woman in the Elijah story, confess Jesus to be a prophet, one who speaks for God. So great a figure had Elijah become by Jesus' day, however, that to think of him was to think of Israel's greatest prophetic figure: so great was he that he should be the one to return to prepare Israel to meet its God.

For Luke, so profound is the link between Jesus and God that what any Old Testament figure, Elijah included, can contribute to clarifying this link would be much appreciated. No one figure tells all about Jesus, but each has traits which correspond to traits of Jesus, and thus are touching points in human experience which can help us appreciate just how full and intimate was Jesus' relationship with God.

Luke was not to be sold short, however, in his claim about Jesus. Jesus was not another Elijah, was not limited to being Elijah returned. Just to take the case of the young men raised to life—one through Elijah, another through Jesus. It was clear that Elijah's prayer to God and his placing himself over the child was in marked contrast to Jesus' direct exercise of authority, without even a prayer to God: "Young man, I say to you 'Arise.'" Jesus has all the power and authority over death within himself; Elijah does not. And this makes all the difference!

Naim has much to say to its visitor, Jesus. One learns much about him here, both because of his exercise of power and because of Luke's way of presenting it as part of his Gospel. Naim gives us an insight into the heart of the One who keeps calling for repentance; at times he will even step beyond the hearts we do not offer him to console us with his power; and this becomes another incentive to turn our hearts to love him and live with him. In Zachary's song of joy at the circumcision and naming of John, Luke had Zachary sing that God will visit his people who "sat in darkness and in the shadow of death" (See 98). At Naim, the people confirm that God has visited them, as, not death's shadow but death itself, was made to yield to Jesus' word of life. May he shine, too, in our darkness and sweep us from the shadow and touch of death. From his love can come only life for us.

Path Leading to the Church of the Transfiguration (Mount Tabor)

Mount Tabor

Rising from the Plain of Esdraelon south of the Galilean Hills to a height of eighteen hundred feet is the majestic and most beautiful of Palestine's mountains, Mount Tabor. Since the top of Mount Tabor is the traditional site of the Transfiguration of Jesus, we must go up the mountain, using the only means available now: a winding road with its many hairpin turns, built in 1954 A.D.

At the top of the mountain we meet an esplanade some thirty-nine hundred feet long and thirteen hundred feet wide, surrounded by the ruins of the fortress wall built about seven hundred years ago by Islamic forces in Palestine. We enter through this wall by what is known as the Wind Gate. The ruins remind us of the many battles fought here to gain possession of this holy site, battles between Christians and Moslems, particularly during the crusades when the Christians tried to recapture what Moslem armies so cruelly took from the poor monks. Today the Greek Orthodox own the property on the left or north side of the road, the Roman Catholics, that on the right or south side. Near the basilica we can see today a large monastery and a house for pilgrims; a tower built in 1955 A.D. after the fashion of a medieval tower is also nearby.

The beautiful Basilica of the Transfiguration is built between 1921 and 1924 A.D. The style chosen for the basilica is called Roman-Syrian, a style of the greatest splendor in the fifth and sixth centuries A.D.. As we enter, we can see two chapels—on the right, one dedicated to Elijah, on the left, one dedicated to Moses. These two chapels are quite a bit older than the basilica; indeed, it is the intention of the architect of the basilica to so construct the entryway or facade of the basilica as to unite the two old chapels with the new basilica.

The basilica is divided into two levels. The lower level is marked by the splendid window of the peacock, the bird which is a sign of the resurrection from the dead. Indeed, the peacock window marks the site of the ancient Byzantine church which stood here to celebrate the Transfiguration of Jesus many, many centuries ago.

With a guide we can go further under the level of the peacock window to see ancient walls and a very old altar brought to light by excavations of this century. On this lower level there are mosaics on four transfigurations of Jesus: the Nativity, the Eucharist, the Passion, and the Resurrection.

The upper level contains a mosaic celebrating the wondrous transfiguration of Jesus, for which this entire basilica is built. There are also striking side chapels commemorating St. Francis of Assisi and the Blessed Eucharist. The alabaster windows of the basilica enhance the sense of mystery and glory that is associated with the Transfiguration of Jesus.

Transfiguration   *Mt 17:1-9; Mk 9:2-10; Lk 9:28-36*

Matthew, Mark and Luke speak of a wondrous change in Jesus' appearance on a mountain. This mountain has long been identified in tradition as Mount Tabor. The change in appearance included a whiteness of garments and generally a gloriousness of Jesus' features which can only be likened to what the divinity of Jesus must look like if it were to break through the humanity which hides it, or to the projected glory of the Son of God in his Coming at the Last Day.

While Jesus' face "glowed like the sun," as Matthew says, Moses and Elijah appeared on either side of him; Luke says they conversed with Jesus about Jesus' departure or exodus from this earth. All scholars understand Moses and Elijah to stand for the two great traditions which make up Judaism and prepare for the coming of Jesus: Moses represents the law, Elijah represents the prophets—and each has much to say in foretelling the coming of Jesus and the particular twist his life took at its end. Thus, the two traditions of Israel spoke with Jesus—seen for a moment in his glory—and discussed with him how these traditions prefigure the way in which he would pass his last days and enter heaven.

To Peter and his friends, James and John, this meeting of Jesus with Moses and Elijah was awe-inspiring; the natural response of these three was fear and reverence, in keeping with his nature, Peter suggested a way to honor these three persons. But before Peter's words lost their force, he and his friends were covered by a cloud, out of which came the voice of God. This voice aimed to impress on Peter, James, and John the unity between God and Jesus, "This is My Son," and went further by asking that Peter, James and John "listen to him." With this, the cloud passes and the three disciples find they are alone with Jesus, the Jesus of their normal and human acquaintance.

This event, has two parts. First, God made visible, if only for a moment, the reality of Jesus' true gloriousness; this is revealed for the sake of the disciples, surely. Secondly, God pointed out once more, for he had said these very words at the Baptism of Jesus, that Jesus is his Son; surely this, too, was for the disciples' benefit. But God added here that, because of this relationship between God and Jesus, the disciples were to listen closely to him, to obey him and believe him. To this listening were added the witnesses of Moses and Elijah; they, too, tried to tell the disciples something which is for their good. What is all this about?

When we look to see where the Transfiguration takes place in the sequence of events given us in the three synoptic gospels, we cannot fail to note that the Transfiguration follows the startling words of Jesus that he would soon die in Jerusalem. Within the larger frame of things, the Transfiguration is one of the very few bright spots, which include miracles, to occur in the gospel structure, once Jesus turned his attention to the imminent pain and grief which await him in the Holy City, the city of the Temple. Given this distinctive placement of the Transfiguration right after the prophecy of death in Jerusalem, scholars come to the conclusion that the Transfiguration of Jesus is a way of revealing to the disciples the reality of Jesus which they would have to trust in mightily when he would, soon, be utterly without any trace of gloriousness. In short, the Transfiguration is meant as an encouragement in anticipation of a time when the disciples would have to call on any kind of strength or encouragement they could find to keep their sanity and wits. Added to this touch of momentary glory is the voice of God and the witnesses of Moses and Elijah, that what Jesus foretold about himself must be believed and not rejected; the very Scriptures of Israel themselves had prophesied for centuries what would be the fate of the One sent by God to bring Israel back to him.

Connected with the prophecies of Jesus about his own fate at the hands of the Jerusalem authorities are Jesus' words about those aspects of being a Christian which entail cross carrying. Someday, Christians would have to stand like Jesus before kings and magistrates; they would be asked to profess belief in Jesus at the cost of their lives. To these, too, Jesus offers the vision of himself glorified, in the hope that this momentary glimpse of the Lord Transfigured into the reality which reveals his power and majesty would encourage his disciples to profess their faith in him courageously. Similarly, Christians would be asked, if not for their lives, at least for death to their sinful selves—in itself a martyrdom, even if undertaken by one's own self. Here, too, in this form of death for Jesus, we are encouraged to think of the gloriousness of the Lord we serve and obey, to think deeply on the rightness of putting our lesser, evil, selves to death so that the greater, truer, better selves might live. It is to bring about life for our better selves, after all, that the Son of God became man.

Here, then, on Mount Tabor, we relive that experience of Peter, James, and John; in this reliving we hope to grow in trust that, despite the pain, ignominy, and apparently absurd death we are asked to undergo out of obedience to Jesus, what he asks is for the best, is for life—that his words are truly the words of life itself.

Faith and Miracles   *Mt 17:14-20; Mk 9:13-28; Lk 9:37-43*

When Jesus and his three disciples left the top of the mountain and gained the plain below it, they ran into an argument and an angry mob. A man had asked the disciples who did not accompany Jesus to the top of Mount Tabor to cure his possessed son. This they were unable to do. And so Jesus was met with the consternation of this group of frustrated people and asked to do the curing. Jesus performed the exorcism, but not without again challenging everyone to faith, the kind of faith that would produce a miracle without recourse to his miraculous power.

Obviously, the story is pitched in the gospels to the audiences among whom Jesus no longer walked. They must trust and show their unwavering faith in order that God work a miracle among them. Moreover, exorcisms can be worked at times only by those who persevere in prayer before God, and prayer which lasts a long time is a possibility only for the person who has strong faith.

Inner Gate to Ruins of King Herod's Palace (Caesarea Philippi)

Caesarea by the Sea

When the Roman general Pompey came into the area we know now as Lebanon, Syria and Palestine, he took control of a small village perched at the edge of the Mediterranean Sea. This village was Strato's Tower, named after a tower which rose over the town as a watchtower and as a beacon for sea travelers. After Pompey and Julius Caesar died, Mark Antony gave the town to Cleopatra, who in turn lost it back to another Caesar, Octavian Augustus, after he defeated her and Mark Antony in 31 B.C. at the famous battle of Actium. In 30 B.C. Caesar Augustus gave the town to Herod the Great, who had been ruling Palestine since 37 B.C.

Herod always had an inclination and great talent for building, and he turned his hand to make the small village of Strato's Tower into a magnificent port city. In honor of Caesar Octavian Augustus, Herod named the newly developed city Caesarea. To distinguish this Caesarea from the inland Caesarea Philippi, we call this city Caesarea by the sea, in Latin *Caesarea maritima*.

It is easily understandable that Jerusalem, the religious center of Israel, was hostile to every exercise of pagan influence; the further one went from Jerusalem, the more likely one was to meet a blending between Jews and Gentiles. Thus whereas Judaea, whose capital was Jerusalem, was devoted so energetically to God and his law and worship, an area like Galilee produced faithful Israelites living very close to Gentiles. In such a situation, the Romans realized that it was best for them to live away from Jerusalem and in an area which had grown more tolerant of Gentiles. The Romans took advantage of Herod's newly built Caesarea and settled the administrators of Palestine and their army there. Thus the normal living quarters of Pontius Pilate and other procurators was Caesarea; only at the great

Jewish festivals—Passover, Pentecost, Tabernacles—did the procurator and his legions come to Jerusalem. These legions then reinforced a small band of troops always billeted in the Fortress Antonia at the northwestern corner of the Jerusalem Temple platform; the Romans thought it necessary to increase the number of military in Jerusalem at these festivals, since the huge numbers of Jews coming to participate in religious rites could evoke the Jewish desire for freedom from Rome.

Pontius Pilate

Today we only glimpse Caesarea's beauty and grandeur. We usually begin a visit to Caesarea by entering through walls which remind us of a castle surrounded by a moat. This wall was built by crusaders, who found a very dilapidated Caesarea from the times of the Islamic invasions of the seventh century A.D. Rather near this entry through the crusader wall was a replica of a stone discovered here with the name of Pilate inscribed on it; this is, then, a very good indication that Pontius Pilate was involved with Caesarea. Indeed, it is archaeologically unique for it is the only ancient stone which bears Pontius Pilate's name. Four areas or sites are important to Caesarea today. Within the crusader walls are the remains of the center of ancient Caesarea—they go down right to the shore of the Mediterranean. To the south of the city center is a still well-preserved theater; indeed, it is used today for outdoor concerts. To the north of the city's center is a famous Roman aqueduct, and to the east of the city center was a hippodrome or racetrack.

Caesarea remained the capital of Roman government in Israel till the Moslems overran it in the seventh century A.D. At Caesarea Eusebius of Caesarea wrote his famous history of the church about 300 A.D.; earlier the famous biblical interpreter Origen had set up his school of interpretation in Caesarea (231–33 A.D.). But more important for our purposes are two significant biblical events which occurred in Caesarea by the Sea: the conversion of Cornelius and the defense of Paul before he was sent for trial in Rome.

The Conversion of Cornelius   *Acts 10:1-11:18*

The Acts of the Apostles devote chapter ten and half of chapter eleven to the episode involving the conversion of Cornelius, a Gentile soldier stationed in Caesarea. The very length of the story shows how important this conversion was to the development of the Acts of the Apostles. How does this story make its significant contribution to the entire Acts?

The way in which the story is told throughout chapter ten shows that the meeting of Peter and Cornelius was a divinely ordered encounter. Thus we cannot attribute to Peter or to any other agency the credit for seeking out Cornelius; indeed, it was very clearly indicated that for a long time neither Peter nor Cornelius really understood what God was moving each of them to do. One's conclusion from this way of presenting the story should be that God's personal decision and guidance brought Cornelius to hear the word of God about Jesus the Savior.

Peter's problem involved not only his wonder just why he was to go to Cornelius, but also his need to realize that a Gentile was as acceptable to God as was a Jew. This latter reality was difficult for Jews of the first century A.D. to accept, for the traditions which had built up around the Jewish religion made it clear how unacceptable, how unclean, the Gentiles were in the sight of God, in comparison to the people of God. Peter's vision in which he learned that all foods are clean was an indication that not only all food, but also all people, were clean in God's sight.

When Peter finally met Cornelius and heard what he had to say, Peter knew both what he was to give to Cornelius and how Cornelius was equal to him. But a further divine intervention clarified the will of God about Cornelius as an apt subject to hear the preaching about Jesus. Even as Peter was speaking about Jesus as judge of all mankind, the Spirit of God descended on Cornelius and his household, as one more sign of God's satisfaction with Cornelius; Peter could interpret this coming of the Spirit as nothing other than the divine sign that Cornelius was to be baptized—for he was in a sense being baptized in the Spirit before Peter's eyes. Thus, in another distinct way God showed his willingness, even eagerness, that Gentiles become fully Christians, on a par with Jews.

Peter was called by his associates to explain in Jerusalem what he had done in the pagan city of Caesarea, for Jews did not associate with Gentiles as Peter had with Cornelius. Thus, the first half of chapter eleven of Acts was devoted to a retelling of the events of chapter ten, but it was a retelling which highlights, once again, the divine intent that Cornelius, contrary to Jewish traditions, be treated equally with the Jews in the divine process of salvation.

In the circumstances of Peter's day, the claim that Gentiles had equal access to calling on the name of Jesus to be saved was an elevated Christianity beyond the expectations history had dictated. Yet it was true that some Christians then found it difficult or impossible to adjust to this new way of looking at Gentiles. For many Jewish Christians, division was to be maintained, even when the new Christianity abandoned other Jewish traditions.

The Cornelius episode has further ramifications. In chapter fifteen of Acts, Peter spoke to a new problem brought by some Jewish Christians against Gentile Christians; when Peter spoke to this problem, he drew his thoughts from his experience with Cornelius. Around the time associated with chapter fifteen of Acts, certain Jewish Christians, noting in Antioch the number of Gentiles joining Christianity, insisted that these new converts be circumcised and obligated to keep the Mosaic law and its traditions. Chapter fifteen represents the answer which turned Christianity decisively from being simply another form of Judaism. Indeed, to ask that Christians be circumcised and made to keep the Mosaic law was a direct affirmation of the belief that circumcision and obedience to the entire Mosaic law were necessary for salvation. This meant that circumcision and the Mosaic law and its traditions were the equal of Jesus in bringing about salvation. In this opinion, Jesus was to be fitted into the system of Judaism which had prevailed for over a thousand years.

As chapter fifteen develops its arguments, it becomes clear that Gentiles would not be forced to be circumcised and to keep the entire Mosaic law as things necessary for salvation. Whatever else the chapter accomplishes, it underlines in its own way what has been a consistent and essential theme of the Acts of the Apostles: that to be saved one was to call on the name of Jesus; all else was to be considered unnecessary, secondary. Anyone today who thinks he was on the road to final salvation while never having been circumcised or forced to keep the entire Mosaic law appreciates the impact of chapter fifteen on his life. In a very short period of history, then, human understanding of what God understood to be necessary for salvation had undergone a significant change; it was no wonder that some people were incapable of grasping the rightness of this change.

The Cornelius episode of chapters ten and eleven laid a foundation for the resolution of the problem posed in chapter fifteen. Peter addressed the problem by citing the lesson he

learned earlier, that Gentiles have as much right to salvation as
do the Jews. Yet he went a step beyond this lesson to draw out a
more pertinent conclusion. If God saw fit to give his Spirit to
Cornelius without having asked that Cornelius be circumcised
and made to keep the entire Mosaic law, then this was to be the
pattern from now on: no Gentile need be circumcised and made
to keep the entire Mosaic law as elements required for salvation.
Immediately after Peter's speech, Paul and Barnabas recounted
to the audience the evident willingness of God to have Gentiles
throughout what was present-day Asia Minor become Christians,
without a one of them having been circumcised and made to
keep the entire Mosaic law and its traditions. Thus, what
happened in Caesarea when Peter met Cornelius was buttressed
by the experience of Paul and Barnabas, and the accounts of
these three men, together with the scriptural argument posed by
James, won the day; Gentile converts to Christianity needed
nothing else for salvation but to call on the name of the Lord
Jesus.

In these rather simple stories of Acts ten, eleven, and fifteen,
we later Christians are helped to understand how Christianity
essentially differs from Judaism and how, step by step, this
distinction became ever clearer. In short, it was to Jesus and
Jesus alone that a Christian looks for grace and guidance,
forgiveness and intercession. All else was perhaps useful, but the
one essential was "to call on the name of the Lord" for salvation.

The Defence of Paul   *Acts 23:23-26:32*

About 60 A.D. Festus replaced Felix as Roman procurator. When
Festus took over his duties, he found St. Paul among the
prisoners in jail in Caesarea. He discovered that Paul was a
prisoner in Caesarea because, Paul claimed, if he had to await
trial in Jerusalem, he would be killed by those avid Jews who
were wrongly convinced that Paul had violated the holiness of
the Temple by bringing a Gentile into a part where he was
forbidden to enter. Indeed, giving credence to the possibility that
Paul would be killed without trial, the Romans had brought Paul
to jail in Caesarea, only to let him languish there for two years;
no one was willing to bribe the procurator, Felix, for Paul's
freedom. Now Festus looks into the case of this Paul and
ultimately agrees to hear Paul's case himself. Because Herod
Agrippa II, great-great-grandson of Herod the Great and ruler of
some of the territories on Israel's northern border, was nearby,

the procurator Festus invited him and his sister, Bernice, to hear this Paul defend himself; after all, Herod Agrippa II did know quite a bit about Judaism and thus should be able to help Festus figure out the intricacies of this Jewish case.

Paul's speech to Festus, Herod Agrippa II and Bernice, and the court was the third and final effort of the Acts of the Apostles to recount of Paul's conversion and mission for Christianity. Earlier, the author of Acts had described Paul's conversion and mission in chapter nine and had Paul tell to a Jewish audience in chapter twenty-two his own story of this same conversion and mission experience. Now, in a sense offering Paul's culminating speech to all of the Acts of the Apostles, Luke has Paul rehearse again the basic cause which explains Paul's Christianity and his determination to give this Christianity to others.

Why did Luke tell this conversion and mission story three times? The answer to this question lies in another trait of the Acts of the Apostles. The Acts has as one of its goals to emphasize that the teachings received by the Christians of 85 A.D. are those given in the lifetime of Jesus. The objection to this claim was that many Christians of 85 A.D. were taught by people who never knew Jesus, who had never been in Palestine. Indeed Paul not only did not know Jesus, but he also opposed Christianity with all his strength; why should he be trusted to convey with accuracy the teachings of Jesus? To answer this objection, Luke three times noted that Paul, even at the moment when he was most unwilling and perverse, was directly chosen by the Lord; with this divine approval Luke nailed down the trustworthiness of Paul.

To recite something three times accentuates its importance. Luke, however, told the story three times with changes of perspective apt for each telling. Thus, in the first account in chapter nine, the reader is simply meeting the event, and is given only some indication why Jesus intervened in Paul's life. This telling explains why Paul began to act as he did and eventually why he became the missionary we discover in chapters thirteen and fourteen. With the telling in chapter twenty-two we are in a different set of circumstances. Here Paul's Christianity was seen as an apostasy from Judaism and from God. Thus the second telling is so worded as to show that, quite to the contrary, Paul was simply carrying out what God himself wants him to do. Thus, Paul was truer to God than those who oppose him.

The third telling of Paul's conversion and missioning highlights both the fact that Jesus directly commissions Paul on

Jesus' behalf and the language of this missioning. Paul's efforts to represent Jesus are painted by Jesus in the broadest strokes, against a world view of darkness and light, the kingdom of Satan and the kingdom of God, in which Paul would bring faith, forgiveness of sins and share in the inheritance of the sanctified. To these words of Jesus was added Paul's own description, that he has said nothing more than was said in the Jewish Scriptures, "The Christ would suffer and, risen from the dead, would proclaim that light shines now for our people and for the pagans, too."

In this way Luke presented the most thrilling and profound analysis of Paul's missionary effort in all the Acts of the Apostles. In this way, too, he offered the justification for Paul's astounding turnabout, from persecutor of the Christians to champion of Christ. This speech, like so many other elements of the Acts of the Apostles, traces the cause of events to the divine will and intervention. The mystery and success of Paul was to be found in God's plan, God's determination to offer himself once again to all mankind, despite the ignorance or pettiness of human beings who try to stop the fulfillment of the divine will. It was here at Caesarea by the Sea that Paul gave the most glowing account of why he became what he became and how profound was the life's work he undertook for God, for the Lord Jesus.

Jacob's Well (Sychar)

Sychar

(Jacob's Well)

Travellers between Galilee and Judaea often stop at a site called Jacob's Well. They pass through a gate and a lovely garden of a church into the church itself, in the midst of which is a venerable well. Much of the church is modern, since its construction dates from the early part of this century, and was delayed by World War I and lack of funds. The ancient water source beneath the church surely goes back to the time of Jacob, the son of Isaac and grandson of Abraham. The present well is about one hundred feet deep, as we can sense from the time it takes an object to hit the water. The water is fresh and good for drinking; it is what is called *living water,* water which comes from running water and is distinct from the water which is gathered in cisterns from rainfalls and becomes brackish and stale after standing a long time.

In St. Jerome's time, 404 A.D., there was already a church here; a baptistry occupied this site before the church . In Jesus' time a town called Sychar was near this freshwater well. One day about noon, Jesus stopped here to rest from the heat, and sent his disciples into the village for food. Alone and resting, Jesus sees a woman coming to draw water from the well; as she begins to draw water, Jesus asks her for a drink. This was the famous encounter of Jesus and the Samaritan woman at the well, told in Jn 4.

The Samaritan People

The Old Testament suggests the origin of the Samaritan people is to be found in the eighth century B.C. population that made up the area of Israel beginning about ten miles north of Jerusalem. Though this northern area had been made up of tribes of Israelites ever since the Israelites crossed the Jordan river under

Joshua, successor to Moses, the destruction of the area's capital city, Samaria, in 722/1 B.C. by the Assyrians drove almost all Jews from northern Israel. The city had been built about 875 B.C. on land bought from a certain Shemer. When the Assyrians conquered it, they, as was their custom, gave to the entire area controlled by the town of Samaria the name of Samaria. Further, as was their custom, the victorious Assyrians deported about twenty-seven thousand Israelites and imported many foreigners; by doing this, the Assyrians hoped to so upset people that they hardly had time to think of revolution. To the Jews of the south, the capital of which was Jerusalem, what they saw to the north of them in Samaria was ultimately a paganized population which worshipped false gods. This was a people to be avoided at all costs.

It should be noted, however, that the Samaritans of today, of which there are fewer than six hundred in the world, three hundred at the foot of Mount Gerizim near the Samaritan well, tell a different history. They say they are descendants of those Israelites who remained faithful to the religion of Abraham, Isaac, and Jacob, even through the time of the Assyrian conquest. The southerners, they contend, are the ones who have fallen away from the true God.

When the southern Jews were permitted by Cyrus the Persian to return to Jerusalem and its surrounding area, Judaea, the Samaritans tried to block the building of Jerusalem's walls; this was an obvious effort to keep Jerusalem a second-rate town and no threat to Samaria just forty miles away.

Once the Jews were settled in Jerusalem and the Jerusalem Temple rebuilt—it was dedicated in 515 B.C.—there were sporadic fights between Jerusalem and Samaria, culminating in Jerusalem's destruction of the Samaritan Temple on Mount Gerizim about a hundred years before the birth of Jesus. History can recount the reasons for the unhealed scars of Samaritans and Jews; on any given day, in Jesus' time, one could sense the bitter antagonism between these two groups. Ironically, it was not Pilate's bloody treatment of Jesus that got him removed from his procuratorship in Judaea, but his bloody massacre of Samaritans.

If we grasp the hatred that existed between Jew and Samaritan, we have the key to understanding what Jesus was teaching in the story about the Jew who was cared for by a Samaritan, when a Jewish priest and a Jewish levite had preferred to leave the half-dead Jew to his own resources (Lk 10:29–37). And we can better understand the astonishment expressed in the story of the ten lepers, cured of their leprosy; it was only one of them who returned to thank Jesus—and he was a Samaritan (Lk 17:11–19).

Jesus and the Woman at the Well   *Jn 4:4-24*

Here we find Jesus quite willing to ask a Samaritan woman for a favor. Even she, sinner though she was according to Jewish and Samaritan standards, recognized the impropriety of Jesus, a Jew, speaking to her, a Samaritan.

John recounts the story of what occurred at Jacob's Well. It was not surprising, therefore, that almost immediately there develops a play on words: here the pivotal word is *water.* Quickly Jesus was identified, for those who can grasp his meaning, as the one who can provide the water that wells up forever in a human being. From a remark of the evangelist in chapter seven, clearly this unending source of water is the Holy Spirit of God, to be given after Jesus has died and risen. The Holy Spirit is the living water, the water that is so much better than any other water on which people look for refreshment, health and life itself.

But the gospel writer was interested in further piercing the identity of Jesus. Jesus was professed to be a prophet, on the basis of his knowledge of the woman whom he has never met. This gave the evangelist the opportunity to make clear the Christian position on worship of God which he championed in the 90s A.D. The Jewish Temple was destroyed by the Romans by 70 A.D. This destruction implied that true worship of Yahweh was not to be found in Jewish or Samaritan temples but in acceptance of Jesus, for with Jesus one was finally worthy to offer God the sacrifice worthy of Him.

The woman knew enough of her religion to respond to the future described by Jesus, a future beyond Gerizim and Jerusalem; it was the time of the Messiah. True to the convictions of the Gospel of John, Jesus told the woman that the person expected at the end of time was already here. It was John, above all other New Testament works, which underlines the presence in this world of characteristics of God's kingdom normally reserved for the world to come.

When Jesus identified himself to the woman who was looking for the Messiah: "I am he," many scholars suspect that

the words "I am he" are meant to recall the words by which
Yahweh identified himself to Moses at the burning bush. To
Moses God said his name was "I am who am," or in abbreviated
form, "I am." The Greek translation of this formula "I am" was
the precise wording that Jesus used about himself here with the
Samaritan woman and elsewhere in John. Was Jesus taking to
himself the name which had come to be associated only with the
God of Israel? In this understanding, Jesus' reply to the woman
was not "I am the Messiah," but I am "I am."

Jesus had said enough to move the Samaritan woman to go
into the village of Sychar to spread the news that a prophet,
quite possibly the Messiah, was at the Well. The townspeople
believed her witness and came to study this impressive stranger.
Jesus acceded to their wishes and stayed with them two days,
when the people said that they no longer depended on the
woman's witness about Jesus; now they believed in him without
needing her as intermediary. This is probably a subtle reference
to how a person in later decades was first introduced to Jesus
through the witness of a preacher, but then was so deeply united
to Jesus that the preacher was no longer needed.

Scholars often wonder at the reception of Jesus by certain of
the Samaritans, at least, insofar as in the synoptic gospels Jesus
has nothing to do with Samaritans in their villages; in Luke, in
fact, Jesus' disciples are rejected when they try to enter a
Samaritan village on their way from Galilee to Jerusalem.

Yet, when we take into consideration the success of the
early Christian preaching in Samaria by Philip, as narrated in
Acts 8, we are aware that for some time before the writing of
John, Christianity found a home in Samaria. Perhaps the Gospel
of John recounted a story about Samaria because by the time of
its writing the Samaritans had found the teaching of Jesus and
his person eminently credible.

When the woman had gone into the village to tell the
Samaritan villagers about this striking stranger at the Well, Jesus'
disciples return with food which Jesus had sent them into the
village to find. They were astonished that Jesus had been
speaking to a Samaritan woman—but then Jesus' sense of
charity broke many barriers others had, even for religious
reasons, erected. They bring Jesus food, which becomes an
opportunity for Jesus to express to his friends the deeper hunger
he has—a hunger for all peoples to know and love his Father
through belief in himself. So ripe was the harvest, so ready are

people to accept true preaching about the real God, the God who alone can save them—if only there were people to bring the saving words of God to those ripe for such harvesting!

Other Samaritan Sites

Such then are the events associated with the well traditionally noted as the well dug by Jacob when he pitched his tents with his family outside the town of Shechem. The ninth century B.C. town of Samaria had succeeded Shechem as the most important city in the kingdom of the north, called Israel, after the division of the kingdom after the death of Solomon. But it was the Shechem of old where we would find the cenotaph of Joseph, brought from Egypt by his relatives after they fled slavery in their exodus. One can still explore, near the Well of Jacob, the remains of ancient Samaria, where such famous people as Ahab and Jezebel lived and died. But not only are Samaria and Shechem near Jacob's Well; so is Mount Gerizim, the famous mountain on which the Samaritans built their own altar to Yahweh, the famous mountain from which were sung the blessings on Israel associated with the covenant made with Yahweh. Finally, the ancient town of Samaria, destroyed in the invasion of the Northern Kingdom by the Assyrians in 722 B.C., was resurrected from the dust and, much later, gloriously renovated by Herod the Great and given a new name, Sebaste, which is the Greek equivalent of *Augustus;* thus, the ancient city was newly dedicated to the famous Roman emperor and protector of Herod the Great: Julius Caesar Augustus.

part 2
Judaea

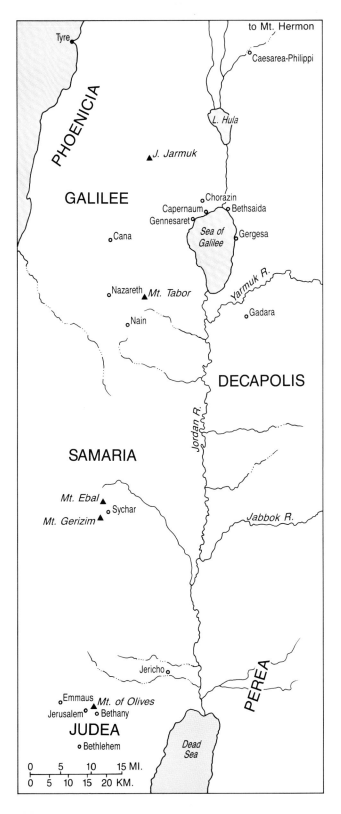

Church of St. John the Baptizer (Ein Karem)

E in Karem

About four miles west of Jerusalem is the little town of Ein Karem. The fame of Ein Karem lies in the tradition that here lived Elizabeth and Zachary and their child, John, someday to be called the Baptizer or Baptist. Here we find two church buildings associated with traditions which honor this town and its environs as holy to Christians: the Church of St. John the Baptizer in the town and the Church of the Visitation very close to the town. To reach the Church of the Visitation, one usually takes a route from the Church of St. John which passes by a spring called, since the 1300s A.D., the Fountain of the Vineyard, which was the meaning of *Ein (Fountain) Karem (Vineyard).* Both churches, though rather updated, have paintings of great worth, and trace their roots to traditions that John and his parents lived in the areas on which the churches were built.

Two major gospel episodes are associated with this small village. The first we shall consider was the meeting of Mary and Elizabeth, called the Visitation of Elizabeth by Mary; the second was the psalm spoken by Zachary, John's father, at the time of the circumcising and naming of his child, John.

Visitation of Mary *Lk 1:39-56*

In Nazareth, Mary was visited by an angel who, to support the message he was delivering to her from God, told Mary that her relative—no clearer relationship can be defined—Elizabeth was to have a child; indeed, though Elizabeth, naturally speaking, could have no child, she was already in the sixth month of her pregnancy. Mary, responding to what she knew would be appreciated help in the last three months of the pregnancy, hurries from Nazareth to reach the "hill country of Judah," about eighty miles south of Nazareth. The Bible does not identify the town Mary hastened to, but tradition says it was Ein Karem.

Elizabeth greeted Mary in words and thoughts inspired by

the Holy Spirit. Under the guidance of the Spirit, Elizabeth said things which no human could have said on her own: Mary was the mother of my Lord; Mary was to be considered blessed, for she believed that what the Lord told her would actually happen. Elizabeth was inspired to understand things she could not naturally understand; the child of her womb leapt at the presence of the newly conceived Jesus. This, too, was a way of indicating to Elizabeth in whose presence she stood.

Mary's response to Elizabeth's inspired words, "mother of my Lord," was a psalm known by the first word in its Latin translation, the *Magnificat,* which means *makes much of* or *glorifies.* The psalm was divisible into three parts. First, Mary acknowledges that God's intervention has freed her from her lowliness and made her one who would be praised for all ages. Secondly, Mary's reflection on what God has done for her turns into a remembrance of the many times God has saved and would save the poor, the suffering, the lowly, the downtrodden, the people traditionally oppressed by the uncaring powerful and rich. Thus, what happened to Mary was typical of God: he was always aware of and caring for the lowly, and Mary's case was just one more example of this awareness and caring. Thirdly, this reflection about God's eagerness to help those whom human beings often oppress brings to mind the ancient fact that God had long ago promised Mary's forefathers, indeed Abraham himself, that he would always come to the defense of his chosen ones.

In looking over the entire psalm, we get the feeling that Mary did not regard her pregnancy as a concern of herself alone. Rather she was once more Israel itself, the people chosen by God yet so often abused and trodden upon. It was a psalm of encouragement: what seems to have happened, that God abandoned his people in their lowliness and poverty, was a misunderstanding; rather, Israel should recall the many times God has intervened on Israel's behalf—and this pregnancy of Mary's was one more example—and Israel should never forget that such interventions were promised at the very beginning of Israel's foundation in Abraham.

Thus the psalm sung by Mary is, in the plan of Luke's Infancy narratives, a strong expression of conviction that Jesus was the flowering of promises traceable all the way back to Abraham; Jesus was the fulfillment of what God had long ago assured mankind: he would intervene and save human beings from the tragic consequences of sin which are summed up in death. Praised would be the virgin mother of Jesus, for all ages, but, as she herself indicated, praised even more would be the God who constantly shows his intense desire to save mankind, no matter what the odds. Jesus was his fullest answer, his fullest saving intervention.

Psalm of Zachery   *Lk 1:57-79*

Some three months after the meeting of Mary and Elizabeth, and eight days after the birth of John, Zachary was asked to give a name to his child. He writes, for he was dumb since Gabriel had spoken to him in the Jerusalem Temple, that the child should be called "John." A strange name, for no one in Zachary's family had ever borne that name. But, as the reader of Luke already knows, God wants the child named John, which means "God was kind, loving." Zachary obeys this divine will. At this obedience, Zachary can speak again, and his first words are words of praise of God. Zachary begins with a typical Jewish prayer vocabulary: "Blessed be God." The first word *blessed* was translated in Latin by the word *benedictus;* hence, Zachary's prayer of praise, a psalm, was called the *Benedictus.*

The first part of the *Benedictus,* about 55 per cent of the hymn, has to do with the coming of Jesus; the second part of the hymn begins with a direct address to the child John, but it also ends with the greater event, the coming of Jesus.

In the first part of the hymn, Zachary was at pains to make clear his praise for the God who has, at long last, brought to reality the hoped-for coming of the Saving Power of God. He mentioned two promises God made in times past: a promise made through the prophets that a savior would appear from the lineage of David, a promise made to Abraham and to all his offspring. The center of the hymn is the explicitation of this promise to Abraham and shows the ultimate reason for Israel's existence: the promise is, concretely, that Israel would be freed from its enemies and rid of all fear. And why this freedom from foe and fear? So that Israel could, by freedom, live a life thoroughly filled with obedience, holiness and worship. It was Israel's deepest calling, its highest perfection as human, to worship God; it was for this that Israel must be free from enemy and fear itself, the things that could in so many ways make Israel unable to fulfill its very reason for existence. From this picture we grasp the purpose and goal of Jesus; he was the savior that makes it possible for human beings to be their very best selves.

Zachary now reflected on the role of his child in this great, unfolding plan of God. John was not the savior, but he has the role of a prophet who prepares for the coming of God and that worship which God deserves. He would do this by moving Israelites to repentance, to free themselves from the state which keeps them from their true purpose in life: the worship of God. This repentance would surely be received kindly by God and so forgiveness of sins could be assured to anyone who repents of those sins. Did John, though not the savior, contribute in some way to the sense of being freed from one's foes? Zachary identified forgiveness of sins as an experience of salvation, an experience of being set free from bondage so that one could be fully human, that is, a worshiper who could worship fully, holily. In this way John was a prelude to the one who would offer the complete salvation, Jesus.

Zachary concluded his praise of God by suggesting imagery which very adeptly indicated the greatness of what God was about to do. Zachary saw mankind living in darkness and under the shadow of death. For ages, these two images—darkness and the shadow of death—have operated in various societies and cultures to depict in image what reason itself cannot fully express. The natural shrinking before darkness and the shadow of death are powerful images of the bondage in which human beings live and from which they cannot ever hope to extricate themselves. All the more, then, we can appreciate the appearance of the sun, warmth and light against darkness and the shadow of death. In this way the role of Jesus was emotionally heightened and we can grasp in a very fundamental way the goodness and joy that should flow from his coming. It was he who would set us on the road to peace, a road once closed to those in darkness and very near death.

Both the *Magnificat* of Mary and the *Benedictus* of Zachary are replete with the sense of old promises now being fulfilled; the very language and thought patterns of the hymns are drawn directly from the Old Testament. Indeed, it was Luke's claim through his Gospel's first two chapters that the Jesus event, which includes John the Baptizer, has long been planned for by God, that Christianity was the natural fulfillment of the words of God throughout the Old Testament. Now was the Savior here; the longing for and promise of freedom to be fully what a human being should be—this was what Mary and Zachary sing about in their glorious psalms in praise of God's merciful salvation.

Jordan River in Galilee

The Jordan River

John the Baptizer   *Lk 3:1-20; Jn 1:19-34*

It was not certain just where John the Baptizer performed his baptisms, but we cannot be far off in looking to the area on the west side along the Jordan River north of the Dead Sea. John the Evangelist identified a site as "Bethany on the far side of the Jordan" (Jn 1:28); but that Bethany has never been discovered. Somewhere in this desert, people of Jerusalem and the nearby countryside were the first to listen to John and repent, as he asked. Soon people flocked to John from farther distances to listen to his message of repentance.

As Luke tells it, the father of John, Zachary, had been told by an angel that John was to go before the Lord, to prepare a people for him (See 190). He would prepare them under the inspiration of the Holy Spirit, who would dwell in John from his very conception. More specifically, John would be another Elijah, who was the greatest of Israel's prophets. Elijah, in the middle of the ninth century B.C., stood alone to defend, within Israel, its worship of the one and only God, Yahweh. Some nine hundred years later, another Elijah, John, would again call Israel to recognize the rights of Yahweh to Israel's obedience. But he would add a new dimension to this call to repentance: Israel must realize that the Lord was "at hand," "near." The message of John thus underlines both the need for repentance and the need for it now, because there was so little time before repentance would not be accepted. It would fall to Christian thinkers of the first century A.D. to find a way to insist on the need for repentance, without arguing that the new age was at hand, was near.

The New Elijah

In speaking of John the Baptizer as the new Elijah, we should be aware of a prophecy spoken by the prophet Malachi and recorded in his writing in the Old Testament. Malachi, in anticipation of the renewal of Israel after its destruction and humiliation by Babylon, looked forward to the coming of Yahweh and the introduction of a new state of things called the kingdom of God, a situation in which the will of God and his love for Israel would dominate. To prepare Israel for this coming, for this new state of things, various figures are foreseen as persons who would appear in time to ready Israel for its God. One of these figures was the "angel of the covenant," another was called "my messenger," and a third was identified as Elijah the prophet who was to come "before my day, the great and terrible day." This prophecy of Malachi, enmeshed with many others, made the people of Israel in the first century A.D. particularly sensitive and initially willing to listen to anyone whose message seemed to be a fulfillment of what the prophecies had foreseen. One should remember the particular twist that Elijah never died; he was taken up to heaven in a fiery chariot. Thus he was destined to come again. This alertness to the prophecies was what accounts for the people's willingness to listen to Jesus, too; perhaps he was one of those spoken of by the prophets? Indeed, as the synoptic Gospels report, people thought of Jesus as "the prophet like Moses, Elijah, Jeremiah, or one of the prophets," all figures which would prepare the people for God's coming; the disciples, on the other hand, think of Jesus as Messiah, another figure who was expected to prepare for God's kingdom.

The Message of John

What did John the Baptizer preach? Certainly, he called the people to repentance; various sources in the New Testament witness to this. But it was Luke who makes more concrete the meaning of repentance. That is, if one was truly sorry for disobedience to the will of Yahweh expressed in the law of Moses, one should set himself to produce deeds appropriate to repentance, to sorrow for sin. Luke gives three examples of the direction these deeds follow. People in general ask what they should do; the answer was simply: "If you have two tunics and another has none, share—and the same goes for food." Tax collectors, who in Israel then had an automatic and justly deserved reputation for injustice, ask in the same vein; the answer is: "Exact no more than was your due." Finally, military police, associated with the Jerusalem Temple, put their question to John; the answer: "Do not intimidate people; do not extort, but be content with your pay!" Though we cannot go further than the evidence allows, we are struck that the deeds appropriate to repentance are all in the area of justice and charity. It was true that Luke's general outlook emphasizes charity and justice, and so what he reports of John was fitted into this format. Yet, it was particularly striking to see the emphasis given to love of neighbor, with no reference made to worship of God, prayer, penance.

The general thrust of John's message, which was repentance and change of life, may lead us to conclude with many scholars that John, at an early age, was trained not at home but within one or other of the religious communities to be then found in the desert regions along the Jordan River or Dead Sea. The now-famous Qumran community at the northwestern zone of the Dead Sea was one of many communities which, in sharp disagreement with the Judaism in control of the Temple and dominating the theology of Israel, separated themselves to live their own interpretation of Judaism found in the documents of the Old Testament. It was not surprising, if John had been a young apprentice in one of these dissident groups, that John would have been sensitized to the theme of many of these communities: that God was coming and demands the repentance of his people in order that he and they may live in harmony and love once again.

But John's greatest contribution to the Christian tradition was his witness to Jesus. John turned people's attention to Jesus: John was only the best man, Jesus was the groom; John must decrease, but Jesus must increase; John considers himself to be less than a slave to Jesus, for John thinks he was not worthy to even loose the strap of Jesus' sandals—the task of a slave. John presented his whole mission as a preparation for the coming of Jesus, not simply as a preparation for the coming of God. John was not the Light, but gave witness to the Light.

John and the Coming of the Kingdom

In this interpretation of the meaning of John, we must reformulate traditional thinking. John was not followed immediately by the coming of God's kingdom. John was followed immediately by Jesus, who, in turn, would bring about the kingdom of God. What eventually distinguished Jesus from John was the realization that, in various ways, Jesus himself was the kingdom of God and not the anticipator of that kingdom. For the power and truth and obedience and life associated with kingdom of God have in reality been expressed in Jesus; indeed, the forgiveness of sins won by Jesus and his entrance into life in the new age witness to the fact that he not only prepares for the new age but was the embodiment of what was to be hoped for in this new age. Those who belong to Jesus share in this new age.

It is to the Gospel of John that we owe the information that some of Jesus' first disciples were disciples of John the Baptizer; these religiously minded men soon found others who were looking for the fulfillment of the prophecies. In a very concrete way, then, John did indeed go before Jesus and prepare his way; John decreased while Jesus increased. That there were to be found disciples of John in 50 A.D., over twenty years after his death, shows that not all John's followers became disciples of Jesus. But the existence of these disciples of John shows that John was a highly regarded religious figure who spoke on God's behalf, and this esteem, in turn, helps explain why John's witness to Jesus was so powerful: John was an admired figure, respected for his integrity and honesty; his witness would instinctively deserve respect and belief. Jesus' own confirmation of the ordinary man's admiration for John further supports belief that John was objective in his witnessing. In this way John served the cause of God and of Christianity in a singular way.

John and Herod Antipas   *Mt 14:3-12; Mk 6:14-29; Lk 3:19-20, 9:7-9*

To look over the sandy desert of the Jordan bed was to look for a figure clad in the poorest garments, which witness, not so much to poverty as to single-mindedness: one thing only mattered, the call to the obedience to God which true and honest repentance promises. That John would offend Herod Antipas was more likely than not to happen. John was not one to be silent about the public and grave sin Herod Antipas, son of Herod the Great and ruler of Galilee, had committed by divorcing his wife to marry Herodias. Herodias had in her own way prepared for marriage to Herod by divorcing her husband Philip in Rome. That Herod Antipas had to deliver the head of John to Herodias' daughter, Salome, seems a cruel fulfillment of his promise to give Salome whatever she wanted in return for a dance. But such were Herod and Herodias; and such was John. Jesus was a bit more adroit than John in avoiding conflict with authority, but in the end he too fell because he would not go back on what he taught and, through his teaching, claimed to be. The fates of John and Jesus, considered on the merely human level, are particularly alike and intertwined.

The Two Baptisms

John, then, was a figure particularly supportive of God and of Jesus. His primary value was as witness to Jesus, but his call to repentance was of immense importance in the saving plan of God. But for all his encouragement of people to return to God, he was clearly distinguishable from Jesus. John's baptism was more like what Catholics call *confession* or the sacrament of reconciliation: to enter the Jordan water—*baptism* means *to be dipped into*—was to publicly confess oneself a sinner and to profess a firm purpose of amendment, to promise a life of deeds befitting a repentant.

The baptism Jesus was understood to bring not only involved repentance for past sins, but assured entry into the people of God and the outpouring of God's very Spirit. There was a newness here, a share in God's life, which was lacking in the simpler baptism of John. From the difference in quality of their baptisms, we can sense the difference in the persons of John and Jesus. It was to Jesus that we owe the life of the Spirit which was the life which animates all that lives in the new age, the age to come.

For all this difference, Jesus praised John as the greatest of the sons of men. The Jordan desert still rings with his piercing cry, the cry of one in the desert: Repent, the kingdom of God was at hand; prepare for Jesus, the Lamb of God.

The Town of Jericho

Jericho

Jericho is famous as the town whose walls were blown down by the horns of Israel at the beginning of its conquest of the Promised Land (Jos 6:1–16). The name *Jericho* refers to three areas. First is the present-day Jericho, pretty and flourishing because of the abundant water supply in an otherwise forbidding desert. Then, quite near modern Jericho is the famous artificial hill whose hidden treasures were made known by archaeological diggings begun in 1867 A.D. This hill covered over at least fifteen layers of cities and towns going back to 7000 B.C. Finally, some distance to the south of the hill are the remains of the Jericho Herod the Great built and in which he died painfully and miserably.

Surely the two events associated with Jesus in the New Testament, a cure and a dinner with Zachaeus, are to be associated with the hill and the first-century town the hill covered. Although Jesus would have walked by the Jericho built by Herod the Great, Herod's city built was really meant for himself and his friends and not for the common man. That Jesus would have been in Jericho at all can surprise people until we realize that the ordinary way to reach Jerusalem from Galilee in Jesus' day was to proceed from Galilee to the Jordan river, then to walk along its banks southward till Jericho, then turn westward and upward—to Jerusalem.

Cure of Blind Man   *Mt 20:29-34; Mk 10:46-52; Lk 18:35-43*

On a visit through Jericho Jesus, praised by crowds who knew of his life, heard a cry: "Jesus, Son of David, have mercy on me!" This miracle gives us the opportunity to reflect on several things pertinent to Jesus' miracle working.

First, there is no record that Jesus ever shirked from working miracles. That he initially refused a miracle for the Syro-Phoenician woman—one from present-day Lebanon, known in the first century A.D. as Phoenicia and Syria—was accounted for by his sense of total dedication to the people of Israel. Jesus did not shy away from working miracles; indeed, he never refused a request and often, without being asked, undertook to work miracles for people whose miserable circumstances never failed to move him.

It was difficult to understand why, despite all this visible show of power, so many people kept asking Jesus for a sign to prove that he was authentically from God. For John, the miracles are clearly the signs by which we are to understand who Jesus was and how intimately related he was to his Father. It was ultimately a mystery why these signs cannot be read properly; people who cannot pierce their meaning are labeled as "of this world," "from below," "blind," "not taught by my Father," "children of the father of lies." For other Gospels, too, there was a struggle to understand the ultimately mysterious failure of so many people to grasp the meaning of the miracles which was so obvious: Jesus' power to cure was the sign of divine approbation of Jesus.

But for all the episodes concerned with miracle working and for all Jesus' willingness to work miracles, it is clear that Christianity is not a religion rooted in this miraculous power. On the contrary, Christianity, compared to other suggested ways of finding life's ultimate happiness, is hardly one that promises physical and psychological, sociological and political peace and joy. Christianity is, ultimately, a religion looking only to conversion to love of God and neighbor: the rest of man's longings might well be fulfilled only in the age to come, after he has left this world. Thus miracles take a very secondary place in Christianity—unless we designate repentance and conversion as miracles. The surest sign of the tenuous relationship of miracle working to essential Christianity is the death of Jesus. If ever a miracle should have saved someone, a miracle should have saved the one most beloved by God—but it did not. The cross revealed not Jesus' power to escape it but his love and devotion to embrace it as something the Father wanted from Jesus. In other words, Jesus occasionally worked miracles, but every moment sought out the will of his Father. This difference in "frequency" indicates what was essential and what was secondary in Christianity.

But we should say more. Many scholars believe that Mark wrote his Gospel to de-emphasize the wonder working of Jesus. Mark seems to have been convinced that his readers needed to understand the full meaning of Jesus, especially that he died painfully, ignominiously, like a fool, powerlessly. To embrace Jesus because of his power is to run the risk of misunderstanding Jesus completely. The fundamental lesson of Christianity is to be found in the cross, the seed dying so that beautiful things might blossom, repentance. One cannot minimize, in this regard, the complete lack of reference to miracles in the entire block of writings attributed to St. Paul.

In a certain sense, the Gospels are a welcome corrective to Pauline theology, for Paul looks for the meaning of Jesus only in Jesus' death and resurrection; the public life of Jesus, as well as his infancy, have no place in the writings of Paul. Christianity, then, is linked closely to the person of Jesus Christ, but we must understand this Jesus Christ to be the one who, above all else, wants my repentance and does all he can to make possible the union of God and man in free choice. Miracle working has its place in this plan. It was an assurance of the love and presence of God, even if a miracle was not worked for all who need one. One was aware, through a miracle, that the thrust of God's love was to make every human being whole. That everyone must wait till the resurrection from the dead for this wholeness does not deny the reality; the miracle which occasionally burst through the laws of this age shouts out the eventual destiny of everyone who belongs to Jesus. This was what the people of Jesus' time failed to grasp: that, though a miracle was not the solution for salvation, it was the sign of what salvation meant—the healing and perfection of the entire human being.

For New Testament authors, a physical miracle is a sign of the deeper salvation to which each person is called. One is supposed to cherish the miracle because it grounds hope that we can possess that spiritual healing which is, alone, the healing necessary for any permanent salvation.

The history of Christianity has shown how God can, for his own good reasons, interrupt the nature of sickness and disease to make a person physically whole. One has the right to say that God loves so much that he would even change the patterns of this life to further the happiness of the beloved. But Christianity argues, in the person of Jesus for whom the one miracle was lacking when he needed it most, that salvation was essentially a change of heart; it was this Jesus came to work in every person, and, with understanding of life Jesus has brought, we can affirm the rightness of freely chosen reunion with God as the essential ingredient to complete salvation. In short, no one for whom a miracle was worked, by Jesus or by another, ever was said to have avoided further suffering, sin, and death. Total salvation lies elsewhere than in physical cure in this life. What was very helpful and consoling was that the physical miracles of Jesus have shown that Jesus was concerned to make us whole and has the power to do it.

Zachaeus   *Lk 19:1-10*

At Jericho one day, as crowds swarmed about Jesus, a very short man had trouble seeing Jesus. He was an enterprising person, and so he finds a tree to climb, a sycamore, one of three wild trees indigenous to Israel; the others are oak and carob. Jesus notices Zachaeus aloft in the sycamore and spontaneously offers to come to Zachaeus's house, if Zachaeus wants this. One must be able to understand the subtlety of what Jesus was doing here to grasp the logic of the story. Jesus was aware of the type of man Zachaeus is. Zachaeus was one of those tax collectors in Israel who grossly overcharged people in the collection of taxes. Everyone knew this, not just Jesus. To say he was willing to dine with Zachaeus was an implicit call on Zachaeus to accept all that Jesus stands for. Zachaeus understands this, for his welcome to Jesus includes what he knows Jesus was most concerned about: Zachaeus was willing to return four times as much to those from whom he has gouged money and to live from now on in fairness to others. The normal penalty for stealing money as Zachaeus stole it from his clients was repayment four times the value of what was stolen; thus Zachaeus was only being fair in his offer of repayment announced to Jesus. Repentance, then, was what Jesus sought, not a meal. His contemporaries could not understand why Jesus would associate with a sinner like Zachaeus. But this story, as so very many others, shows the unflagging determination of Jesus to offer each person the essence of salvation, the opportunity to repent, to reestablish one's friendship with God. This union restored, it follows with the most rigorous logic that the divine love and power would make thoroughly whole, indeed thoroughly new, the newly-won beloved of his heart.

Entrance to a Cave in Bethlehem

Bethlehem

Birth of Jesus   *Lk 2:1-21*

Jesus was born in Bethlehem. Mark and John do not refer to
Jesus' birth in Bethlehem; Luke and Matthew inform us of the
role Bethlehem played in the story of Jesus. Though Matthew
does not explain how the Holy Family came to be associated
with Bethlehem, Luke was very clear: a census was ordered by
the Roman emperor, Caesar Augustus. To comply with this order
meant that each Jew had to go to his ancestral home town to be
counted for the census; thus, although Joseph lived in Nazareth,
he had to travel to Bethlehem, the town of his forefathers, to
register for the census. Since Joseph's wife was pregnant, he
evidently preferred to have her with him than to leave her at
home. Through these circumstances Joseph and Mary arrived in
Bethlehem.

We can explain in purely human and historical terms why
Joseph and Mary are in Bethlehem when she was about to
deliver a child. Yet another world of influence was to be
considered here: the world of God and of his plans for the
salvation of the world. According to the Scriptures God wants the
world saved by a person who comes from the "line of David." If
David was anointed king of Israel, the greatest king of Israel, the
anointed, which means *messiah* and *Christ,* would be a
descendant of David; more specifically, he would even be born in
the town in which David was born, where David was king for
seven years before moving to Jerusalem. Thus, while Joseph
found himself in Bethlehem out of obedience to a royal edict, the
plan of God, which overarches all human devising, was fulfilled in
having Jesus born of the line of David even in the town of David.

Strangely enough, neither Matthew nor Luke spends time
telling of the birth of Jesus or the moments which led up to it. At
best Matthew states that Jesus was born, and inserts this
sentence between the angel's message to Joseph which occurred
some short time after Joseph noticed that Mary was pregnant,

and the coming of the magi, which probably occurred over a year after Jesus was born. Luke, on the other hand, tells of Joseph's being turned away from the usual places where a traveler could spend a night—this was close to the time of Jesus' birth; and Luke describes the visit of the angel to shepherds on the evening of the day of Jesus' birth. But this was all that Luke associates with Bethlehem, for the next story in the Infancy narration describes an event in Jerusalem forty days after Jesus' birth.

Thus the New Testament has little detail on the actual birth of Jesus. Why this was so was not quite clear. Perhaps there simply was no more information available to the gospel writers. But it was more likely that the birth of Jesus, like the rest of the Infancy narratives in both Matthew and Luke served a purpose different from what we expect. Let us discuss this reason for a moment.

In the scientific study of the Gospels, scholars believe that Mark's was the first Gospel and was read by Matthew and Luke. One implication of this opinion was that Matthew and Luke were not content to simply pass on Mark to their readers; each evangelist decided to write his own Gospel, though basing it on Mark's work and using Mark generously as a source for himself. From this perspective we must say that both Matthew and Luke, each in his own way, expanded Mark's basic outline and series of stories by beginning the Gospel with something new: Matthew and Luke decided to begin with stories about Jesus' infancy.

But there is a further implication here. The Gospel of Mark is an attempt to organize individually developed and transmitted stories into a narrative, beginning with the appearance of Jesus as an adult and ending with the death and resurrection of Jesus. This then was the essence of the gospel, this was its core. It was the adult Jesus—preacher, teacher, and wonder worker, opposed, betrayed, tried and killed, raised up on the third day—who forms the center of the gospel; it was his words and deeds which proclaim good news to all mankind.

From this point of view, the childhood stories are not at the center of the gospel story, but serve as an introduction. The Infancy stories are meant to convey to the reader a sense of the meaning of Jesus before the adult Jesus steps onto the stage as central actor. One of the great difficulties of Jesus' own contemporaries is that they had no "introduction" to Jesus such as what the Gospels of Matthew and Luke presents to their readers. The Gospels, in the light of the resurrection at the end of Jesus' earthly ministry, can reconstruct the life of Jesus by hindsight; they can also provide stories to introduce this contruction, stories influenced by what the writers came to know after the entire life of Jesus has been lived. Thus, the infancy stories are not at the center of the Gospel narrative, but prepare the reader to understand Jesus and his words and deeds as best as possible. This is the contibution of literature, an improvement over historically having to come to grips with Jesus over a few minutes' or hours' or even months' time. In other words, we readers know more about Jesus before he ever began his life of ministry than many of his contemporaries ever concluded about him after spending a long time with him; this is the gift of the infancy stories, this is their purpose. Let us investigate, then, what the Bethlehem stories have to tell us about the future adult Jesus.

There is throughout the Gospels a recurring question about the origin of the Messiah, of the Blessed One of God: from where would he come? At times, and in some Jewish circles, the Messiah was to have no known origin, and this underlines his uniqueness and mysteriousness. He is from God; to say that he is from one particular place would only undermine the supernaturality of the Messiah who was from nowhere on earth.

Most Jews of Jesus' time, however, understood that the Messiah should come from David's line, and presumably from David's town. When Herod the Great, at the prodding of the magi, asks his own wise men, "where was to be born the King of the Jews?" the answer he receives points directly to Bethlehem. And this answer was drawn directly from the Jewish Scriptures. Thus, that Jesus was born here in Bethlehem was to link Jesus with the plan of God that foretold an identifying characteristic of God's holy Messiah; the reader already knows the messianic qualification of Jesus before he ever does or says anything messianic.

This effort of the Gospels to locate Jesus' Davidic origins explains the genealogy of Jesus with which Matthew begins his Gospel. Jesus was clearly identified there as son of Abraham and son of David. Genealogically, we can trace Jesus' roots backward through Joseph to David and to Abraham. Of course, Matthew wanted not only to show how Jesus related to David; he wanted also to intimate that Jesus was the one who fulfills the promise made to David, that, if there was to be a king on the throne of Israel, that king would be Jesus, born from the line of David. Likewise, when Matthew specifically notes that Jesus was son of

Abraham, he means us to see in Jesus the fulfillment of the promise God made to Abraham, that through his offspring, Jesus, would all the nations of the world be blessed.

Both Matthew and Luke take time to explain more precisely the relationship of Jesus to David; they would not have had to do this, if the conception of Jesus had been simply normal. But the conception was not normal. Joseph qualified as Jesus' father only in the legal sense; God, though not having sexual intercourse with Mary, was emphatically said to have caused Jesus' existence and qualities on the analogy of fatherhood. Thus the relationship of Jesus with David was a bit more tenuous than we might hope; yet in the legal sense and as legal heir to David, Jesus qualified as son of David.

Visit of the Magi   *Mt 2:1-18*

Another way of saying that Jesus was son of David, heir of the promise made to David, is to say that Jesus was king of Israel. This was exactly what the magi sought: the king of Israel. To understand better this story of the magi and their quest, we should review for a moment the meaning and activity of magi.

A *magus—magi* is the word's plural—is essentially a wise man; the origin of magi seems to be the area of present-day Iran and Iraq. Such a wise man was a public servant whose task was to study every possible source of information which might bear on the happiness of the kingdom to which the magus belonged. In particular, such a wise man would study to be able to find out about, and perhaps influence, the future, that most significant yet most elusive part of time. If the king could only control the future, at least through knowledge of it, how successfully he might plan his efforts for the stability and peace and prosperity of his kingdom! The wise man was hired to learn, to be able to control all factors which might determine the happiness of the kingdom.

Star of Bethlehem

Though in our civilizations we have limited the sources of knowing the future more so than in earlier ages, we do acknowledge the influence of the heavens on human activity and we still claim that many parts of nature, if understood properly, reveal the directions in which the world was destined to move. It was not surprising, then, to find the magi or wise men of the first century A.D. looking to the heavens in eternal vigil for signs of what the future of the world would be.

To complete this picture, we should realize that the heavens often were divided into zodiacal parts which were meant to fit a similar division of the earth. Moreover, planets and other heavenly bodies were ascribed to powers and gods. Thus the planet Mars was a planet which signified war. All this has bearing on the story of the magi, in the following fashion.

If we admit that our astronomical records show no appearance of an unusual star at the time of Jesus' birth, we can still point to a unique convergence or lineup of planets as they relate to earth. That is, only every 805 years do Jupiter, Saturn, and Mars come so near one other and Earth that we can call them *lined up* in relation to Earth. The last time this lineup occurred was in 1604 A.D.; one earlier than that was in 799 A.D.— and the one before that happened in 6 B.C., the time now believed to be the birth year of Jesus. If we suppose that Matthew, for a reason which we would investigate in a moment, termed what was really a rare convergence of planets a star we should suppose the magi thought in this way: *Mars* signifies *warrior*; *Jupiter* signifies *king.* In what part of the heavens did this convergence take place in 6 B.C.? It happened in the zone of Pisces, which generally stood for the Hebrew people and had connotations of the "last days of this age." Jupiter, too, was god of the people who lived in the area in which Israelites found themselves for centuries. All this should yield the following interpretation: a king of power was born for the people of Israel. Thus it was quite proper for the magi to inform their own king of the revelation of the heavens that there was born a king of the Jews. And it follows that this king would prudently send representatives and gifts to the king of Israel, in an attempt to assure and solidify good relations with his own kingdom, for now and in the foreseeable future.

But why would Matthew substitute a star for the triple-planet phenomenon? The answer seems to lie in Matthew's desire to use the Jewish Scriptures to elucidate the meaning of Jesus—we are talking, after all, of a simple substitution of means of a heavenly revelation. An ancient prophecy spoke of Israel's leader as a star which would lead Israel to freedom and peace; the *star* was symbol for God's appointed leader for Israel. Thus to link this old prophecy with the heavenly phenomenon witnessed by the magi, Matthew substituted *star* for the rare triple-planet phenomenon.

The magi learned of, and in their own way announced, the birth of the king of the Jews. In search of this child born to the throne of Israel, they stirred up the fear of Herod the Great, who ruled Judaea from 40 B.C. to 4 B.C., "and all Jerusalem with him." Though Herod ultimately directs the magi to Bethlehem, he hopes that through the naivete of the magi he can kill the child.

The magi are led by the star to the place where Jesus was to be found. This place was called a house, thus indicating that the animal shelter, in which Jesus had been born, had been abandoned. Here the magi gave Jesus gifts of gold, frankincense, and myrrh. Each of these gifts was a present suitable for a kingly person. Because of the three gifts, people concluded that there must have been three magi. Because of the ability of various precious scents to cover up odors in a society which was unable to bathe and wash with necessary frequency and because of the costliness of myrrh, which as an ointment used with wrapping cloths would give the body a dignified burial, both the myrrh and the frankincense were understood as very valuable gifts destined for royalty.

The point of the Herod and magi story lies not only in the recognition that Jesus was king, deserving the prostrations of the magi; it was a preview of the larger history which runs from the public life of Jesus to the time of Matthew. The opposition of Herod and all Jerusalem together with the acceptance by the magi was a type of the eventual rejection of Jesus by Jewish leaders and his acceptance by the Gentiles. Thus Matthew does not simply underline Jesus' kingship; he was also prepares the reader for the greatest of ironies: the king was rejected by his own and welcomed by the foreigner.

Grotto of the Nativity

To complete this application of the New Testament to Bethlehem, we must pause for a moment to contemplate the building and grotto of the Nativity of Jesus. Luke alone gives us any hint about the circumstances of Jesus' birth. It was the call to register for the census that brought so many visitors to Bethlehem that Joseph could find no room in the overnight resting place used for times when Bethlehem was crowded with visitors. It was not a unique experience that Mary and Joseph would spend a night, out of necessity, in a cave which had the depth to protect animals from cold and robbers. Nor was it unique that a child was born outdoors, or perhaps in a cave. For all that, it was deeply sobering to actually have such a series of events happen to any young mother, father, and child. If there be any reason behind the statement that Jesus could have chosen whatever society and whatever level of society he wanted for his incarnation, we can only stand in wonder at the choice he made for himself, for his mother, and for his father. This was the Messiah, the Lord, the Savior, the King. We can only conclude that, if the choice was intentional, it was a choice somehow for our benefit, for our instruction. The adult Jesus would speak of love of the Father and trust in him to such a degree that all the things of the Father's world lose their attraction; they are good, but he was very good—never to be substituted for by them. He spoke in this way and he lived in this way, a constant corrective to our tendencies to put our trust ultimately in the things God made rather than in God himself.

Ironically, it was this puzzling preference for poverty that made Jesus accessible to the poor, to all mankind. His deeds of power would impress people as would his wisdom; but his poverty showed him the equal of the poor and gave him access to them, to resolving their deepest needs and desires. If Jesus was to share human life, he seems to say, he would share it in a way that makes him intelligible to all mankind, approachable to all mankind. But above all he would so live life that no one would have any doubts about what makes him tick: from his earliest moments, he wants only his Father. Jesus never showed dislike for the things his Father had made, but he had to let his love burn fully, and it was this love which pushed all else aside so that he could have, in his poverty, the richest union he could imagine: union with his Father, uninterrupted by possessions and desires for them.

Slaughter of the Innocents   *Mt 2:16-18*

A story connected with the infancy of Jesus depicts the slaughter of the innocent children of Bethlehem. Herod the Great had sent the Magi to find the child Jesus, but was frustrated in his final goal, for the Magi under divine guidance returned to their own country without speaking with Herod again. Herod, incensed and eager to do away with Jesus, King of the Jews, ordered his soldiers to kill every young boy under two years of age in the region of Bethlehem. Jesus escaped this massacre; he went to Egypt, under the direction of God through an angel.

The story of itself suggests several questions. Why do we

never hear again of this slaughter, whether in the New Testament
or in other literature of the first century A.D.? Was it right that
Jesus should allow others to die for him as he escapes? Where
did Joseph take his family—to Egypt, yes, but where? After all,
they lived there for some time. Where did Joseph and his family
live in the Bethlehem region when the soldiers of Herod were
sent to kill the children? Surely, if the children even one and two
years old were killed, Jesus was assumed to be quite possibly
that old; surely, he was no longer living in the cave of Bethlehem
associated with his birth.

None of these questions has a sure answer, except that now
we assume Jesus to have been about a year-and-a-half old when
this slaughter occurred. This means, practically speaking, that if
we are right in our calculations that Herod the Great died shortly
after his attempt on Jesus' life and about 4 B.C., we should put
Jesus' birth at about 6 B.C. But the main conclusion should be
one that reinforces much of Gospel study: a story was told out of
a tradition; the tradition made sense of many details, but the
story told out of the tradition ignored many details to emphasize
one. Of the slaughter in Bethlehem, we can only presume that
Matthew has organized his story telling to show the divine
guidance directing and protecting the life of Jesus and to show
that, even in such a bizarre event as this, Jesus fulfilled yet one
more detail of the plan spoken of by God through his various
prophets of Old Testament times. Other questions, which are
admittedly raised by the story–telling, are of no concern to the
author; what was of concern was clearly stated or arrived at by
analysis of the details given. This was as surely a part of the
method of writing here as in the rest of the Gospel. We are
forced, by the very manner of writing, to concentrate on what the
author wanted the reader to grasp—and not on other things the
author thought extraneous to his narrative.

The slaughter of the children of Bethlehem not only
underlined the reaction of Herod and his hangers-on to Jesus, it
also showed Matthew's concern to relate Jesus' life and being to
Old Testament sayings and events. The reason for this
association is very simple: if Jesus was from the God of Israel, he
must be shown to fit into the plan of that God and not be shown
to be a foreign substance grafted onto a history unnatural to it.
Jesus emerged from the Old Testament as its completion and
fulfillment; he was not a reaction to the Old Testament, but its
perfection. The constant concern to show him fulfilling Old
Testament texts witnesses to the absolute necessity that he be

shown to conform to the one will and plan of God, inaugurated so many centuries ago, for the salvation of Israel and of the world.

The particular Old Testament text fulfilled in the story about the slaughter of the children concerns Rachel, who weeps for her children. This Rachel was one of the two freeborn wives of Jacob; from her, and from the other freeborn wife and from two slave born wives of Jacob, came the twelve sons of Jacob. Since these twelve sons gave birth to the twelve tribes of Israel, and gave their names to the tribes, Rachel can be understood to be the mother of Israel.

In giving birth to her last son Benjamin, Rachel died. She was buried where she gave birth, just east of Jerusalem. Many centuries later, when Israel was being taken out of Jerusalem eastward toward conquering Babylon, Jeremiah in a poetic style imagined that Rachel could see from her tomb the procession of captives, of her children, forced into grim slavery in Babylon. As they passed by her tomb, she wept (Jer 31:15).

As often happens in the establishment of religious sites, the tomb of Rachel over the years was identified as being in an area south of Jerusalem, more exactly, between Jerusalem and Bethlehem; we pass it today as we go from one city to the other. Since this area was identified in Matthew's time as the tomb of Rachel, Matthew saw the propriety of applying the prophet's words to Rachel watching from her grave the slaughter of her children of Bethlehem. Thus, an ancient tradition having to do with Rachel's burial was used by a prophet in the sixth century B.C. to describe the poignancy of the Babylonian exile—and then used again by a writer of the first century A.D. to describe yet another suffering of Israel. In seeing the aptness of this quotation for an event of Jesus' childhood, Matthew stresses that, though the quotation was fitting for the suffering undergone in sixth century B.C. Israel, the quotation comes to its fullest significance as it was seen to rightly fit the circumstance surrounding the life of Jesus. It was not the sixth-century prophet who foresaw the Jesus event in his own words, but he said the words which would have their full meaning realized once the Jesus event had come to pass. In short, God had been talking of things through his prophets, sayings which were fully understood only when the events they spoke of finally happened.

What then does Matthew see of value for his purpose in the story of the children of Bethlehem? This story shows God's protection of the One sent to save all mankind, and it shows how

Jesus was spoken of by God centuries before he was born. Jesus completes the Old Testament, and the Old Testament had for centuries been looking for him and gives him meaning.

Basilica of the Nativity

It is time to turn our attention to the basilica of the Nativity, beneath which is the traditional cave in which Jesus was born and laid in a manger. To enter the basilica we must bend very low, for the doorway is not high; the reason for the lowness of the door was to keep out of the basilica animals like horses and camels, though we may, with Chesterton, see the aptness of one's lowering oneself to enter the place where God made himself lowly and welcomed the lowly. This small door was made about 1500 A.D.; above it we can still see, before bending down to go through it, the outline of the pointed arch of the entrance built by the crusaders about 1100 A.D., and above that was to be seen a cornice of the entrance built by the Byzantine emperor, Justinian, about 535 A.D.

   Having passed through the low door, we enter the vestibule of the basilica and move directly to the ancient door (1277 A.D.) which leads us into the main body of the basilica. The basilica in which we stand is a tired, old building, the scene of many—often violent—changes. It is essentially the same basilica built by the Emperor Justinian, who intended to restore to its former glory the original basilica built here by the Emperor Constantine about 330 A.D. In rebuilding of the basilica almost destroyed by Samaritans in 529 A.D., Justinian installed a new floor about thirty inches above Constantine's floor; today, at certain easily reached spots, we can still see the remains of the Constantinian floor below the Justinian floor. Another change by Justinian is visible after we walk the length of the basilica and stop at the end of the last set of pillars. Originally, Constantine had built an octagon at the end of the rows of pillars; this octagon, with a high altar in the middle of it, stood over the cave in which Jesus was born. Justinian did away with the octagon shape and extended the sides of the church so that the length of the church now intersected with the new width of the church to form a cross; right below the point of intersection was to be seen the holy cave of Jesus' birth.

   On the way to this intersection, we pass mosaics and frescoes decorating the walls above the pillars of the main aisle of the church. As we walk up the central aisle, we notice, high up on our left, the ruins of twelfth century A.D. mosaic busts of Jesus' ancestors, and long inscriptions which highlight the decrees of the ecumenical councils of Constantinople, 381 and 680 A.D. On the upper wall on our right as we walk up the main aisle from the entrance can be seen mosaic fragments depicting the famous and ancient churches of Antioch and Sardica, as well as portraits of Jesus' ancestors and frescoes commemorating some provincial councils of the Church.

As we stand at the intersection of the main aisle and the cross aisle, it is apparent that many Christian religious groups worship at the altars about the sanctuary. Indeed, just as the outside of the entire basilica was blocked on three sides by the convents of Franciscans, Greeks, and Armenians, so we can expect that these groups have certain rights regarding space in the sanctuary originally Constantine's but remodeled by Justinian. Depending on the decisions of the day, we look to these various altars and side chapels for the entrance by which we descend to the complex of caves below, one of which was the holy site of Jesus' birth. By and large, most of the caves have been starkly, but respectfully restored and marked as to their significance. But we should look particularly for the cave of St. Jerome, the patron of all biblical scholars, who came to Palestine in 382 A.D., at the age of forty-six, and settled here at Bethlehem to pursue his interpretative studies and translations into Latin of the Sacred Scriptures. From here St. Jerome politely disagreed with people like St. Augustine.

The sacred cave of Jesus' birth has undergone many changes. The Roman Emperor Hadrian, about 140 A.D., tried to dedicate an area sacred to the Christians to the god Adonis, and the sacred cave itself was turned into a place of weeping for this Greek god. The first change has to do with smoothing walls and ceiling to make what was once a rough cave a respectable place of veneration. The second change was the establishment of altars to distinguish the place of birth, which has a star imbedded in the marble flooring, from the place of the manger. Later a third altar was added in honor of the stopping of the Magi. If we look directly at the altar over the star, we need only look over our right shoulders to see the altar of the manger. To honor these spots marble slabbing was used, which further removes us from the sense of being in a rough cave.

One further notes the fifty-three lamps lit to honor the site of Jesus' birth, clearly an addition of later ages and tastes.

Nineteen of these lamps belong to the Roman Catholic Church. One cannot ignore the blackened walls; the blackness was in part due to the fifty-three ever burning lamps, but in greater part because a fire broke out and scorched these walls and ceiling in the last century. Thus, although white marble covers the floor and walls, we are strongly impressed by dark and dirt. And we may not be strongly attracted to the leathery asbestos wall coverings. Yet, these were precious in their day—1874 A.D.—sent by the president of the French Republic.

Finally, we become aware that there is no outlet from the cave, thus no entryway visible by which the Holy Family entered and exited the cave. One must use one's imagination to lift from the cave the entire basilica above and to open the cave at the end opposite to the altar of Jesus' birth. From here we can see the stars and look over the valley where the angel spoke to the shepherds. (See 124-28.) In this fashion we may begin to get a sense of how Palestinians, today as well as in ancient times, used caves for houses, whether permanent or transitory. It was not impossible that what Joseph found for his pregnant wife was a house of a poor family who had divided its dwelling into an inner room and a room entered from outside. Often enough, one of these rooms would be large enough to take in a few animals for the night. And it would not be unlikely that a poor family would accept an equally poor family for a night of emergency.

Whatever the precise circumstances of Jesus' birth, the most powerful of lords, the one to whom all the world's lords do homage, was laid to rest on straw in a stone cave near the small town of Bethlehem—far from the palace of kings. Why should he be one of us? Why should he be one of the poor among us? Such was the mystery of Bethlehem and the assurance, too, of this cave—that his love for us, including those who are not loved by us or anybody else, was inestimable.

Shepherds' Field   *Lk 2:8-20*

Just east of Bethlehem, on the road from Manger Square through Beit Sahour, are the fields which evoke the memory of the angels' visit to the shepherds on the night of Christ's birth nearby. With the help of Canada, a chapel was erected in 1954 A.D. here to the memory of the shepherds and their vision; this Barluzzi chapel has the shape of a nomad's tent and enjoys Noni's lovely frescoes. Most visitors go to this chapel to spend some time in thinking about the event that happened in these fields. But it was not surprising to learn that throughout these fields are traces of towers, monasteries, chapels—dating back to the fifth century A.D.—which served earlier Christians contemplating the visit of angels to shepherds.

Given interpreters' penchant for seeing symbolism and analogy, type and fulfillment between the Old and New Testaments, today's reader of the Gospels can expect to be reminded in this Bethlehem incident how the shepherds fit into a larger picture and expectation. Indeed, it seems to many that the shepherds stand for those faithful Israelites who for centuries waited with patient hope, "in darkness and in the shadow of death," as Luke puts it, for a divine light to shine and set them free (Lk 1:79; Is 9:1). They are particularly poor, corresponding to poverty of the Holy Family now passing a terrifying night in childbirth in a cave nearby. To these poor the messenger of God himself spoke words that prophets and kings longed to hear, but never heard. To those faithful, deprived for so long of the good news, was now given the proclamation. The shepherds thus combined those two qualities which particularly attract God: the faithful, watchful Israelite who in his poverty still longs for and trusts in God.

Matthew presumably chose a different kind of person as the first recipient of the good news that "a king was born in Israel." Yet he was not actually far from Luke's preference. For the wise men, though they are probably court figures and bring royal gifts to Jesus, are not themselves kings. They are not poor, but they are not members of the Chosen People, either. Rather they represent of another kind of poverty, the poverty of the Gentile who lives perpetually in darkness of folly and estrangement from the true God; he may be physically well-off, but to know his darkness of soul and the corruption of his life lived apart from God is to know a truly poor person. One cannot deny that God loves deeply every human person, but some kinds of poverty move his fatherly instincts in particular haste. A parent understands this situation. It was the shepherds in Luke's story which move God to announce the good news to them first.

To them came a messenger of God and the glory or brilliant light of the Lord; no cause for fear, but reason for greatest of joy, for it was very good news the angel brings. Luke everywhere, especially about Jesus' resurrection, emphasizes what one sees and hears as grounds for belief. Thus here the angel gave two signs: the words he speaks and the sight of a child wrapped in swaddling clothes and lying in a manger. It was important, then, that Luke include in his following verses that the shepherds did in fact see the "child lying [wrapped] in the manger." This discovery led them to give credence to the message of the angel, to try to understand what these words mean. In this way, Luke shows how Christian faith is linked to words and deeds, to hearing and seeing.

What the angel announced was nothing less than the longed-for news, news worthy of the Angel of the Lord, who in the Old Testament brought mankind the best of news. The message, a message of joy for all the people, was simple: a savior was born who was nothing less than Christ Lord, a descendant of the shepherd and king, David. How Jesus is savior to each individual is known only in the depths of an individual's heart and soul. Luke's effort here was to bring out elements of that saving which are understandable and experienced by all. This savior is Messiah. He is, therefore, the one who would bring about the shift of entire ages, from this age we move with him to the age to come. With him we move from pain and unhappiness and grief and trial and deprivation and death; God promised to do this, then indicated that he would anoint "one of us," born as the child of David, to introduce this change of the ages—through and in this anointed one, this Messiah, God would act. Little did the Old Testament think that this Anointed One is actually the divine son of the divine Father, inexplicably become man and named Jesus, born in a Bethlehem cave!

For St. Paul, Jesus was ultimately anointed, that is, designated, to bring about the change of ages by his death, which ends death, and his resurrection, which begins life with God without end. For Luke, who knew this Pauline understanding of Jesus, Jesus was not only Son of David, but heir of the throne of David. This image must be understood as that of a person who receives authority over others to bring all the benefits of a kingdom which individuals cannot provide for themselves. In this sense of king, Jesus becomes a servant, for his purpose in life was to mediate to all people as much of the good things of God as he possibly can, things which no person could provide for himself. Thus, when Jesus saves, he saves with kingly power over our enemy, Satan, in order that, having saved us, he can now provide us with all the goods of God's kingdom. Thus Jesus both snatches us from this age and governs the distribution of the many gifts of the age to come.

Jesus was also described as Lord. This, too, was a title of

dignity and royalty, for it was David's Lord who was to sit at God's right hand in glory—as Jesus did after his Ascension, which was the logical sequence to his Resurrection from the dead. But "Lord" also means to say that we who have given ourselves over to many lords in our lives—as human beings have done for centuries—can now identify the Lord designated by God himself to whom we can commit ourselves for the benefits of life which we thought other lords would give us if we served them faithfully. Even more, the most powerful lord of our lives, Death, can now be rendered powerless once we throw in our lot with the Lord Jesus. Indeed, we would die, we would suffer the little deaths which lead to the final separation of soul from body; but the foreverness of Death was now removed by our Lord who was greater than the tyrant whom we cannot overthrow ourselves. Again, Jesus, whose name signifies one who "saves," serves us in his lordly power, as he removes from us so many tyrannies and false lords so that we may enjoy the life and power and love of the one true Lord.

It was indeed a happy message which the angel of the Lord brought to the shepherds. It was reasonable that Luke follow the angelic message with a host of angels in chorus singing a song which proclaims that God, pictured as living in the "highest" heaven, is given glory by all his creatures acknowledgment of the great act he has done in the birth of Jesus, a song which also announces that God, who so generously has offered Jesus to mankind, thus gave mankind the peace which union with Jesus should bring about. Glory and peace—two effects most befitting the good news and reality of the birth of Jesus.

The shepherds must follow the direction of the angel, for the good new was too good to miss. The results of their doing what the angel bade them do were three. First, they pondered over the words of the angel as they look at this child—how would this child be savior, Messiah, Lord, source of great joy for them? To their ponderings are added those of Mary who, on top of all else that has been told her and has happened to her, must make sense of the words of this band of shepherd strangers. Secondly, Jesus was good news and the fulfillment of hopes the shepherds know are part of the lives of their friends and neighbors. How can they not, therefore, tell them this good news? The relationship of hope and fulfillment between what a person longs for and what Jesus was moved the shepherds to tell people about Jesus. Thirdly, the shepherds gave glory and praise to God for what they saw he had begun in this little baby. They recognized God in this birth and praised him for what he had done.

The shepherds knew that the Jesus event was rooted in God and was the flowering of God's love. We shall have to see how the adult Jesus' contemporaries interpreted him in this way. Thus we realize again that the infancy stories of Jesus are, on the level of story-telling, an introduction to the adult drama which would unfold very soon. The reader, through hearing the story of the shepherds, knows so much more than do Jesus' contemporaries. May this infancy story, like all the others, give strength and understanding to faith—and glory to God and peace to mankind.

Tomb of Lazarus (Bethany)

Bethany

At the foot of the eastern slope of the Mount of Olives lies
Bethany, famous in the New Testament as the village of Martha
and Mary and their brother Lazarus. Indeed, even today we can
visit a tomb traditionally considered to be that of Lazarus; near
the cavelike tomb is a modern church commemorating not only
the raising of Lazarus to life, but other stories of the Gospels
which speak of Mary and Martha. Bethany was also famous as a
village in which Jesus passed many nights, presumably often
with Martha, Mary and Lazarus, especially when Jesus was in
Jerusalem at Passover time—Jesus taught all day in the Temple
area, then retired in the evening over the top of the Mount of
Olives to Bethany. Indeed, on his way from Bethany to Jerusalem,
Jesus cursed the fig tree for not producing fruit as a symbol of
his rejection by Israel, often symbolized as a vine or tree. And he
encouraged his disciples to have faith like his own, faith that
"can move mountains."

Mary of Bethany   *Lk 10:38-42; Jn 11:1-44; 12:1-8*

There is some confusion about the person of Mary, sister of
Martha and Lazarus. According to John, at a dinner in Bethany
sponsored by Lazarus and his sisters before the Passover, Mary
anointed Jesus with ointment, pure nard (Jn 12:1–8). Her act was
interpreted as a prophecy of death for Jesus, foreshadowing the
real embalming of Jesus with ointment. Mark, too, tells of an
anointing just before the Last Supper (Mk 14:3–9), but does not
identify the woman anointing as Mary, nor does the dinner at
which Jesus was anointed take place in Bethany in the house of
Lazarus and his sisters, but rather in the house of a certain
Simon the leper. Matthew follows Mark's lead in this narrative
(Mt 26:6–13). Luke, however, was conspicuous for his not
mentioning the Bethany anointing at all, even though he tells the
story otherwise just as Mark does; rather, Luke tells a story of

anointing much earlier in his Gospel, a story placed in the house of another Simon, a Pharisee, not a leper, and involving an unnamed woman who was clearly a repentant sinner, a state of soul never ascribed to Mary, sister of Lazarus.

Who might this woman be who plays such a prominent part in a story which occurs in Galilee? Many scholars think that Luke's next verses (Lk 8:1–2) identify this woman as Mary, called Magdalene, from whom seven spirits had been driven out; many scholars, too, suspect that the story of anointing appearing early in Luke (chapter seven) was somehow identical with the anointing mentioned in Mark, which took place in the house of Simon the leper and just before Passover, and with the anointing mentioned in John, which took place in Bethany in the house of Lazarus and his sisters, just before Passover.

So appears the evidence which leads scholars to various hypotheses about the anointing of Jesus, ascribed in John to Mary at the time of a dinner in her house in Bethany. It remains dubious that Jesus would have been anointed twice just before his Passover dinner. Yet it is not easy to say which tradition is historically accurate and which comes from misunderstanding or rewriting to emphasize a symbol. Nor is it easy to say that Luke's rendition of an anointing is a retelling of Mark's story, with Luke adding and deleting from Mark's story to fit Luke's own purposes; nor is it easily assumed that the sinful woman of Luke's story is Mary Magdalen, for, though Mary was possessed by seven demons, possession itself was not cause for saying that she was a sinner. Ultimately, we are left with the traditions of Luke, Mark followed by Matthew, and John, with only guesses about how they might relate with one other. Bethany, then, does not easily lose its identity as a place where Jesus was prophetically anointed for his death.

Bethany was also known in the New Testament as the place where Jesus said his famous words to Martha, "Let your sister be; she has chosen the better part and no one should take it from her" (Lk 10:38–42). Martha, we recall, had urged Jesus to nudge Mary to help Martha with the preparation of a meal for Jesus; Mary preferred to listen to the Lord. Indeed, the circumstances of the event described in this story about Martha and Mary are not fully reported and thus Martha's position was not fully attended to. One was asked to consider the value of Mary's inclination and determination to "listen to the word of the Lord." The story was geared to emphasize her listening to the Lord; it reaffirms what appears in many other explicit and implicit statements of the New Testament about the supreme value of attention to the Lord above all else. Indeed, as Jesus said earlier, "The one who listens to my word is my mother and brother and sister" (Lk 8:19–21). Throughout Luke's entire work, the Gospel and the Acts of the Apostles, Luke calls his reader's attention to appreciation of Jesus' role as Teacher, the Son who knows the mind of the Father and reveals it to us. It is this teaching of the Lord which the eyewitnesses and witnesses to the Lord spread throughout the Mediterranean world in the middle of the first century A.D.

For John, Jesus is the Word, who, when spoken, expresses the mind of God the Speaker and to whom we all attend precisely because we enter through the Word made flesh into the very thoughts of God for us. It is in the nature of the Gospel that attention to the Lord's word is praised and encouraged.

Raising of Lazarus   *Jn 11:1-44*

Perhaps Bethany is most famous in John's Gospel as the place marking the miracle of Jesus' raising Lazarus, his dear friend, from the grave. The miracle is itself stupendous; indeed, it is the last of Jesus' works or signs. After this miracle, John's story leaves the world of Jesus' signs, the world of his public life, to bring the reader into the profoundly mysterious world of Jesus' betrayal, crucifixion and resurrection. The Lazarus story was the last of the signs meant to prepare us for entry into this part of the Jesus event; as such, it was an anticipation of Jesus' own leaving the world of the dead for the life in God's presence.

From the way the story of Lazarus is told, we clearly see how the signs, and particularly this sign, fit into the purpose of the Gospel of John. The purpose of the Gospel was clearly stated in the verses which originally ended the Gospel: "There were many other signs that Jesus worked and the disciples saw . . .These are recorded so that you may believe [or: continue to believe] that Jesus is the Christ [Messiah], the Son of God, and that believing this you may have life through his name" (Jn 20:30–31). All the signs Jesus worked from John 2–11 should promote belief in Jesus as Messiah and Son of God; the raising of Lazarus clearly shows Jesus giving life, which, as the Gospel argues, was the effect of belief in Jesus as Messiah and Son of God.

An important distinction must be made, however, concern-

ing "life." At the time of the creation of the world, God
shared life with creatures, life, which, as John's Prologue (Jn 1:4)
indicates, came to creatures through the Word of God. Once the
world had broken its bond of friendship with God, this life
suffered several adverse effects, not the least of which was
domination by Satan or "Darkness" and the universal necessity
of death. Thus, because of sin, there existed a type of life which
was without God. This was not the kind of life which Jesus, the
source of life, since he was the Word made flesh, came to give.
Jesus came to give people the power to be children of God, to
free people from the control of "Darkness." The Word is the
source of God's gift of life and this life was light. It is important
to realize that, for John who tells the Lazarus story and for all
the New Testament writings, the "life" worth striving and hoping
for and already shared in was only "life with God." Thus, though
Jesus clearly performed a great act of power and mercy for a
friend who was bound by Death and the cause of great sorrow
for his sisters, Jesus did not give him that life which Jesus really
has come to give. Lazarus, in short, was not freed from dying
again, nor was he freed from the little deaths that precede the
final dissolution of body and soul. His rising from his tomb, then,
was only a sign of that greater, that true life which was the result
of our belief that Jesus was the Messiah, the Son of God, the one
through whom God has decreed that true life, unencumbered by
sin and its effects, should be given. To believe in Jesus was
already to free ourselves from sin; in time we would be freed
from all sin's effects and life with God would be lived to its
fullest.

From what I have said about the relationship of this miracle
to the purpose of the Gospel, it was clear that John has written
his story to explain

1) why it was Jesus who said so authoritatively that "Your
   brother would rise again";
2) why Jesus identified himself as the "Resurrection," faith
   in whom would allow us to escape death forever in favor
   of life forever;
3) why Jesus was so openly confessed by Martha in very
   significant terms: "I believe. . . you are the Christ, the Son
   of God."

John was not interested, here as elsewhere, in establishing a
psychological development of Martha so that the reader can see
how she arrived at her confession; her role was to stir up the
reader to respond properly to Jesus' declaration that he was "the

Resurrection." The sign Jesus now works serves to confirm his declaration of his meaning for human beings; most of them would be called on to believe, without the benefit of a confirming miracle.

The raising of Lazarus is a wonderfully told story about a wondrous miracle. As a miracle story it brings home to the reader how deeply into the depths of corruption Lazarus had gone; yet not so far that Jesus could not bring him back. In its wider interest the story also answers the objection that, if Jesus really loved Lazarus, he would have saved him before Lazarus died. From the work of Jesus, we gather a true impression of how much Jesus really loved his friend and learns a theological truth used often in the New Testament and thereafter to make evil in God's world intelligible: this present suffering would in time be shown to be for good. The story also retains in several ways the precious remembrance of Jesus' actual responses to the human suffering and fate of his very dear friends. John's entire effort in his Gospel aimed at piercing the humanity of Jesus to reveal his oneness with the Father, to reveal the Jesus of Nazareth to be God the Word made flesh. At times, however, John has left behind traces of the humanness he sought to penetrate—and we are all the more blessed for that. Finally, the story is good drama, as it leads the reader through a variety of empathies till the story ends with the glorious words: "Free him and let him go."

The story of Lazarus can be read as a complete story, yet it is clearly integrated into the larger gospel story by John. Immediately after the miracle at Bethany, some who heard of it decided to get rid of Jesus, who should die rather than be allowed to continue to the point that people might, appealing to Jesus as their protector, try to overthrow Roman control of Israel—an attempt, verified in the tragic suppression of the Jewish revolt of 67 A.D., seen as foolhardy. Indeed, not only does John record that Jesus was marked for death from this miracle on, but Lazarus himself soon was tagged for death, for he stood as the incontrovertible sign that life, in all its forms, flows from the source known as the Word made flesh called Jesus.

Bethany, amidst its few remains, was the physical site of the sign most clearly asking for belief that Jesus was the source of the fullness of life.

Chapel of the Ascension (Mount of Olives)

The Mount of Olives

The Ascension   *Lk 24:50-53; Acts 1:9-11*

To enter the area of the Ascension of Jesus to heaven is to pass, first, through a wall which surrounds, secondly, a small building used in some times past as a mosque. At ground level within this sometime mosque a rough piece of rock is visible. An old tradition says that Jesus left this world from this rock, and claims are made that we can even yet see the imprint of one of his feet on this rock. To picture this rock in Jesus' time we would have to mentally remove the building that houses the rock and the wall that surrounds the building. Both the mosque and the wall were built in the eleventh or twelfth century A.D. The Muslims graciously allow Orthodox and Latin Christians to celebrate liturgies here on their Ascension days.

The mountain on which the rock of the Ascension is found is known in the New Testament as the Mount of Olives, for on its lower western flank flourished many olive trees. The Jewish Scriptures portrays God, the great Lord, coming from the east, like the sun reaching out over the Jewish world each dawn. (Ez 43:1–2.) Hills would be leveled and valleys filled up, so that this great King would enjoy an entry into his city befitting him. Thus the Mount of Olives would be divided from east to west and the valley of Kidron, which separated Jerusalem from the Mount of Olives, would be filled in, so that God could approach his city in stately ease. From this mountain, then, would come judgment on Jerusalem, when God comes at the end of time to purify his city. The picture of Jesus, returning as he had left, suggests that Jesus was identified as the one who would fulfill this role expected of God: Judge at the end of time.

The Mount of Olives is famous for several sites. Just over the top of the mountain and out of sight of Jerusalem is the gospel town Bethany, the home of Martha, Mary and Lazarus. About halfway down the mountain on its western side facing

Jerusalem is located a fitting spot to commemorate the weeping of Jesus over Jerusalem. Farther down the same slope, near the bottom of the mountain and across from Jerusalem, is the garden area where Jesus agonized over his imminent suffering and where he was captured. Indeed, to move from the Galilee and northern Judea to Jerusalem usually meant that one, after following the rather flat edges or bed of the River Jordan southward to the north end of the Dead Sea, turned westward at Jericho to climb upward towards Jerusalem, finally reaching the top of the Mount of Olives before descending to cross the Kidron Valley at the base of the city's eastern wall. The man who enjoyed the kindness of the Good Samaritan would have passed a route like this, from Jerusalem to Jericho over the southern end of the Mount of Olives. Such then is the significance of this mountain, so near the holy city of Jerusalem, a mountain which watched the growth of the city of David into a major capital under Solomon, which saw David flee from his opponents and the Judeans pass into and return from exile in Babylon.

But what of the event which has crowned its top? What is to be understood of the Ascension of Jesus? According to the thinking of Jesus' time, ascension represented a mode of entering the presence of God, a manner of leaving this world for the life with God. Thus, though ascension is the term used for this aspect of Jesus' life, we must really concentrate on the result of that movement into God's presence. For Jesus, this entrance was a return; moreover, it was a taking of a position at the right hand of the Father, the position of God's Favorite, the position indicated as that belonging to David's Lord, as the famous words of the psalm had said, "The Lord [Yahweh] said to my Lord: 'Sit at my right hand; I would put your enemies under your feet as your footstool.'" (Ps 110:1) In essence, then, the metaphorical language of moving upward from this earth to God's dwelling in the heavens conveyed the conviction that Jesus has not only risen from the dead but also reached the terminus or last goal of Resurrection and Ascension, that is, the sitting at the right hand of his Father.

Luke's two renditions of Jesus' return to the Father—at the end of his Gospel and at the beginning of his Acts of the Apostles—differ in their details. So different are they, indeed, about the time of the Ascension, that one is not quite sure how to justify both accounts as accurate reports of what actually happened: the Gospel gives the impression that Jesus ascended on the day of his Resurrection, which is the impression given elsewhere in the New Testament, whereas the Acts of the Apostles indicates that Jesus ascended to the Father forty days after his Resurrection. Since Luke would more than likely not contradict himself in such a matter as this circumstance of timing, he probably meant the account in the Gospel to be emphasize that continual movement from death to life to the right hand of his Father, a movement all in one sweep in the nature of things, whereas the definitive departure of Jesus from his disciples was delayed till Jesus had taught what he thought his disciples needed for the time when he would no longer appear to them after his Resurrection. But there is more to these two renditions than just a difference of time; let us look at them more closely.

What characterizes the Ascension in the Gospel is the joy and glory emanating from the narration. This is a wonderful moment, the culmination of Jesus' life on earth, the visible sign of Jesus' innocence before the world and his chosenness before God. The disciples rejoice in this ending to the events of the life of Jesus. Jesus is not only revealed as Messiah by virtue of his Resurrection, but he is known to be Lord by being taken up to the right hand of the Father. Luke hopes his reader would enter this joyfulness, as the painfulness of the crucifixion recedes before the joy of glory.

The Ascension in Acts conveys a different sense. Here the disciples are rather confused and hesitant; they realize that, with the passing of the one they knew to be Messiah, the chances that the Kingdom of God, to be introduced, they thought, by the Messiah, is to be a reality at all seemed rather slim. Thus, the aspects of joy and glory are missing from this version of the Ascension. The key to understanding this version lies not simply in the story telling, but also in the position of the story. We are not at the end of a book, but at the beginning of one.

The Ascension is not merely the culmination of Jesus' life; it opens a period which, from the perspective of the disciples, was uncertain and threatening. Only knowledge given by the Pentecostal Spirit would calm the disciples, and they do not as yet have that knowledge, nor experience of the Spirit. Luke intentionally underscores the need of the disciples for Jesus' guidance by describing Jesus as teaching them for forty days beyond his public life, and he underlines the disciples' diffidence to show how clearly dependent they are on the Spirit poured out by Jesus for whatever good they accomplish in the days and years to come. The disciples, then, at this juncture of Acts were nervous and unsure of the future, so to show the reader that whatever good happens, that good was the result of God's intervention and protection and inspiration; the departure of Jesus here leaves behind, not a group joyful at his conquest, but dependent on the goodness of God for their eventual progress.

The story of the Ascension, then, has three elements as the New Testament develops it. First, there is the certain proclamation that Jesus, visibly crucified to death, was not a criminal, but had been raised up and taken by God to himself, to the position of God's Favorite, Secondly, the return to the Father has been described in terms fitting to the triumphant closing of the life of Jesus on earth, a life not confessed by all to be glorious and the expression of God in Jesus. Thirdly, the telling of the Ascension, when it serves the purpose of opening up the apostolic age, shows how that age's heroes were dependent at the departure of their Lord on his continued guidance and intervention, not the least of which, as Acts goes on to show, was the outpouring of the Holy Spirit as the primordial inauguration of the apostolic activities of witness to Jesus as savior of the world.

This place, then, commemorates a departure—and an assurance that those left in "this world" would enjoy the comfort and protection, the guidance and encouragement and inspiration of the Lord who resides in "the world to come," till he comes finally to take all of his with him to eternal happiness. We rejoice in his glory, hope for his return, and count on his presence in so many situations over which we would have no control unless he is with us.

Pater Noster Church *(Our Father Church)*   *Mt 6:7–15; Lk 11:1–4*

On top of the Mount of Olives is a compound whose center is the Our Father Church. This church is a complete restoration about 1874 A.D. of an earlier church established by the crusaders about 1160 A.D. The crusaders named this church the Pater Noster Church. But not only is this the site of a crusader contribution to Christian memory; the church of the crusaders lay close to the church Constantine had erected in honor of the events of the Mount of Olives, particularly that of the Ascension of Jesus. The Greek word for *olives* is *elaia,* so we are not surprised to hear this Constantinian church called the Eleona. The Eleona forms that third church of a trinity devoutly wished for and erected by

Constantine: the Eleona, the Church of the Burial and Resurrection of Jesus, the Church of the Birth of Jesus in Bethlehem.

The present church was built in the last century and presents to the visitor a series of over sixty tile plaques, each with a version of the Our Father in a different language.

In the Gospels Jesus taught the Lord's Prayer twice. One version occurs in Matthew as part of the Sermon on the Mount, situated in Galilee. The other presentation of the Our Father is found in chapter eleven of Luke; it was probably of this Lucan situation that the crusaders were thinking when they erected this Church of the Our Father on the Mount of Olives. No doubt the crusaders chose this mount because the story which immediately preceded the words of the Our Father is the story of Jesus dealing with Martha and Mary (Lk 11:38–42); though Luke only located this Martha-Mary story in a village, it was natural enough that the crusaders concluded that, since Martha and Mary lived in Bethany, the village must have been Bethany; so the story immediately following the Bethany story must have taken place on the Mount of Olives, on whose slopes we find Bethany. Today scholars may agree that Luke's story about Martha and Mary took place in Bethany, but they would be reluctant to agree that the Our Father of Jesus, as it is located in the sequence of Luke, occurred on the Mount of Olives. For chapter eleven, where the Our Father appears, seems to put Jesus in the Jerusalem area much too soon before the explicit statement in chapter nineteen that he had arrived there, especially when Luke notes that "Jesus went through towns and villages teaching, making his way to Jerusalem." (Lk 13:22.)

The Our Father of Jesus appears differently in Matthew and in Luke. Luke reported only half the petitions of the Our Father which are to be found in Matthew's rendition. (Compare Mt 6:9–13 with Lk 11:2–4.) Moreover, the circumstance which prompted Jesus to give his prayer is distinctive in each Gospel. In Matthew, Jesus wanted to discourage his disciples from abusively long prayers, to which some of the religious leaders in Israel were accustomed; and so, Jesus gave the Our Father as an example of a prayer which was both brief and contained the essential expressions characterizing a people's relationship with God. In Luke, on the other hand, Jesus gave the Our Father to his disciples in response to their request that he teach them to pray, as John had taught his disciples.

Comparison shows differences in the two versions of the

Our Father, yet substantially and essentially they are quite similar. We attend to this substantial agreement, for herein lies Jesus's own suggestion of our approach to God.

Matthew	*Luke*
Our Father in heaven,	Father,
may your name be held holy,	may your name be held holy,
your kingdom come,	your kingdom come;
your will be done on earth	
as it is in heaven.	
Give us today our daily bread,	Give us each day our daily bread,
and forgive us our debts,	and forgive us our sins,
as we have forgiven those who are in	for we ourselves forgive each one
debt to us.	who is in debt to us.
And do not put us to the test,	And do not put us to the test.
but save us from the Evil One.	

The fundamental relationship between God and human beings, as it is laid down in this prayer, is that of father and children. Every religion has, through name giving and title giving, favorite expressions for God; these names and titles reveal the views religious people have of the saving power and loving care exercised for themselves and for the world. From this point of view, the Christian is asked to consider the all-powerful and only God as father. The Christian should apply to God all the positive meaning human beings attached to this figure. The Christian is also asked to approach God in imitation of Jesus, who rarely spoke of God in any term but Father, and never addressed God in any term but Father. Finally, the dominance of the view of God as Father forces the Christian to recognize all others, especially cobelievers, as children of the Father, brothers and sisters under one Father.

In guiding us to consider God as Father, Jesus made an inestimable contribution to each person's self-understanding and value before the eyes of the world, he opened up to us the secret by which we can understand the dominant motivation of God's relationship with us—he approaches us in the best sense of Father. It is a constant source of wonderment that the Being we know as the one and true God wants us to understand himself as Father; for thousands of years human beings more easily have understood God as Power, Authority, Lord and awesome Master, Judge, than they have accepted him as Father in the concrete circumstances of their lives. Yet this is the title Jesus knew is best to address to God; he lived with God as his Father, and urged us to do so, as well.

It is typically Jewish that the mention of God's title, *Father,* should elicit an immediate expression that God's name be held holy by all creation, in all times and places. Isaiah had long ago known the picture of the heavenly beings unendingly calling "Holy, holy, holy" before the throne of God, and the tradition of Israel is replete with the call to Israel to be alert and attentive to the holiness of God, to reverence him as holy, the source of all holiness. It is not surprising, then, that the first words from the lips of those who address the Father are a wish or prayer that God's name be kept holy. It may be surprising, however, that one's first thought before God is not of one's own needs, but of concern to see that the name of the Father be kept holy.

The entire New Testament is a witness to the basic framework in which the appearance of Jesus took on its first meaning; the New Testament witnesses to the expectation of, and longing for the kingdom of God. By this image of kingdom, Israel summed up its tradition in which what goodness and happiness and peace it knew under David and Solomon would be once again granted to Israel—in even greater lavishness than before, if possible. Having suffered disasters of severe magnitude after the time of David and Solomon, the high points of their history, Israel looks for restoration to that position of Chosen One where it would know the dazzling effects of God's love when it is no longer impeded by Satanic and human folly. Jesus, then, urges his followers to pray to God for that form of existence, still out of our grasp and ultimately ours only if God grants it, wherein God, the source of all happiness, like a king controls human lives, and wards off every grief from our lives.

Typical of Matthew, who retained in his presentation of Jesus strong accents of the original climate of Jesus' dealings with a Jewish society, Matthew developed here what the Jewish Scriptures considered to be the essence of God's reign: the dominance of God's will which is the key to human happiness. Not that Luke ignored the need for following the will of God; on the contrary, he emphasized it, but under the more Gentile form of obedience to the teaching. Jesus himself had always been devoted to the fulfillment of the will of his Father, as had the bitter lessons, preserved in the Old Testament, encouraged him and his contemporaries to be. Jesus weighed his devotion and love for God by his obedience to God; he can only hope that the confidence he had in the effects of obedience to the will of his

Father would be understood and sought for by his followers. Heaven itself is traditionally preserved as the model for earth, for in heaven the will of God dominates all relationships and the effect is supreme harmony and happiness. This could be our circumstance, in the view of Jesus, if only the will of God were obeyed here as in heaven. Adam had shown us the results of disobedience, results for which we still pay, not only in dying, but in weakness which makes us prone to continue the separation from God which Adam had begun. Jesus appeared as the second Adam in that he fixed on obedience as our key to reunion with God and ultimately lived up to his word as he accepted in total trust the will of his Father that he die. It is in this absolute trust in the goodness of God to those who obey that he urges us to pray that the will of God be supreme on earth. Indeed, others, besides God, have historically dominated the world or parts of it; what has history taught us of such dominance, if not that where the will of God is obeyed, there is our best chance for happiness? The ever-present model of the peace and joy which obedience to the divine will brings is that heavenly world which we often glimpse; if only what causes such peace and joy there rules us here.

One of the most striking relationships Jesus drew for his disciples is the connection between worldly needs and trust in God. Almost to the point of being considered naive exaggeration, Jesus's encouragement that we learn trust for our daily needs from the way God has provided for birds and lilies has become a monumental challenge to all Christians. What seems to have been the original preoccupation of Jesus calling for abandonment of worry in his finding that people looked so much to their own devices for their happiness that they failed to realize the part God played in his role of Father in the concerns of his children. To protect against losing confidence in the Father, and not to lead us to think we should be unconcerned about the necessities of life Jesus calls us to reflect on the logical implications of God's fatherhood for us. That we slowly, perhaps imperceptibly, shift our hope for true happiness to the things of this world, particularly to money, is to turn to idol worship, and it was against this shift that Jesus urgently preached.

The words of Jesus, which suggest that God would fulfill our needs, represent a logical conclusion drawn from God's desire to be known as our Father. The history of Judaism and Christianity has long had to contend with this conclusion in a world where, in fact, God's intervention and provision for his children is not as constant or as dramatic as we might wish. Yet, this sense of God's absence in one's time of need has never been accepted as an indication that we should understand God to be, or be made up of, evil. Jesus never wavered in his confidence in the love God has revealed for him, nor would he let us waver in this trust. For Jesus, God was fully good—unlike the gods as perceived by other thinkers in societies of the past; it follows that good must be his intention always for me. If he is my Father, how can I be in need? The problem of evil, in short, must be resolved inasmuch as possible without harm to the belief which was the foundation of Jewish and Christian analysis of reality: that God is good, that evil does not proceed from him. That we have progressed to understand that God might permit evil or need or suffering, without willing it directly on us, for our good is a step taken without harming our remembrance of God as good.

Within this context Jesus encouraged us to think of ourselves, of our needs, and to ask God and no other deity for daily help, daily provision, our daily food. Petitioning God thus keeps me within the traditional awareness of God as source of my total well-being and Father of me, his child. Should God my Father not provide what I cannot provide on my efforts alone, I do not turn elsewhere to things which I begin to consider as more trustworthy for bringing me happiness than God.

A second concern is a request for forgiveness of sins, that God forget, as Matthew's version puts it, our debts to God. This was the constant prayer of Jesus's memories back to his earliest days, and it occupied the minds of many Israelites and was one of the essential petitions rising daily from the Temple in Jerusalem. Jesus encouraged his disciples to make this petition their own; in this way we can remain attentive to the reality of the relationship which exists between the Father and his children.

Both Gospel versions of the Our Father make the request for forgiveness of sins rest within an acknowledgment of the disciples' forgiveness of others. It is not necessary to review the teaching of Jesus regarding his follower's willingness to forgive, to love his enemy. From our awareness of that teaching we can understand why Jesus would see it as so reasonable that we ask for forgiveness with the frame of mind that he is willing to forgive and does forgive those who have hurt him. In human thinking it makes no sense that an unloving person expect love. Jesus capitalized on this human way of thinking. Not that we are forgiven only because or if we forgive our enemies, or that we are forgiven in the manner in which we forgive our enemy—we are simply reminded that it is only reasonable that forgiveness by God occurs in the context of our own willingness to forgive others. Ultimately, what is at stake here is conversion, something which God longs for, but which can only occur if we are willing to undergo it; to say that we do wish to return to God—a process which essentially entails forgiveness—is to imply that we now approach the world of God as he sees and desires it. But to approach the world this way is to be forgiving, to be, in other words, what God wants to be for all people. To be in his image and likeness is to relate to him and his as he does. We hope for that forgiveness which we know is at the heart of God; it is only logical that we seek to be one with him, and to be like him: forgiving.

In Jesus's religious world, there existed as the result of many prophecies, an expectation that the change from "this world" to the "next age" would involve, unhappily, an exercise of power by Satan which could only be called traumatic; Satan, realizing that this was his last opportunity to control God's world, would wage a struggle worthy of his nature and the stakes for which he fights. Since in Jewish thinking God himself cannot be defeated or harmed by Satan, the struggle at the end was a struggle worked out within God's creation, the product of his love and thus dear to him. Destroying it was next best to destroying God. Everyone can expect to be part of this final struggle, particularly the faithful who are singularly objects of Satan's hate and treachery. To be protected from the eventual test of one's fidelity to God in these extreme circumstances is the final request of the Our Father. Who can hope to withstand the mighty power of him who said to Jesus, "All these things [kingdoms of the world and their glories] are mine; I will give them to you." (Lk 4:6 and Mt 4:9.) It is the common understanding which Jesus reflected here: only with God's intervention can we hope to escape the confrontation with Satan which we fear. At another moment St. Paul would assure us that God would provide us with what is necessary to overcome any temptation put in our way; this is an assurance that our petition against the Evil One and his ultimate machinations would be gladly heard.

The Our Father sums up the relationship of God to those who believe in him and hold steadfastly to him. Jesus asks us to think of God as our Father, to approach him in this way and to look to him, as our Father, for the blessings which pour from a Father's heart. The Our Father Church serves to remind us how we have come to understand the world in which we live as the world of a Father and his children—and we thank Christ for this precious understanding of reality.

Dominus Flevit Chapel   *Lk 19:41–44*

About midway down the western slope of the Mount of Olives, within the ruins of a cemetery with burial materials going back to the first century A.D., is a lovely chapel with a grand view of Jerusalem, particularly of the area where once stood the Temple of Jerusalem. This chapel lies close to the ancient route usually followed by travelers coming from Jericho and the north end of the Dead Sea to Jerusalem. Though we cannot be sure it marks the exact spot, it causes us to pause for a moment to remember that Jesus, according to Luke, wept over Jerusalem's fate as he moved down the last half of the Mount of Olives, seated on a colt of an ass, about to enter Jerusalem—for the first time in the synoptic gospel tradition. Jesus was riding on this colt, which itself was walking in part on garments, cloaks, thrown before it by joyous crowds; in Jesus' ears were the exhilarating words of his disciples: "Blessings on him, the King, who comes in the name of the Lord! In heaven peace and glory in the highest heavens!"

Jesus' disciples, then, were guiding their master the last few hundreds of yards and making of this walk a triumphal entry of Jerusalem's Messiah, Jerusalem's King; they did this, as Luke explicitly remarks, because of "all the miracles they had seen" (Lk 19:37). This notice by Luke intends to show the grounds on which the disciples, and others, praised Jesus; it shows how little they were prepared for the coming moments of suffering and death when Jesus failed to exercise those powers by which he had so successfully overcome all enemies including Satan up till now. Jesus had warned his followers of what would happen once he had entered into the stronghold of those who plotted against him, but his disciples "did not understand him when he said this; it was hidden from them so that they should not see the meaning of it, and they were afraid to ask him about what he had said" (Lk 9:45). The disciples knew only that the miracle worker was about to enter Jerusalem; he was the blessed one, coming to take possession of the city belonging to the One who had sent him, the city that would be the most bitterly contested ground in history.

In contrast to this welcome was the attitude of some Pharisees in the crowd; they could only respond, "Master, silence your disciples." Such had been their reaction throughout the lives of Jesus and John the Baptizer; the Pharisees could accept neither, despite one's being so different in approach to humans from the other. It is interesting at this point of the narrative to refer to what most scholars think to be one of Luke's sources, the Gospel of Mark. Mark also narrated a wonderful reception of Jesus as he approached Jerusalem, describing Jesus as the Messiah in the minds of those welcoming and accompanying him. Immediately following the sullen remarks of the Pharisees, however, Mark told the story of Jesus' cursing a fig tree, a symbol of God's turning from Israel, traditionally symbolized in the Old Testament by a vine or a tree, for its unwillingness to bear fruit at the preaching of repentance by those authorized by God who is coming. Luke, it seems, eliminated this cursing story in favor of a different expression of divine reaction to the rejection of Jesus and John: the forecast of the destruction of Jerusalem.

Jesus wept for Jerusalem, the site of God's dwelling for centuries, where his Name and his Glory dwelt. Jewish thought regarded all the world as organized to form rings emanating from and leading to the holiest of places, the Holy of Holies, the private quarters of earth's King and Israel's covenant Partner. Jesus wept for the imminent destruction of city and Temple which would soon reject him and suffer the tragedy of "one stone not being allowed to stand on another" (Lk 19:44). One cannot fail to hear in Jesus' words the former pleas for attention addressed to their contemporaries by prophets such as Isaiah and Jeremiah. Nor can we miss the Old Testament manner of thinking that pierces human events to show that the real cause of joy or sorrow rests in the reaction of God to Israel's attention to him. Thus, Jerusalem would be destroyed, but not because the Roman army was stronger than Israel's army or because other human factors favored a Roman victory. Such causes of the destruction of Jerusalem were secondary, for God could manipulate them as he had done so many times in his defense of his chosen ones. Jesus pointed to the radical cause for the destruction of Jerusalem: ". . . because you did not recognize your opportunity when God offered it!" (Lk 19:44.)

In formulating this reason Jesus squarely identified himself as one more of a long line of those who pleaded for Israel's attention to its relationship with God before it was too late. It soon became a major defense of Christianity that its Lord should have been recognized as continuing, indeed, fulfilling, the call of God to his people over the centuries. And Christianity, because it accepted Jesus as Lord sent by God, soon and inevitably identified itself as a true continuation of the Chosen People; it saw itself as responding positively to the call to repentance and fidelity with a faith characteristic of Abraham, a faith which God rewarded with the promise of blessings.

Jesus wept for Jerusalem, for his people. Jerusalem was the city *par excellence* of Jesus' forefathers, the center of pilgrimage three times a year for all Israelite males (See 195), the Sion hymned in psalms and the symbol of God's union with Israel. Given his history, Jesus' weeping at what he knew would come to pass is not surprising. Sobering to Christians and to Jews are the words of John's Prologue which sum up succinctly this sad break in covenant friendship: "he came to his own, and his own received him not" (Jn 1:11).

There is no doubt that the destruction of Jerusalem was a great tragedy. Yet the Scriptures did not perceive such suffering as the worst effect or pain to result from breaking friendship with God. No, the worst effect, visible in all physical sufferings visited on Israel, was God's simply allowing Israelites and Gentiles as well, to follow the path they chose to live freely alienated from him. There is no greater punishment than that, for the simple withdrawing of God, at our choice, from human life is to set in motion and give sway to all the forces which will destroy ourselves. Human beings left to themselves is the greatest tragedy, as Scripture sees it, for in this state are contained all the potentialities for suffering which we can inflict on ourselves and others.

Jesus's prediction of the destruction of Jerusalem occurred not only on the western slope of the Mount of Olives. Soon, during his teaching days in the Temple area itself, not far from the front of the Temple building proper, Jesus again predicted the state of "one stone not resting on another" (Lk 21:6). This particular prediction, within the walls of the Temple area itself, and founded on the Marcan prediction of the destruction of the Temple and of Jerusalem as its source, was aimed, however, not as justifying the divine reaction to Israel's disobedience, but as the circumstances in which Christians should be brave and trusting; it is all part of the divine plan by which the infidelities of all this world, this "age," will be brought to an end and replaced by an "age" in which the divine goodness will have its way. Then, there will be a presence of God which will render all creation fully happy, as God alone can do it. Till then, we remain faithful as God, admittedly through pain at times, overcomes his enemy, Satan, and all under Satan's power. We trust in God and realize that our own purification to becoming our best selves is a miniature of that cleansing which must take place so that God may fully and forever bless all the world.

The Lord's weeping, ultimately, is a weeping over the inability of human beings to respond to the one person who can free them for total happiness, over human preference for "living in darkness and the shadow of death" (Lk 1:79—drawing on the seven-hundred-year-old words of Is 9:1). To this doomed city Jesus now descended.

part **3**

Jerusalem

NEW TESTAMENT JERUSALEM

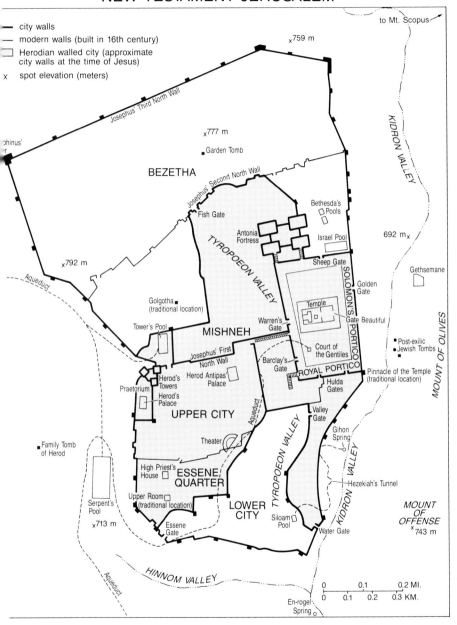

city walls
modern walls (built in 16th century)
Herodian walled city (approximate city walls at the time of Jesus)
x   spot elevation (meters)

to Mt. Scopus

x759 m

Josephus' Third North Wall

x777 m

Garden Tomb

BEZETHA

Josephus' Second North Wall

Fish Gate

KIDRON VALLEY

Bethesda's Pools

Antonia Fortress

Israel Pool

692 m x

ohinus' r

x792 m

Sheep Gate

Gethsemane

Aqueduct

TYROPOEON VALLEY

Golden Gate

Golgotha (traditional location)

Tower's Pool

MISHNEH

Warren's Gate

Temple

Gate Beautiful

SOLOMON'S PORTICO

Court of the Gentiles

Post-exilic Jewish Tombs

Josephus' First North Wall

Barclay's Gate

ROYAL PORTICO

Pinnacle of the Temple (traditional location)

Praetorium

Herod's Towers

Herod Antipas' Palace

Hulda Gates

MOUNT OF OLIVES

Herod's Palace

UPPER CITY

Valley Gate

Aqueduct

Family Tomb of Herod

Theater

Gihon Spring

TYROPOEON VALLEY

KIDRON VALLEY

Hezekiah's Tunnel

High Priest's House

ESSENE QUARTER

MOUNT OF OFFENSE x743 m

Serpent's Pool

Upper Room (traditional location)

LOWER CITY

Siloam Pool

x713 m

Essene Gate

Water Gate

HINNOM VALLEY

0   0.1   0.2 MI.

0   0.1   0.2   0.3 KM.

Aqueduct

En-rogel Spring

Olive Trees in the Garden of Gethsemani

Gethsemani

Practically at the bottom of the western side of the Mount of Olives in the Kidron Valley is a most holy site, the place of the arrest of Jesus and of the prayer of Jesus before that treacherous arrest. The site itself, long venerated by Christians, is marked today by a noteworthy church which includes in its garden ancient olive trees reminiscent of the olive grove in which Jesus, as Luke notes, prayed through the night after teaching in the Temple area by day (Lk 21:37). So old do these olive trees appear that we might suspect them to be the trees which mutely watched the terrible events of that night nearly two thousand years ago; though it is not likely that an olive tree would live so long, it is quite possible that these present olive trees do come ultimately from ancestors which witnessed the pain of that night.

The church marking this holy site, called the Basilica of the Agony or, more recently, the Church of All Nations, was begun in 1919 A.D. and consecrated in 1924 A.D. The basilica is readily visible because it stands overlooking the Kidron Valley to the steep eastern wall of Jerusalem. Very easy to see are the three great arches in the front of the basilica which separate the four statues on high of the evangelists and their symbols. Matthew is symbolized by the young man; his Gospel begins with a genealogy of a young man. Mark is symbolized by a lion: his Gospel begins with a mention of a voice, identified later as a lion, crying in the desert. Luke is symbolized by an ox: his Gospel begins in the Temple, where sacrifices were carried on—and the ox is the animal par excellence of sacrifice. John is symbolized by an eagle: like an eagle, the Gospel of John, and particularly the Prologue, soars to the heights.

Above the arches and the evangelists is a great triangular mosaic, whose theme is the Jesus in glory offering of his sufferings and those of the world to the Father. Thus the basilica invites us to reflect on what the evangelists have reported about the tragedy begun with betrayal in this garden area, the tragedy which ended in nothing short of the sitting of Jesus at the right hand of his Father in glory. The church itself is, however, a pattern of this movement from tragedy to glory, for when we enter it, we enter from the garden of sorrow, and pass time in a dimly lit place of prayer, an interior meant to stir up in the visitor the grief of that terrible night. Only after this can we exit into the light of day whereby we can rejoice with Jesus in glory.

Within the basilica we must let our eyes become accustomed to the darkness. There is one place of light here and that is centered on the large rock, surrounded by a metal crown of thorns. This rock traditionally has been considered the rock on which Jesus knelt for his prayerful moments, apart from his disciples, just before he was arrested.

So impressive is this interior that many nations donated money to its building and preservation; these benefactors are remembered on the ceiling of the basilica by representations symbolizing each nation. As we stand about the middle of the basilica facing the altar and look up at the right third of the ceiling, we can discern the symbols of the United States of America. Notable also in this church construction are the windows of alabaster, the small cupolas which remind us of Byzantine art, the mosaics of the cupolas executed by Italian artists and the lovely mosaic floor on which we stand.

The mosaic floor particularly deserves comment. It is an exact representation of the mosaic floor of the church built when Theodosius (379–93 A.D.) was emperor of Constantinople, and called "elegant" in a document written by a pilgrim in the fourth century. A.D. Beneath the covers of the floor is the mosaic flooring of the original Theodosian basilica—a precious archaeological remain. We are, by virtue of this identical flooring, in touch with a long tradition of veneration at this spot; and we can add that between the modern church and the Theodosian basilica there was built here, too, a small church in the time of the crusaders, a church dedicated to St. Savior. Here, then, Christians have come for many centuries to share in the sorrowful event of that night almost two thousand years ago; the vestiges of these Christians allow us to share our moment with them.

Grotto of the Agony

Before considering the significance of this revered site in accord with the Gospel presentations, a word should be said about the grotto which can be found once we exit from the Garden of

Gethsemani and follow the road towards the Grotto of the Virgin, not many yards from the olive grove of Gethsemani. This grotto, between the Grotto of the Virgin and Gethsemani, is called the Grotto of the Agony, but is actually the place of the betrayal and arrest of Jesus, the place where Jesus went with his disciples to meet the betrayer and his accomplices. This area thus contains three places connected with the sorrowful events of this night: the olive grove, known as Gethsemani, the place where Jesus prayed apart from his disciples, and the place of the betrayal of Jesus by Judas. We can trace worship services at the grotto and at the site of the agony at least to the fourth century A.D.

The Gospel stories about what happened at Gethsemani can be divided into two parts: what happened to Jesus before his arrest, and the arrest itself with its attendant circumstances. John does not report the suffering Jesus underwent; Matthew, Mark and Luke in various ways ask their readers to consider carefully the degree of fear Jesus suffered at the realization of what his Father was about to ask from him. Yet, even John conveys some of this suffering in the one verse he gives to its reality at an earlier point in his Gospel: "Now my soul is terrified—and what should I say? 'Father, save me from this hour.'" (Jn 12:27.)

The Agony in the Garden   *Mt 26:36-46; Mk 14:32-42; Lk 22:39-46*

In the stories of Matthew, Mark and Luke, two elements are the backbone of the narratives: the call to the disciples to pray lest they enter a temptation which they cannot resist and the prayer of Jesus to his Father. Indeed, the three Gospels follow the same format to introduce the suffering of Jesus and conclude with the call to attentiveness, watchfulness, prayer. The concern of these reports is as much to report the exhortation to the disciples as it is to tell the story of Jesus' moments in the Garden. In this way the reader, a disciple of another generation, is asked to be attentive, to watch, to pray when it is obvious that suffering in association with the Lord is to be the disciple's lot. While Luke goes furthest in detailing the physical effects of Jesus' mental anguish, all three agree that the suffering of Jesus here is unparalleled in the life of Jesus as they have reported it thus far. Here we receive an insight into the human reality of Jesus. His was a struggle between survival and obedience and his whole being was convulsed by it; his was not purely an intellectual struggle, but a torture which brought him to ask for freeing from suffering. The reader finally has a glimpse of the psychological struggle Jesus had to undergo in wrenching himself into obedience.

There are many values in these reports. The nearness of the reader to the terrible moment of his Lord is one. Another is the bitter contrast between one person struggling for his life, to be the best he can be before his Father, and the weariness and inattentiveness of his closest friends, so physically close and so psychologically distant. A third value is the awareness of the seriousness of the sin for which Jesus must suffer. For, if Jesus has freed us from our sins by his death, we can already sense, through his terror in the garden, how thoroughly evil must be those desires and actions which sinners find pleasurable and desirable.

In short, Jesus' suffering is the central aspect of these Gethsemani reports, and the disciple finds strength in his own loneliness to imitate the Master who, even in this decision to obey to the death, goes before him. But the story of Jesus' struggle is bracketed by attention to the disciples, warnings to the reader of how disciples might associate themselves with the Lord, warnings that the disciples, like the Master, must pray in the face of suffering, pray for strength to endure and, above all, that the will of the Father be done.

We should not overlook that the entire expression of Jesus' soul-rending prayer is set against his view of God as his Father. In suffering, the disciple must always know the One who controls the world as Father, despite the conflict which we sense between fatherhood and a father's permitting a child to suffer and to die. Jesus saw the decision of God in his regard as the decision of his Father. The problem of suffering must be resolved, if it can be resolved, within the context of the father-son relationship, not by the abandonment of it.

Capture of Jesus   *Mt 26:47-56; Mk 14:43-52; Lk 22:47-53*

The second part of the Gethsemani story has to do with the capture of Jesus. All four of the Gospels narrate the basic elements of this event: Judas, the betrayer, knew where to find Jesus, and he found him there; Judas betrayed Jesus; his disciples trie to prevent the capture by recourse to weapons and Jesus rejected that intervention; Jesus marveled that his capture must be done in darkness and silence, when he could just as easily have been captured in daylight right up in the Temple area where he taught openly; Jesus is bound and led away.

Clearly, the evangelists not only give details, but also present the conspiratorial style of the authorities as a sign that Jesus really is a victim of injustice; indeed, if the ordinary people, the listeners of Jesus, knew of what was happening, they would violently oppose Jesus' arrest. Thus, into this story of the capture is built an apologetic or defense of Jesus' innocence, a dominant theme of the Gospels from their very beginnings.

Matthew adds to these basic elements of the capture story the words of Jesus by which is explained the desire of Jesus that his disciples not fight to defend him; first, people who fight by the sword would die by it, and Jesus did not want this to happen here; secondly, given that God is Jesus' Father, surely the Father would be moved to defend his son if it were right—but Scripture indicated that defense is not the proper course of action, and Jesus wanted Scripture to be fulfilled. Indeed, Scripture must be fulfilled and Jesus' life was guided by the need for that fulfillment; he understood when all others did not that the words of God spoken in the Jewish Scriptures are to be cherished and lived out, for in obedience to that Voice Jesus became perfect Son of his Father.

Further, Matthew follows Mark's text by citing Scripture which prophesied that the "Shepherd would be struck and at that moment his sheep would be scattered." In this way, even the abandonment of Jesus by his disciples appeared predictable. Matthew, above all others, welcomes the Old Testament texts which are fulfilled in Jesus' life; by them, the events of Jesus' life are made intelligible and the events bring to a close the Scriptures which foretold them.

Mark is unique in telling his readers that, among those who fled the scene of the capture, there was an unnamed young man. Many interpreters have suggested that this young witness is the author of Mark.

Luke, too, has something to offer in this story which is not accentuated by others. Luke concludes the story by noting that "this is your hour; now is the exercise of the power of darkness" (Lk 22:53). Many interpreters see this sentence as the completion of what was said at the conclusion of the Devil's temptations just before Jesus' public life began: "and having finished tempting him the devil left him till another opportune moment" (Lk 4:13). Thus, they understand Luke's presentation of the temptations of Jesus as a prelude to the time when the satanic power will have its full, destructive way with Jesus. The capture of Jesus is what we were waiting for, ever since the Devil left off his attempts at controlling Jesus through temptations.

Jesus Identifies Himself   *Jn 18:1-12*

When we turn to John, however, we not only find this or that aspect of the capture of Jesus to be a contribution of a Gospel; with John we have a different approach to the entire scene. Here no agony of Jesus is reported; with the approach of the captors, Jesus knew all that was about to happen. Having told us that, John reports that when Jesus identified himself to those who sought him, they fell back to the ground, motionless until Jesus bade them move. What is the meaning of this strange encounter between Jesus and those who have come for him?

When Jesus identified himself to his captors, he was answering their reply to his question, "Whom do you seek?" Hearing them answer, "Jesus of Nazareth," Jesus responded with the deeply significant words, "I am," (Jn 18:4–8). These two words are, of course, on one level simply words affirming that he is Jesus of Nazareth: if he is the only one they are seeking, they can let the others go. But the Greek of these words, *ego eimi,* are famous as the abbreviated name of God (See 87). Thus in Johannine irony, Jesus identified himself as "I Am," and the captors showed the proper response: they fell back to the ground and did not rise until Jesus told them to. What is the point of this rather strange account, especially when we realize that its strangeness is intentionally accentuated by John as he lifts us to this higher level of seeking and understanding?

This particular slant to the capture story seems to be an affirmation of what had already been stated in another, earlier part of John, that Jesus lays down his life and takes it up again, that no one takes his life from him. Thus, what might appear to a reader as impotency by Jesus who, captured, does not free himself now is understood as a willingness on Jesus' part to submit himself to these captors. He wills this laying down of his life; they do not take it from him unless he wants it to happen. The power behind this is the power of that Person revealed to Israel as "I Am." If we understand, then, who Jesus is, we can appreciate the truth that Jesus died only because he permitted others to control him; he is not, ultimately, subjected to the power of others; they, in reality, act only as he permits them to act. Here, then, in the depths of what appears to be weakness is revealed the true identity of Jesus, and such a revelation is the abiding concern of the person who wrote John.

Finally, we might note that, in the moment of the disciples' attack on Jesus' captors, it is Luke who reports that, when the ear of the high priest's servant had been cut off, Jesus spent a moment in this tense and sorrowful scene to heal that servant, his enemy. In his own sorrow Jesus taught the love of enemy, a major concern of Jesus as Luke presents him and his teaching.

Such, then, are thoughts which recall the significance of Gethsemani, of the moments of grief, terror, injustice, sorrow, abandonment, divine revelation. We stand in awe at our own physical nearness to them in our presence here today.

The Pool of Siloam

The Pool of Siloam
(Siloe)

The Pool of Siloam is about fifty-two feet long, about fifteen feet wide, and three feet deep. In the fifth century A.D. here stood a sizeable church with three aisles in honor of the miracle Jesus worked here. The church enclosed with four porticoes the pool where the sick of Jesus' time, especially the lepers, washed in hope of freeing themselves from their sicknesses. The church was destroyed in the seventh century A.D. and no one did any more to build another church or shrine. Thus the pool stands as a mute witness of the first century A.D., when Jesus used these waters to cure a man blind from birth.

The Tunnel of Hezekiah

The pool is snuggled against a hillside which curves around the east side of the pool. If we were to tunnel into that hillside, working our way southeast through the hillside, we would reach fresh water flowing from the Spring of Gihon on the other side of the hill. Such a tunnel was actually dug about 700 B.C. at the command of Hezekiah, king of Jerusalem.

Hezekiah, unable to encompass the Spring of Gihon within the eastern walls of the Jerusalem of his time, had a tunnel built so that the Assyrian enemy would not know how the Israelites got their water supply; surely they did not venture out of the city walls! But water flowed silently through a tunnel of 583 yards to the pool within the city walls and behind the hillside, into the Pool of Siloam!

It was a remarkable feat of engineering: two groups of workmen with pick axes, shovels, and carefully calculated directions started out, one from the spring side of the hill and the other from the pool side. A plaque placed in the tunnel commemorated the remarkable achievement of these men; it is now stored in the Classical Museum of Istanbul.

Ever since Hezekiah's time, water has flowed through his tunnel to fill the Pool of Siloam. Today we can walk through the ancient tunnel connecting the Fountain of the Virgin, the pool where the waters of Gihon gather, and the Pool of Siloam.

Feast of Sukkoth

The Pool of Siloam had an important liturgical function to play in the time of Jesus. At the time of the Feast of Sukkoth or Tabernacles, or Tents, occurring sometime in September-October, water was brought from this pool to the Temple of Jerusalem with great trumpet blasts; there it was poured together with wine into a tube beside the Temple altar which allowed the water and wine to flow, ultimately, into the Kidron Valley. This liturgical action was partly thanksgiving for the harvest of what was grown over the summer, which depended on water received in the springtime and kept in wells, and partly petitioning of God that he would provide water for the growth of the newly planted seeds to be harvested in the next spring from March through May. During the Feast of Sukkoth Jesus identified himself as the source of the water which quenches all thirst. (Jn 7:37; See below, 195.)

Cure of the Man Born Blind   *Jn 9*

But for Christians the most famous event associated with this pool is the cure of the man born blind. The cure itself is as simply told as it is marvelous. So marvelous was it that the blind man, once cured, could say that no one had experienced such a miracle as this since the beginning of time (Jn 9:32). Looked at this way, we see that there is much more to be told to the reader here than just the fact of the miracle, wonderful as it surely is.

The context of the miracle is very significant. Jesus had just argued, for the length of two chapters, with "Jews" as they are designated at this point of the Gospel; indeed, great pessimism had set in at the end of chapter six as many followers of Jesus began to leave him, and chapter five itself contains seeds of exasperation as Jesus tries to defend his curing a man on the Sabbath at the Pool of Bethesda. Chapter nine, then, continues the cause for antagonism, for the cure through the waters of

Siloam was a cure worked on the Sabbath. But we must also be aware that the cure has to do with blindness and sight, qualities which each side of the Jesus debate—Jewish Christian and Jewish Non-Christian—claimed for itself and attached to the other. It is not surprising that the cure story ends with the self-condemnation of the Pharisees who claimed they could see and needed no help like blind people. Moreover, the following story, on good and bad shepherding, is a fitting conclusion to the lengthy attack on the Jewish leaders mounted through the chapters of John. Thus, in this context we see a great deal of the acrimonious feelings expressed which separated Jewish Christians from Jewish non-Christians at the time of the writing down of this Gospel.

The interchange between the cured man and the Pharisees is very instructive—and certainly meant to be, for much more time is spent on it than on the working of the cure itself. So many excellent defensive arguments are made here, particularly the appeal to the fact: I was blind; he told me to wash and I see. Against this realism there can be no denial that Jesus is from God. The healed man can only conclude that Jesus is a prophet; later he is offered the opportunity to believe in Jesus as Son of Man. The Pharisees are prevented from belief in Jesus on two counts; first, Jesus worked this miracle on the Sabbath and this, for the Pharisees, was an act defying the Law of God to keep holy the Sabbath by not working; secondly, the Pharisees do not know where this man Jesus is from. That is, they know he is from Nazareth and therefore no special messenger from God, for "nothing good comes from Nazareth,"—indeed most prophecies indicated that the Messiah of God would come from Bethlehem, and Jesus, as far as they knew, did not come from Bethlehem.

Two elements of this interrogation by the Pharisees should be noted. First, the man's parents sense they will be expelled from the synagogue if they are judged to be defending their son's views about his cure. They will appear to defend the proposition that Jesus is the Messiah (Jn 9:22). For many scholars, what is said to be a fear in Jesus' time was actually the fear in John's time. The Pharisees of 85 A.D. had indeed moved to exclude the Jews who believed in Jesus from the synagogue services which Jews who believed in Jesus normally attended. This excommunication from prayer together accounts for the acerbic tone which the Gospel portrays, for the Gospel is an attempt to defend the Christians of John's time by arguing, chapter after chapter, that Jesus is the Messiah, the Son of God, that through belief in him we will have life everlasting (Jn 20:31). continuation of the chosen people; the impression the opponents want to give is false, caused by ignorance and blindness which, when willful, will not encourage God to have mercy and teach anew the truth about Jesus. At every step, then, the Gospel of John wants to pierce the meaning of events to reveal the truth they contain about Jesus, thus justifying the belief of the Jews of time in Jesus.

A second point should be made here. The Pharisees ultimately throw up their hands and drive the cured man away; they do this because he is, when all is said and done, a sinner and as such his witness is no good, even deceptive. This is the kind of argument the Pharisees and non-Christian Jews could easily make when forced to listen to the faith statements Christian Jews make; why believe them, for they do not follow Moses any longer, they are sinners. Again, we are brought into the contemporary scene of John and his community as it faced the arguments of the nonbelieving Jews surrounding them.

Three particular final points should be made here. First, the story of the blind man begins with an assessment of the cause of his blindness: either he was responsible or his parents were responsible for this blindness, and the responsibility flowed from their sinfulness. Jesus overturned human thinking here, which is quite prone to seek the cause of sickness in sin. Jesus saw suffering rather as the opportunity to show the great love of God, for God is the One who circles ever vigilantly to pick up the pieces Satan has caused by his destructive ways. This is just one of the many answers Scripture offers to the problem of evil.

Second, the man's blindness suggested two thoughts to Jesus. First, blindness makes him think of night, and of death. Jesus would undergo death, would enter night, but only when the Father indicated the day and the hour. Till then, Jesus worked while the light lasts, that is, while he was given life in which to work. Secondly, while he worked, he not only enjoyed light; he was the Light, the Light of the World. He is the one by whom everyone else can see. Without him, we enter into the darkest of nights, where we see nothing as real any more.

Third, at the end of the story about the blind man now able to see, Jesus revealed himself to be the Son of Man, and immediately spoke of judgment. (See above, 167.) Judgment is a role of the Son of Man as portrayed in the Book of Daniel which introduces us to the image of the Son of Man. In the vision of Daniel told to us in chapter seven of the Book of Daniel, God, under the form of the Ancient of Days, hands over the judgment of the world to "one like a Son of Man." Thus, Jesus, who understood himself to be the Son of Man seen by Daniel, immediately said that he had been sent into the world for judgment. His judgment, however, is peculiar; it depends on acceptance of Jesus. If we accept Jesus, we obviously have seen the truth of things; if one, who claims friendship with God and thus thinks he sees rightly—if he rejects Jesus, he condemns himself and clearly is blind. Sadly, Jesus could argue that the blindness of the Pharisees, before this and other miracles, resulted from their stubborn refusal to recognize the truth of what he has done and of who he is; their blindness was not by chance and so the judgment of them was *guilty*. They wanted to be blind.

St. Stephen's Gate

S t. Stephen's Gate

The only gate that pierces through the eastern wall of today's Jerusalem is found near the northern end of the eastern wall. It is called by various names; for instance, it received the name of the Lion's Gate after the Six Days' War—above the gate two beautifully sculpted lions greet visitors entering Jerusalem from the east—and at times it was called the Sheep's Gate, for sheep were bought and sold nearby. But the gate has also long been called St. Stephen's Gate, for the area outside this gate is the traditional location of the stoning of St. Stephen (Acts 7:55–60).

St. Stephen is considered the first martyr of the Church; his feast day in the Church's liturgy occurs on the day after Christmas, a symbol of his nearness to Jesus as the first of his martyrs. The story of Stephen has many interesting highlights to which we now turn our attention.

Original Ministry of the Deacon Stephen   *Acts 6:1-7*

We do not know where Stephen came from. He appears in the Acts of the Apostles as one who solved a particular problem which bothered the earliest Christian community in Jerusalem. The problem involved the distribution of food to widows, a good deed which Jews had long practiced and which the first Jewish Christians continued for their own widows. It seems that, by the time Luke mentions the Christian widows in the Acts of the Apostles, they were of two types: widows native to Palestine and whose language, customs and culture were that of Palestine, and widows who, though Jewish, were quite recent arrivals in Palestine, with language and cultural background of the Mediterranean areas where they had spent almost all their lives. Given the diverse backgrounds of the widows, it is not surprising that they divided themselves into two groups along cultural lines. This division that raised the need to bring them food in two different areas of Jerusalem. For whatever reason, it is brought to our attention in Acts 6:1 that the community was not caring very well for the recently arrived widows. This failure, when brought to the attention of the full Church, lead to the appointment of seven men, who themselves were not native to Palestine, to see that the distribution of food fairly reached all widows, not just the native widows of Palestine. Of the seven men appointed to resolve this problem, two played still further roles in the Acts of the Apostles: Stephen and Philip, who is active in Acts, chapter eight.

When the seven men were selected by the Christians who are not native to Palestine, Peter and the other Eleven laid hands on them and thus appointed them to their responsibility. They are to *serve,* and the Greek word used is *diakonein*; it is easy to see how the term *deacon* comes from the Greek word. Though the noun is never used, only the verb, Stephen and the other six are often called the first deacons of the Church; they continue to serve as the founding fathers of the newly vitalized diaconate in the Catholic Church and ground the historical basis of deacons seen in Christian churches throughout the centuries.

Preaching of Stephen   *Acts 6:8-7:53*

But Stephen quickly moved from a rather limited public function of distributing food fairly to widows to a fame or notoriety as preacher and defender of Christianity. As we might expect, he specialized in discussion and argument among Jews who, like himself, had spent the good part of their lives outside Palestine and had only recently immigrated to the Holy Land of their forefathers. Stephen was evidently a thorn in the side of those with whom he debated in the synagogue in Greek; they finally could bring him to a trial where, as in the case of Jesus, false witness against him played a part.

Stephen gave a long speech at his trial in defense against the accusations Luke reports to us. The accusations have various wordings, but their essence is that Stephen made speeches that Jesus said he would destroy the Temple and change the customs of Moses. In short, Stephen spoke against God and Moses (Acts 6:14). In thinking about these accusations, we must ask whether Jesus ever did say he would destroy the Temple and change the customs of Moses.

Jesus never said he would destroy the Temple, but he did say often that the Temple would be destroyed. And, though he never said he would change the customs or laws of Moses, he

certainly adjusted, eliminated, tightened up various laws of
Israel's tradition. Stephen summed up some of the main thrusts
of Jesus' teachings. One has only to remember that the Stephen
story is told by Luke about ten to fifteen years after the actual
destruction of Jerusalem to realize how truly fulfilled were the
claims Stephen made about the Temple and about the changes
wrought by Christian reflection on what laws God really wanted
human beings to obey.

The speech of Stephen is long, the longest of any person in
the New Testament except Jesus. The speech essentially claimed
that the Temple in Jerusalem would be destroyed because the
Jews have rejected Jesus. This rejection implied a rejection of
willingness to listen to the Holy Spirit who recommended Jesus
in his quiet conversation with the souls of the Jews; this
rejection of Jesus was also seen as the culmination of many
rejections of God's prophets, so that what happened in Jesus'
case was just one more visible manifestation of a long-standing
hardness of heart and stiffness of neck towards the will and
messengers of God. But the speech also explained the
destruction of the Temple as the logical response to the deafness
of a people who, from their very beginning, were called to
worship God in this Temple; by their rejection of Jesus, they
rendered their worship of God—the very reason for their
existence—unacceptable. Moses was once, as Jesus would be,
the intermediary between God and Israel; when the Israelites
gave up on Moses when he was gone up to Mount Sinai, they
gave up on God as well and worshipped the golden calf. Now
they have given up on Jesus, and, in giving up on him, they are
rejected by God who stands by Jesus.

Death of Stephen   *Acts 7:54-60*

The Jews did not like this speech, and ground their teeth in
anger. But Stephen only provoked them more when he reported
a sudden, immediate vision of Jesus standing, of all places, at the
very right hand of God! The report of the vision was the
culmination of Stephen's effrontery. He was accused of
blasphemy in assigning to Jesus some kind of identity with God,
and was brought out of the city for a stoning to death, the
punishment ordained for blasphemy. Luke described Stephen in
terms that we could hope to imitate: he commended his spirit to
the Lord Jesus and prayed for his persecutors (Acts 7:59–60).
Standing by, holding the coats of the stoners, was a young man

named Saul. He would have a giant part in the story of the Acts of the Apostles, but only after he joined the Christians he first learned to despise.

Jewish Christians of the Diaspora   *Acts 8*

The brief story of Stephen fits into a larger framework given by the author of the Acts of the Apostles; it is to this framework we now turn. The Stephen story introduces us to a group of Christians of which we had hitherto not been aware. These are Jewish Christians, but different from the Jews who were born in Israel and grew up with and were the audience for Jesus. With these people we have the beginning of that element of Christianity which ultimately abandoned many essential elements of traditional Judaism. They were not Gentiles, but they seem to have been the Jews who most warmly welcomed the Gentiles into Christianity, and into a Christianity free from many aspects of Judaism maintained by Christian Jews. These Christian Jews like Stephen left Israel and began to spread the name of Jesus elsewhere, especially in Antioch of Syria. Today, Antioch is named the most supportive of first-century Christian communities evangelizing the Gentiles of present-day Turkey and Greece. It seems that Antioch was willing to support as well a Christianity which had abandoned circumcision and obedience to the total law of Moses as requirements for the Gentiles to be saved. Though the Acts of the Apostles tells of this changeover from a first Christian community which held to Jewish laws and practices while believing in Jesus as savior to a later Christian community which believed in Jesus as savior, but abandoned so much of ancient Judaism as not obligatory for salvation—though the Acts of the Apostles describes this changeover as a peaceful development, clearly it was not so peaceful for many individual Christians. Our Christianity seems logical to us now, without much of the practice and law of Israel and usually unnecessary grounded in belief in Jesus; but what is logical to us, and evident to boot, was not so clear-cut and logical to many people in the first century A.D.

It is to present the proper understanding of what faith in Christ implies that Luke shows, in the Acts of the Apostles, how Christianity developed properly, logically: step by step, we are shown how the Church became a predominantly Gentiles Church and how God revealed, step by step, the shape of the Christianity he wanted. The ultimate design finally becomes clear; it is worthwhile to realize that it began to emerge for the first time with the appearance of Stephen and those like him. He is part of a vast divine scheme which has given Christianity the fixed shape and form it knows today.

Changing the Customs of Moses   *Acts 6:14*

A last point should be attended to. Stephen was accused not only of speaking against the Temple, but also of speaking against the customs of Moses. His speech answered the accusation about the destruction of the Temple, but did not really touch on the latter accusation having to do with Jesus' changing the customs of Moses. Was this latter point ignored?

No, it was not ignored, but it needed much preparation on Luke's part before it could be simply and forcefully answered. That is to say, Luke finally dealt with the accusation in chapter fifteen, when he made it clear that Gentiles and Jews, as well, need not think of circumcision or obedience to the total law of Moses as necessary for salvation, for they were all saved through the grace of the Lord Jesus (Acts 15:11). But to prepare for this church decision in chapter fifteen, Luke must first introduce concrete examples that God has accepted the Gentiles and forgiven them their sins and given them the Spirit without asking that they first be circumcised and commit themselves to living the law of Moses. These examples start slowly with the conversion of the Samaritans (Acts 8:4–8), develop through the stories of Peter's conversion of the Gentile Cornelius and the many conversions of Gentiles in the journey of Paul (chapters thirteen and fourteen) through Turkey. With these stories in place, Luke resolved the question in chapter fifteen rather easily: no, Christians need not be circumcised and keep the entire Mosaic Law to be saved; belief in Jesus is the one essential for salvation.

But how is it that the first accusation against Stephen regarding the Temple could be resolved in one speech, whereas it took Luke some eight chapters to handle properly the second accusation on changing the law of Moses against Stephen? Probably the answer is that Luke wrote the Acts of the Apostles after the destruction of the Temple by the Romans in 70 A.D.; thus, the challenge to the Temple was a dead issue by the time Luke wrote and could be treated summarily in one telling speech. But the change from Jewish to Gentile church was not so simply resolved even by the time of the writing of Luke and Matthew. The problems of relating Christianity to Judaism, of relating God's traditional will to the meaning of salvation in Jesus—had many thorny debates to resolve. The urgency of this problem, which still agitated certain elements of Christianity, caused Luke to be so thorough in his description of it and its solution.

To stand at St. Stephen's Gate, then, is to remember a profession of belief in Jesus, even to the shedding of blood, and to recall the great movement of which St. Stephen was a beginning and integral part. We have profited from both these difficulties, and we have profited especially from the way in which Luke has presented both realities in his Acts of the Apostles.

The Pool of Bethesda

The Pool of Bethesda
(Bethzatha)

St. Stephen's Gate is located at the northern end of Jerusalem's eastern wall. If we enter St. Stephen's Gate from the east and proceed no more than a hundred yards, we reach the entry on the right to the compound which contains the Church of St. Anne, the headquarters of the White Fathers and—most important for our present purpose—the ruins of the famous Pool of Bethesda. In Jesus time it was called the Sheep Pool because nearby were the sheep market and the Sheep Gate, now called St. Stephen's Gate. *Bethesda* means *House of Mercy;* beneath a building containing five porticoes were two reservoirs which fed the Asclepieion or healing baths to the east. Still visible are the ruins of this building which sat over the curative waters. The building was as a trapezoid and divided, the north half from the south half, by a wall running east and west. Thus the building would have only four exterior walls, but have five walls and walkways in all for the sick to use. Over this east-west wall a church, whose ruins can still be seen, was built in the fifth century A.D.

The waters which served this pool flowed both before Jesus time and after it; the waters are well attested to in ancient documents which also witness to the worship of deities supposedly healing through these waters. Whereas Israel attributed the stirring of the waters to the hand of Yahweh's angel, other peoples, at other times, praised here the divine intervention of other gods, particularly Asclepius and Serapis. The Romans under Hadrian would eventually build a shrine here to Asclepius, the famed god of healing.

Jesus Healing

The healing of the man in the curative waters of Bethesda, a man ill for thirty-eight years, is the second cure told us in John and the third of the signs the evangelist wished to present to his readers. The Gospel narrative stressed three elements: the miracle, the Sabbath occasion of the miracle, and Jesus's reflection on his union with "My Father." Let us look briefly at each of these three elements of the Johannine narrative to appreciate better what happened in the healing days of Bethesda.

The Cure   *Jn 5:1-9*

The gospel story describes briefly the few details which provide the basic circumstances for the miracle of Jesus. A man lies helpless near the curative waters, helpless indeed for thirty-eight years. On seeing the man and realizing how long he had suffered, Jesus concluded that the man did want to be cured and instinctively asked him if his conclusion was right. The man said "Yes," but, not realizing that Jesus would perform a miracle, explained why his desire for health has never reached fruition: he had to be helped into the pool, and he had to be the first to take advantage of the waters when they stirred. He had no one to help him, and "someone else always gets to the waters before me."

The story emphasizes the helplessness of the man so that the reader can appreciate the intervention of the Lord. Jesus, confirmed in his conclusion that the man wanted help, waited no further and certainly did not use the normal procedures outlined by the sick man; Jesus did not help him into the pool, nor did he put the man into the waters at the right moment. The Lord simply told the man to leave, to take his bed and go. Whatever respect and awe the waters deserved is to be transferred to Jesus; he cured the helpless of thirty-eight years—and he did it because he initiated the conversation which ended in healing.

The miracle was astounding, for it was total and immediate: the man got up and with his mat he walked away. Moreover, the physical cure is succeeded by Jesus' encouragement that the man sin no more, "or something worse may happen to you." Both of these statements are typical; the first is typical of the New Testament perception that miracle working is always secondary to the call to repentance. So it is not at all surprising, indeed it is to be expected, that the story should include the

exhortation to greater healing, the turning away from sin.
Miracles are notably invitations to that total restoration which
involves the forgiveness of sins; the power and authority over
evil expressed in the miracles is ready to be used by God in the
deeper healing of that part of me which is most dangerously ill
and threatening to destroy friendship with God. The difference
between miracle working and spiritual healing is this, that God
can intervene and cure one physically without God's being
called on, but he will not heal one on the spiritual level without
one's agreeing to it. However powerful his grace to heal and
forgive, he will not exercise it to take away free will. It is
precisely this free choice that he ardently seeks.

Holiness of the Sabbath   *Jn 5:16-18*

The Gospel expands this marvelous cure to make it one of
several deeds Jesus performed "on the Sabbath." For the Jews of
Jesus' time there were very many activities which over the
centuries had been evaluated as "works," that is, actions which
should not be done on the Sabbath, actions which included even
walking beyond a certain limit: why would a person walk far on
the Sabbath, unless he was en route to business? Jesus found
reason to ignore commands against his curing actions; he did not
consider them forbidden on the Sabbath, but rather saw
commands against them as man-made rules, not contained in the
law of Moses.

But his continually working miracles on the Sabbath could
only mean that inevitably he would be challenged for his
disobedience and, inevitably, his lack of conformity would be
added to other reasons which ultimately issued in a plot to get
rid of him.

The charge against Jesus, that he worked miracles illegally
on the Sabbath, is too widespread an accusation in the Gospels
to be doubted as a historical difference between Jesus and his
contemporaries. It serves to point up the actual area of intense
disagreement between Jesus and his opponents: Jesus clearly
had a different understanding of the will of God and lived by it
and taught it. This "understanding" and the implicit claim to
uniqueness that lay behind it brought Jesus to the cross.

To see why his opinion was not simply an "opinion" but a
serious misleading of the people, we need only rehearse the
reasons for the tragedies of Israel's history at the classical times

of its sufferings: the Assyrian and Babylonian conquests and destruction of Israel and Judah. The Jewish Scriptures are a resounding witness to the belief that Israel's suffering and humiliation resulted from disobedience to the will of God, fostered by the doctrines of false teachers. It is not surprising that those who felt responsible to protect Israel from disobedience and its consequences should suspect Jesus for his "distinctiveness." But suspicion alone is not sufficient to explain the seeking of Jesus' death; the Gospels inform us of other factors, such as jealousy, unwillingness to repent, haughtiness, which entered into the final decision to hand Jesus over to crucifixion. Whatever be the many motivations which are detectable in the handling of this Jesus, clearly the objective foundation of the terrible disagreement was the difference in understanding of the will of God for Israel, a difference which ultimately would keep Israel God's Chosen One, or separate Israel from its Lord. Thus, not only what Jesus did, but the fact that the healing at Bethesda occurred on the Sabbath make more understandable the violent antipathy Jesus very quickly met from the religious leaders of his people.

Jesus' Union with the Father   *Jn 5:19-30*

John took the opportunity provided by the miraculous work of Jesus at the Pool of Bethesda to present the reader with a lengthy reflection of Jesus on "his work." Jesus' first claim is that he goes on working as does his Father. This statement, by which he implies that he works any and every day, Sabbath or not, for the good of people as does his Father, incenses some of his hearers, for they see in this comparison of himself to his Father a claim to being God's own son and the equal of God; more specifically, Jesus claims sonship because he has the characteristic of God: we can tell who is son by looking to see if a person exhibits the traits of one he calls "Father." Such is the understanding of those who hear Jesus claim that he works as does his Father.

Jesus' lengthy statement about himself was rooted in his relationship with the Father; the kind of work he did reflected nothing less than filial intimacy with the Father. Two works in particular are singled out for attention: the work of giving life and the work of judgment. But these are only two of the works which are transferred to Jesus because of the relationship peculiar to Jesus and the Father; whatever the Father does, the Son does as well, for does not the love of the Son move the Father to teach him to imitate the Father?

The relationship of Jesus to the God of Israel indicated that Jesus would exercise the work of giving life and the work of judgment. But whereas these works were considered, from a temporal point of view, to take place only at the end of this world, Jesus indicated that the one who believed in him "has now eternal life," and has already passed through judgment or even avoided it, since judgment is used here in the sense of *condemnation.* Thus Jesus already gave life and judged; these works he learnt from his Father, who made him the source of life and the supreme judge.

It is interesting to note that, in referring to himself as judge, Jesus described himself as Son of Man. This title draws its significance from the seventh chapter of the Book of Daniel, wherein the judgment of the world is handed over by God to "one like a Son of Man." By the end of his discussion of this vision, Daniel had identified this "Son of Man" as Israel, for Israel, after suffering at the hands of its enemies, will be placed, as the Chosen of Yahweh, at God's right hand to judge its enemies. But here Jesus identified himself as this person who, after suffering, would exercise the role of supreme judge at the world's end. For the believer two moments are signaled here and are of importance: the life flowing from response to Jesus by which one can be said to have avoided judgment and have eternal life now, and the eventual being raised from the dead, the rising to fulness of life. *Life* in John always means *life with God.*

The Witnesses to Jesus   *Jn 5:31-47*

Having justified his work on the sabbath by claiming to work as the Father does and in imitation of the Father, and after claiming that he as Son has been given two works usually associated with the Father, that of giving life and that of supreme judge, Jesus anticipated the question about the legitimacy of his claim to sonship. He argued that five witnesses point to the validity of what he has claimed. First, there is John the Baptizer, who gave "his testimony to the truth." Though John is not said here to have given witness to Jesus, we can see in John's call to repentance the signal that the source of life, the supreme judge is at hand. Secondly, there is the witness of the cures or works exercised by Jesus: are they not symbols or signs of life-giving and judgment? Is not the one who worked these signs, such as the cure of the invalid at the Pool of Bethesda, the source of life and the supreme judge? A third witness to Jesus' true identity is the Father himself, whom however no one will hear or pay attention to who is not first willing to commit himself to Jesus.

Two other witnesses, classical at the time of the writing of the Gospel of John in 95 A.D., are the Scriptures in general and Moses, the author, as it was believed in Jesus' time, of the first five and most authoritative books of the Jewish Scriptures. In these two cases time is spent on the reasons listeners of Jesus refused to accept the witness of the Scriptures and of Moses: "you have no love of God in you," "you refuse to believe what Moses wrote." Here we have an appeal of Jesus to the pregnant words of the Jews' own Scriptures, but it is an appeal made over and over again throughout the New Testament writings and is a basic method of appealing for belief in Jesus, as the first Christians made sense of Jesus as the fulfillment of the Scriptures.

Thus Jesus' speech at one moment of his life served also as a defense of the Christian community's claim that Jesus is recognizable as Son of the Father—if we would only pay attention to the words of John, the deeds of Jesus, the word of the Father himself, and particularly the Scriptures in general and the Mosaic books in particular. It is a speech ultimately aimed at defense, a speech of apologetics. Yet it also contains statements about the identity of Jesus which can feed the lives of those already convinced that Jesus is the Son of the Father, the source of their life.

How deeply the reader has been led into the mystery which is revealed in the work of mercy Jesus did for the lame man at the Pool of Mercy, the mystery of Jesus as source of life, Judge of the world, Son of the Father!

Ascending the Steps to the Dome of the Rock

The Temple

Several stories from Jesus' life and from the lives of the apostles occur in the sacred area of the Temple of Jerusalem. As we enter into this sacred area through guarded gates, we must try to reconstruct the scene of two thousand years ago. The large trapezoidal stone area we stand on today is roughly the size of the Temple area or precinct of Jesus' time. If we put our backs to the middle of the western wall enclosing the whole area, we stand against the wall which served as the back wall of the Temple building itself. The building thus extended from west toward the east, without reaching as far as the eastern wall.

This Temple building was divided into three parts or rooms. The room furthest to the west, against the western wall, was the Holy of Holies, or the holiest room; here was Yahweh's most private quarters, and only one human being, the high priest, could enter here—and only on one day a year, Yom Kippur (the Day of Atonement). The room due east of the Holy of Holies, the middle room, was the Holy Room; here were to be found such sacred things as the table of the twelve breads, representing the twelve tribes of Israel, and changed daily, the menorah—a seven branch candlestick—and the altar of incense. In the third part of the Temple, its most eastwardly part, was the huge altar of sacrifice and the great bowl of washing for priests offering sacrifice. This area, where sacrifices were burnt, was open to priests and to the men of Israel.

Eastward still of this area was the courtyard in which the women of Israel were allowed to enter to worship Yahweh. This entire Temple area, from the Holy of Holies to Courtyard of the Women of Israel, was raised up higher from the vast stone floor of the trapezoidal Temple area or precinct which was larger than a football field. Gentiles were allowed into this general area surrounding the Temple building itself on three sides, but they were never to climb the steps to enter any of the sections of the

Temple building itself; these were reserved solely for the women, the men, the priests, the high priest of Israel. Thus, a geographical scheme reveals the nearness each type of person could enjoy with the God of Israel.

The plan of the Temple and its great surrounding area followed palace architecture: a large area for the king's subjects to gather in, his own house which was made up of a porch area—altar of sacrifice area, a private area—altar of incense area, and the most private quarters reserved for the king only—the Holy of Holies area.

The entire area of the Temple and its platform was under the control and direction of the high priest, assisted by about eight chief priests and a Temple police force. All matters of the Temple were attended to daily by priests and Levites. The Levites took care of all music and singing at daily and special sacrifices and looked after the cleanliness of the Temple area. The ordinary priest worked only about eight weeks of the year in the Temple; thus, priesthood was only a temporary pastime, part-time work, which was supplemented by a regular job for the rest of the year.

Walls surrounded the entire trapezoid of the Temple. Overhangs, supported by columns, often three or four abreast, were built inside the north, east and south walls so that people could walk or sit within the Temple precinct even in inclement weather. Though the entire area surrounding the Temple building proper was open to Gentiles, the north half of the area was where one could find the selling of animals for sacrifice and the changing of coins. Coins had to be changed, for one could not buy materials to be used in holy ceremonies with Hellenistic or Roman money sacred to the genius of the emperor.

The Temple Treasury

Many nations kept their national treasuries, as well as their Temple treasuries, within the well-protected Temple area. The Temple treasury was probably kept on the level below the platform of the Temple area. However, in the court of the women of Israel, there were horn shaped tubes for goodwill offerings.

The Temple treasury was probably to be found below the platform on which we stand is, for the entire platform or precinct is flat, not because the contour of the land beneath is flat, but because the platform rests on a series of columns which compensate for the natural unevenness of a mountain top.

History of the Temple

Solomon was the first to construct the Temple on a platform supported by columns; though the Babylonians destroyed Solomon's Temple in 587 B.C., the reconstruction about 480 B.C. followed the same pattern. When Herod the Great began the enlargement and embellishment of the Second Temple (480 B.C.), he too depended on the scheme of platform held up by columns. Indeed, to enter the Temple precinct or general area, one climbed the south side of the hill on the top of which the Temple was built; one enters at a lower level, climbs steps within the basement under the Temple platform to come out, eventually, on the Temple platform itself. Truly, one *goes up* to the Temple. It was in this lower or basement area that we think the Temple treasury was to be found.

One other building of note should be mentioned, in connection with the New Testament stories. The building which housed the meetings of the Sanhedrin is thought to have either abutted the south wall of the Holy of Holies or be found just some yards south of the Holy of Holies. The Sanhedrin was the highest ruling body of Israel, made up of wealthy men or elders, the chief priests, and scribes or interpreters of the Scriptures, to the number of seventy; the high priest, by virtue of his office, was president of the Sanhedrin. A formal trial of Jesus by the Sanhedrin would have occurred in the area adjacent to the south wall of the Temple building.

What do we see on this platform today? We will comment on only three things. First, the walls surrounding the entire esplanade are the construction of Suleiman the Magnificent about 1535 A.D., but they are surely built on the foundations laid by earlier Temple constructions. The gorgeous Dome of the Rock, in the center of the entire esplanade, dates from 691 A.D., although many repairs and gifts have added to its beauty and tradition. The most recent restoration of this Dome of the Rock occurred between 1958 and 1964 A.D. Then the roof, which "shines like gold," was applied: it is a special aluminum bronze alloy. Often this building is called a mosque, but it is not formally that kind of building. It is rather a memorial of the rock beneath the dome, the rock from which Mohammed left this earth for heaven. This is the third most holy shrine of the Moslem world; third only to Mecca and Medina. The rock many think not only was visited by Mohammed in his "Night Journey"; it also is thought to be the rock on which the altar of sacrifice was built as part of the Temple building of the God of Israel, and it is thought, too, to be the spot on which Abraham was willing to sacrifice his beloved son Ishmael at the command of God. Thus, though the Dome of the Rock is of great importance to the Moslem world, it stands over a rock which is peculiarly sacred to the Jewish world.

The third site on the Temple esplanade to be noted is the building, a true mosque, at the south end of the platform. The name is the el-Aqsa mosque, an adjective which means simply "the farthest [Temple]." This mosque indicates the "far distance" Mohammed had come from Arabia before his ascent into heaven. To this day the el-Aqsa mosque is used by Moslems, especially on Friday, the day which is holy to Moslems.

Jesus' Childhood

To review the events of Jesus' life which are associated with the Temple of Jerusalem, we can follow a threefold scheme. First, we treat of those events connected with Jesus' childhood, then we look at one situation of Jesus' public life which John relates, and finally we consider a series of stories associated with the last week of Jesus' life on earth. After this review, we recall the use made of the Temple area by the early church.

Apparition of Gabriel to Zachary   *Lk 1:5-22*

It is in the middle room, the room of the "holies," that we should place the appearance of the altar of incense at the usual, daily afternoon worship service. Here was first revealed the plan of God which has salvation as its goal and in which John's role was clearly defined. The son of Zachary and Elizabeth, a miraculous son, would be filled with the Holy Spirit from conception, so that he might prepare a people for the God who comes, so that he might go ahead of God to ready a people for him, so that he could call for repentance of Israel as did the mighty ninth century B.C. prophet, Elijah, Israel's greatest prophet.

Presentation of Jesus and Purification of Mary
Lk 2:22-38

In the Court of the Women, east of the altar of sacrifice and the room where Zachary heard the angel Gabriel speak, was the place where Jesus and earlier John were "presented" to God and Mary and Elizabeth was "purified." What, exactly, are the *Presentation* of Jesus and the *Purification* of Mary?

To understand the need for presenting Jesus, we must go back into the history of Israel—to the time of the Freeing of Israel from Egypt. To convince Pharaoh to let God's People go free, God worked several wonders; the last of these was the killing of every firstborn male, human and animal, in Egypt. Technically, this killing affected Israelite firstborn males, too; but God gave Israel a way out of this slaughter: if Israel would mark their doorposts with the blood of the lambs cooked for their last meal in Egypt, the Angel of Death would "pass over" their houses without killing their firstborn males. Hence the term "Passover Feast."

Ever since that fateful night of slaughter and salvation, Israel was to remind itself of God's saving of the firstborn males by bringing every firstborn male of every birth into God's Temple. This child was understood to be alive because of God. It was a time of great gratitude and intense remembrance of the saving God.

Besides the Passover and Exodus, this celebration has another important meaning in Israel's life. Israel grew accustomed to annual harvests as it settled down in the land of Israel. Sensitive to the role of God in providing fruitfulness, Israel grew into the habit of offering to God the first fruit of any harvest; it also offered to God the firstborn of animal life, as well. Usually, this first fruit or firstborn was eliminated from human use; in practice this meant that Israel would destroy the first fruits or first animal. Clearly the firstborn child, too, should be considered a gift of life. Hence, there was a ceremony developed whereby the human life that opened the womb should be recognized as God's; but rather than destroy the firstborn human life, a substitution of some animal was made. Nonetheless, Israel maintained through the various obligations of religious ceremony an awareness that life—all life, but especially that first life which first opens the womb—was truly the gift of God and as such belongs to him. Life at all levels was cherished in Israel, but particularly appreciated was the life which began the fruitfulness of human, animal, and grain life.

One can go a step further here. One must be careful, in emphasizing the ceremony surrounding the life which opens the womb, to realize that the dedication of the firstborn is, in its own way, a dedication which includes all life which follows it. This is the thinking behind such a description of Jesus as the "firstfruits" of mankind. Not only was Jesus the "firstborn" of Christians, but as dedicated firstborn he includes in his dedication all those who come after him. As firstborn of those risen from the dead, he consecrates as part of his rising the others who will be born into eternal life with God. Thus, all life was consecrated to God, but it was done through the special firstborn who was visibly given to God, or for whom a suitable substitute sacrifice was offered.

Jesus, then, was presented to God in his Temple as a continuation of gratitude for the saving of life at the Exodus; without that Angel of Death "passing over" the Israelite houses no future Israelite would be born, unless it would be in abject poverty in Egypt. But Jesus was also presented in gratitude to God for the fertile womb through which the precious gift of life begins to flow.

For Mary, this day of Jesus' Presentation, was a day of Purification. In Jewish law, all waste products of the human body are considered unclean. This uncleanness is, of course, related to health; and in very early times, if not so generally as today, to be unclean was to be a source of sickness and death for others. Hence, one who was unclean must be put out of the community, that is, excommunicated. And if he proved to be unclean for human association, how far should the unclean person remove himself from the presence of and association with God? Even in Jesus' day, these physical uncleannesses were considered cause for exclusion from worship of Yahweh—unless one was purified by a religious ritual or ceremony. Mary, like any mother who has given birth, had bodily waste associated with giving birth; thus, she, on the appointed day, must undergo the ritual of purification.

In citing these various ways to be unclean, which was also the effect of eating certain kinds of foods, there was no intent of implying that one incurred guilt by uncleanness. Mary was not guilty of anything; she was simply impure. Perhaps an example in the extreme is in order. If you are riding on a train, and the person sitting next to you dies and falls against you, you are, through touching a dead body, unclean, and in need of a cleansing or purifying ceremony. Clearly, you are not guilty of any sin—but you do need to be cleansed, nonetheless, according to the Old Testament's way of thinking. In the same way, Mary, though guilty of no sin, must be purified, according to the Law of Israel.

The more we realize how ingrained in Israelite consciousness was this understanding of *clean-unclean,* we can understand how radical was Jesus who eliminated all but moral uncleanness as a reason for excluding a human being from worship of God. "It is not what goes into a man that makes him unclean, but what comes out of him—from his heart." From this perspective we can specially appreciate how a leper felt who was cleansed from his leprosy; he was not only physically cured, but now he or she could take a place among the rest of Israel to worship God as one was created to do.

The last story we shall consider from Jesus' childhood is the one told about Jesus at age twelve being lost and found in the Temple. This finding would probably have occurred in the Court of the Women or under the covered walkway along the eastern wall of the Temple compound.

The story is recognized today as very important, for it is meant to sum up the fundamental aspect of the infancy narrative in Luke. What precisely is this fundamental aspect? To understand Luke's infancy stories we must look to Mark, the source from which Luke wrote a good deal of his Gospel. Mark begins with the incomplete sentence: "The beginning of the Good News of Jesus, Christ and Son of God." For Luke, this brief statement of Jesus' identity, really a profession of the gospel writer's faith, was to be improved. Luke makes this improvement by having an angel of God, Gabriel, inform the reader that this child will be Son of David and Son of God. But, in what sense "Son of God," for Mary has never had sexual intercourse with any man? "The Holy Spirit will come upon you and the power of the Most High will cast its shadow upon you; therefore, the child will be called both holy [because of the Holy Spirit] and Son of God [because of the power of God]." Thus, though God was not said to have had sexual intercourse with Mary, he does enter the creation of this child to such a fundamental degree that he can be called Father and the child called Son of God.

So, if Mark professes Jesus to be Son of God, Luke has made clear that this sonship was unique to Jesus, for only in his case do we know that God, on the analogy of father, was the cause of his very existence. An angel has said this; it must clearly be the result of God's choice—the conception of Jesus was part of the will of God.

Jesus and the Teacher of the Law   *Lk 2:41-50*

Before allowing the childhood of Jesus to pass, Luke tells a
closing story of Jesus' youth which caps the prime element we
have been describing. Jesus had been a part of the passover
pilgrimage which so many Jews made annually to celebrate the
Feast of Passover in Jerusalem. On the return home, Jesus'
parents could not find him and so retraced their steps, anxiously
searching for the child everywhere they had been with him
throughout the feast of the Passover. It was in the Temple area
that they found him, and the most likely spot was against the
eastern wall of the Temple area—Solomon's Portico. Here Mary
and Joseph find the child who was described as sitting among
the learned teachers of Israel, listening to them and asking them
questions, no doubt about the law of Moses, the one subject
worthy of debate among the learned in the Temple, and
providing answers, too, for Luke says that they who heard him
were astounded at his intelligence and his replies. Jesus, in other
words, while not exceeding the limitations of a twelve-year-old,
prepares the reader for the marvel of the adult Jesus, the teacher
of Israel; it was as teacher that Luke prefers to present the adult
Jesus, and it was through teaching that Jesus was fundamentally
savior for Luke.

But the culmination of this finding story lies in the response
of Jesus to his parents. Jesus cannot understand why his parents
did not know exactly where to find him; where else would he be,
if not in the house of his Father? Is not that where we would look
for any twelve-year-old, in the house of his Father? Jesus'
response was a test, a test to see if Gabriel's words to Mary
about Jesus as Son of God were fully understood. His words sum
up the lesson Luke wants his reader to grasp very well before
Luke begins the description of the life of the adult Jesus. Like
Mary and Joseph, the reader can only ponder in his heart the
profound significance of this Jesus, Son of God; he does not deny
that he was son of Joseph, but must always be aware that in a
fundamental sense the Father of Jesus was no one other than
God. Now, the Holy Family moves off to Nazareth, but we stand
in this Temple area still listening to the words reverberating off
the eastern wall of the Temple compound: is God not my Father?

Adult Career of Jesus

According to Mark, Jesus goes to Jerusalem only once in his
adult life, the time when he dies; Matthew and Luke follow this

scheme of Mark. But John is not based on Mark; John has Jesus visit Jerusalem several times before that fateful visit which ended in his death. It is to one of these visits to the Temple area that we now turn.

Jesus at the Feast of Tabernacles   *Jn 7-8*

John speaks, in chapters seven and eight, of Jesus' visit to Jerusalem for the Feast of Tabernacles. Tabernacles, Passover and Pentecost are the three great Pilgrim Feasts in Judaism. Tabernacles was an annual celebration, held in the fall of each year about September-October, to commemorate the harvest of the crops planted in the previous spring and grown all through the summer and fall. The feast is called *Tabernacles,* or *booths,* or *tents,* simply because, to take advantage of daylight for the harvesting, everyone moved out into the fields and spent the entire day there; they would build booths or tents or tabernacles in which they could have lunch and noonday rest, if need be, without having to leave the fields.

Among the liturgical symbols associated with the Feast of Tabernacles are two very important ones: water and light. Why water, at a harvest? Because, first, there should be gratitude expressed for the water gathered over the previous winter into cisterns to be used for irrigation of the summer crop at a time when rain does not fall at all in Israel. But, secondly, harvesting makes one aware of the dependency on water, and so one's thoughts and prayers turn to the future: to the need for water after this harvest is over, so that the newly planted crop may be abundant for the upcoming spring harvest of Passover and Pentecost, and so that much rainwater of wintertime can be stored to support the future summer crop. Water meant life, especially for those living in or near the desert. In brief, this was a solemn moment when Israelites turn to God to confess their need for water and their dependence on him for that water. In this context Jesus cries out to the many pilgrims milling about the Temple compound that he will provide water which will last forever, water which will sustain life forever.

The gospel writer interprets this water for us: it is the Holy Spirit of God which will act in a life-supporting role, as does water. To receive this, we must believe that Jesus can give it. In this way, belief in Jesus assures us of that which prevents death forever. With this water there is no more anxiety about finding the source of life: God's very Spirit is that life source.

It is worthwhile, at the mention of the Holy Spirit here, to call attention to a fundamental aspect of Christianity. It is the Spirit which sustains and supports life, the Spirit who will be given, according to the plan of God, only after Jesus' mission ends in death. The roles of Jesus and the Spirit in the Father's plan are not to be confused. The Spirit gives life after Jesus' death, but gives it only if we believe in Jesus. To receive the Spirit is to have believed in Jesus, the Jesus who has his mission precede that of the Spirit and to whom is not given the mission of "water which supports life forever." Thus, while Jesus was on earth, the Spirit was not given; after Jesus was gone, the Spirit was given, but only if we believe in Jesus. Thus, the Spirit is the one for whom Jesus looks, but when the Spirit comes, we must believe in the "departed" Jesus to have the Spirit.

Thus, when we stand on the Temple platform and imaginatively watch the liturgical procession enter the Temple area with water drawn Siloam, we can hear the words of Jesus to anyone who will listen: "I have the water which, if you will believe in me, will be given to you to sustain your life forever." Jews prayed for water here; Jesus gives all that they long for.

But another symbol is associated with Tabernacles: light. Why is this? Given the time of year of this Feast of Tabernacles, one is very much aware of the shortening days and lengthening periods of darkness. Darkness is linked in many cultures with evil and fear, and so it was in Israel; darkness was also linked with the imagery associated with the night of Exodus from Egypt, a night lit only by the guiding light of Yahweh in his effort to save Israel from slavery and death. It is not surprising, then, that at this feast time, in anticipation of the winter, Israel liturgically reminds itself that Yahweh is its true Light.

Each day of the eight-day feast, another huge candle was lit in the Temple area. By the eighth night, eight huge candles blazed with such light that ancient testimony says that all Jerusalem could see by the light of the candles of Tabernacles.

It is against this liturgy that Jesus identifies himself as the Light. Isaiah had earlier referred to Israel as the light for the rest of the world, the light by which the Gentiles could find their way out of darkness to the true God, Yahweh. Jesus transferred that image to his followers in his Sermon on the Mount in Galilee. (See above, 50.) But here he takes to himself the role of primordial light; he is the one who will lead mankind to Yahweh, a mankind which will otherwise remain, as Luke says, in darkness and under the shadow of death. Once again, we strain to hear the echo of these words of comfort amidst the din of the pilgrim crowds moving in this Temple area.

Last Week of Jesus's Life

The third set of events centering on the Temple occur during Jesus' last week of life. For convenience's sake, let us divide these events into three occasions.

Palm Sunday   *Mt 21:1-9; Mk 11:1-11; Lk 19:29-38*

Palm Sunday—As Jesus reached the top of the Mount of Olives just to the east of Jerusalem on his way to celebrate, with so many others, the feast of Passover, an enthusiasm grows, an expectancy. From the way he has acted throughout his ministry, was he not the one we expect to come to take possession of the holy city and Temple of Yahweh? Indeed, as if to fulfill the prophecy, Jesus calls for a donkey on which to ride down the mountain and ascend again up to the southern gates leading into the Temple area. In doing this, he likens himself to the one prophesied by the prophet Zechariah:

"Rejoice heart and soul, daughter of Zion! Shout with gladness, daughter of Jerusalem! See now, your king comes to you; he is victorious, he is triumphant, humble and riding on a donkey, on a colt, the foal of a donkey. . . . the bow of war will be banished; he will proclaim peace for the nations." (Zc 9:9–10.)

This action of Jesus also reminds the scripture writers of a prophecy of Isaiah: "Say to daughter Zion: 'look, your savior comes . . .'" (Is 62:11.) Finally, a psalm indicates a liturgical welcome in store for "the stone rejected by the builders," but made by God the most important stone:

Blessings on him who comes in the name of Yahweh! We bless you from the house of Yahweh. Yahweh is God, he smiles on us. With branches in your hands draw up in procession as far as the horns of the altar. (Ps 118:26–27.)

These Old Testament texts imply that Jesus comes to Jerusalem as the Messiah king, representative of Yahweh, who brings blessings and prosperity to his Holy City. As though to carry out the image to its fullest, Jesus was pictured as coming onto the Temple platform to survey the entire area, before retiring for the evening at a place outside the city. He was like a master surveying his property.

A small difference should be noted that separates Luke from his source, Mark. Mark says that Jesus enters Jerusalem and the Temple; Luke notes that Jesus enters the Temple only. Scholars regard Luke's omission of the reference to Jerusalem seriously. They take it to imply that, for Luke, Jesus has already given up on Jerusalem; he already recognizes it as the city of death for Him. Jesus, then, as far as Luke was concerned, went directly to the Temple area and spends his time there, symbolically leaving the city to its chosen fate.

Associated with Jesus' arrival in the Temple area and seen as part of his religious sensitivity was Jesus' action of cleansing the Temple. Rather than say that Jesus cleansed the Temple—he did not touch the Temple buildings themselves—we should say that Jesus drove out of the Temple area—probably within the Royal Portico, or on the steps leading through the Huldah Gates or at the exit in the Court of Gentiles—those who, by their authorized business and trade enterprises dealing with exchanging money and selling sacrificial animals, created an atmosphere which was harmful to the reverent worship of Yahweh, whose presence should be felt "throughout his house and yard." Purifying the Temple area had long been, in Judaism, an expectation; it would signal the approach of God. Purifying the Temple was an annual part of the Feast of Tabernacles. John the Baptizer was identified as one whose task was to "prepare a people" for God. Jews long had expected that the Temple area, too, would be purified of all elements unworthy of Yahweh. Many saw Jesus' cleansing of the elements harmful to the sensitive worship of Yahweh as a sign that with the coming of Jesus God himself was near.

Unfortunately, there was no reasonable way of resolving the contradiction between John and the synoptics about the time in Jesus' public life when he did this startling action on the Temple grounds. Telling this story early in Jesus' public life, however, gives John the early opportunity to speak of the destruction of another Temple and the resurrection of that Temple in three days.

Some people argue that Jesus could not have acted in the Temple area in the way the Gospels say he did. All we can say in response is that: first, such an action is not inconsistent with prophetic acts in the tradition of the Middle East, and it was understood to be an act of a prophet (or someone claiming to be a prophet); secondly, such an action is not inconsistent with the character or personality of Jesus as it surfaces through the stories which often hide it. Jesus never physically hurt anyone; but bitter criticism, as well as prophetic violence, were consonant with his personality and self-awareness.

Controversies at the Temple   *Mt 21:23-23:39; Mk 11:27-12:40; Lk 20:1-47*

Jesus spent some days before the official beginning of Passover in the Temple area. Several episodes associated with these days of teaching anyone who would listen to him have a quite palpable air of controversy and tension. After these episodes and their acrimony and bitter contesting and challenging, Jesus' newest enemies—the elders and chief priests—resolve to put Jesus away permanently.

As Mark, who gives the basic scheme to Matthew and Luke for these days, reports, Jesus is faced with challenges, final challenges from each of the groups which oppose Him; chief priests and elders, Pharisees and Herodians, Sadducees and, finally, scribes. Let us look at each one of these stories for a moment.

As Jesus was walking in the Temple, chief priests, scribes and elders faced him with the question which went to the heart of his being: Where do you get the authority to do what you do and say what you say? Jesus' answer is famous for its cleverness, for its putting the aggressors on the defensive: by what authority did John, the one respected by all the people, do what he did and say what he said? If you will answer me, I will answer you.

But Jesus' answer is not merely a clever tactic. There is a profound reason John was rejected by the leaders of Israel, and it is the very reason Jesus will be rejected by the same leaders. Jesus' fate, when all is said and done, is no different from that of John the Baptizer or that of many a prophet before them. Why, in other words, would a Jew not be willing to repent; everyone else knew in his heart of hearts that John was right, that God deserved repentance. And the same was felt about Jesus. Why would the (presumably) most religiously sensitive people in Israel not respond to the call to repent? The result is the well-known standoff; Jesus will not answer them, because they will not answer him first. But the deeper question hangs in the air: why is asking for repentance wrong?

A bit later, still in the Temple area, the now-famous question was put to Jesus by Pharisees and Herodians, supporters of

Herod Antipas, ruler of Galilee, and then present in Jerusalem: "Is it permissible to pay taxes to Caesar or not?" Once again, Jesus' answer is extremely clever, for he avoids the horns of the dilemma by affirming full loyalty to God, no matter what human powers demand. By this affirmation of loyalty to Yahweh, Jesus presents himself to be just as faithful to Yahweh as Pharisees. Thus the hopes of the Pharisees and Herodians were shattered. Jesus' reply does not allow them to call him a traitor to Israel, for he affirms God's rights over what is His; at the same time, Jesus does not foment revolt, for he is willing to give to Caesar what Caesar has a right to. Does Caesar have a right to anything in Israel? Well, is not his name and picture on the coin? It must be his! What bothers Jesus most, in all this argument, is the hypocrisy of those who question him. Would that they, who fight so strongly against Caesar's domination, really and truly give to God the things that are his; it is hypocritical to fight Caesar on the pretext of wanting to serve God alone—and then not serve him.

A third group Jesus meets in the Temple area is the Sadducees, people he has rarely encountered in his public life in Galilee. Sadducees, like Pharisees, probably trace their roots to a time before 150 B.C. Unlike the Pharisees, the Sadducees believed that only the first five books of the Old Testament, those written by Moses and called Torah, were truly Scripture of God; the rest of the Old Testament was of great value, but not the source of Yahwistic faith as was the Torah. Limited to these five books and using a conservative approach to interpret them, the Sadducees concluded that there was no life after death revealed by God; thus, they never believed in an afterlife with God, and challenged anyone who claimed that an afterlife was real.

If we understand how irritating to the Sadducees was Jesus' belief and teaching that there will be a resurrection from the dead, we will understand the real thrust of their challenge to Jesus. They constructed an extreme possibility out of a Mosaic law to ridicule the possibility of an afterlife. The Mosaic law provided for the continuation of a man's property after he has died childless and thus without an heir. The Sadducees concluded that the man's wife, having complied with the Mosaic law by marrying six other relatives besides her original husband, would, if raised from the dead, be faced with seven husbands in the afterlife. The Mosaic law was not responsible for putting the woman and her seven husbands into this awkward situation;

rather, belief in an afterlife has done this. The conclusion should
be, according to the logic of the Sadducees, that one surely
doubts the existence of an afterlife.

Jesus' answer to this problem was twofold. First, we must
realize that the need to find a means of continuing the property
of the dead man is the result of the man's dying. What of a
situation in which the man never dies again? Logically, the man
will not have to be replaced by his relatives, and so they will not
be "husbands" to his wife. Secondly, in his words to Moses at the
burning bush, God identifies himself as the God of Abraham,
Isaac and Jacob. Is this identification to be understood to say
that God is God of dead men? Rather, the words are better
understood to mean that God, if he is truly God of these men, is
God of men who are living; what would it mean to be God of
people who no longer live? Would not God's words have been: "I
am God of those who used to live," if Abraham, Isaac and Jacob
were, in Moses's time, really dead?

Finally, the Scribes approach Jesus in the Temple area to
quiz him on what was one of the main abilities of any teacher of
Israel. The law of Israel, together with all its interpretations, was
a complex body of knowledge; it was often felt that some factor
unified all these laws, something which gave each individual law
its meaning and direction, so that one could see clearly how
each law flowed from one source and leads back to the same
source. The scribes, those professional interpreters of the law, in
this sense *lawyers,* put this challenge to Jesus: "What is the
greatest law?"That is to ask, what law grounds every other law
and gives meaning to every other law? Jesus answers that one
law grounds all other laws: love of God with all one's heart, soul,
strength. But, before they can answer him, he insists on noting
that the second law is love of neighbor as oneself. Thus for Jesus
all laws of Israel are somehow simply concrete expressions of
love of God and love of neighbor. Certain observations should be
made about this response.

First, Jesus is not satisfied to answer the scribes with "the
first and greatest"; he insists that his full answer includes the law
of love of neighbor. Secondly, the scribe who had put the
challenging question to him, had only praise for Jesus.
Significantly, Mark here concludes his account of public life of
Jesus: "And after that no one dared to question him any more."
Thirdly, the separation of Christianity from Judaism, for decades
a most thorny problem, was grounded in this response of Jesus,

The norm, where Jesus' own words were not available, was Jesus' central principle: all laws governing human action must flow from and lead back to love of God and love of neighbor. It is in this Temple story where we find the basis for all Christian decisions about what is moral and immoral. It is against the mind of Jesus that all decisions must now be tested.

Matthew absorbs these four challenge or controversy stories of Mark into a larger framework which is characterized as much by these four stories as by parables of impending judgment for those who do not obey God's law and for those who reject Jesus; also in the Jerusalem Temple area Jesus delivers one of his most caustic and bitter denunciations of the Pharisees and scribes we have on record. Truly, we are at the summit of acrimony between Jesus and his enemies; the next step can only be drastic, the death of Jesus.

when Christianity had to ask itself what of the Old Testament laws were to be kept by those who profess Jesus as their Lord.

Before leaving the challenges hurled in the Temple area, we should note two brief episodes. First, though no one wants to ask Jesus any more questions, he wants to ask one. It is a question which Christians would use often in later debates of the first century A.D. in defense of their belief. Traditionally, the Messiah was considered by many to surely be a son of David. This meant, implicitly, that David was his superior, as ancestor is to descendant. Jesus puts this understanding to a test. Using one of David's own psalms, Jesus notes that David refers to someone as "my Lord." Such a statement by David, Jesus suggests, raises more than one question. First, clearly this Lord is alive to David and thus not someone who will come many centuries after David's death. Secondly, David implicitly admits he is subordinate to this Lord, no matter how tradition has emphasized the Messiah's dependence on David. Thirdly, this Lord sits at Yahweh's right hand, obviously the place of God's favorite, of his beloved. Who is this?

Jesus also calls his disciples' attention to something. A widow had just put into one of the trumpet shaped donation receptacles two small coins. What are they worth? As money, not very much. As representing all she had, it was a sum worth more than what the rich had donated. The lady's action served as an example of the total giving which God deserves. Many scholars think this story is the prelude to what is to follow: the total giving of Jesus to his Father, the giving of a life, if necessary.

Prophesy of the Destruction of Jerusalem
Mt 24:1-51; Mk 13:1-37; Lk 21:5-36

The final Temple episode we consider here is the teaching of
Jesus regarding the destruction of Jerusalem. Jesus' disciples,
getting ready to leave the Temple esplanade one day before
Passover began, noted in wonder the beauty of the Temple and
its surrounding buildings. When we realize the kind of housing
most Israelites were accustomed to in these times, it is certainly
understandable that the gold, silver, precious wood and
hangings, bronze and marble would simply astound the person
who had never seen the likes of this in his entire life.

Jesus' reply to their wonderment chilled their enthusiasm
for the Temple's beauteous grandeur: "A day will come when one
stone will not be left on top of another." By itself this gloomy
prediction fits into a pattern of forecasts about the future of
Jerusalem and Israel: destruction is predictable because the
hearts of the inhabitants are hard. And this pattern is simply a
contemporary reaction to a traditional disobedience of Israel:
earlier sufferings on a national scale were attributed to the
rejection of God's will and the call of prophets to turn back to
the right way before the dire, irreversible moment of tragedy is
reached.

But the disciples of Jesus do not rest with this ominous
prediction, which they had heard in other forms before. They
ask, with a certain prudence, when this destruction will happen
and what signs should they look for in advance, so they and their
dear ones can be forewarned and can avoid the gravest of the
sufferings.

Interpreters have for many centuries studied Jesus' lengthy
reply to his disciples' twofold question: when? what signs? The
eternal hope is to uncover from Jesus' words the precise
calendar time for both the destruction of Jerusalem and for that
which Jesus calls attention to after the destruction of Jerusalem.
All efforts have failed—despite the ingenuity of countless
intelligences. This failure suggests of itself that there really was
no calendar date and time predicted by Jesus for the end of the
world, or, for that matter, for the destruction of Jerusalem. In
answer to the disciples, Jesus used a form of speech usual for
prophets: imagery traditional in such situations of dire
prediction, language which is very imaginative, language which is
dictated by a conviction of impending disaster without claiming
to predict the exact circumstances or time of the disaster. The

point at issue, for the prophet, is nothing but the assurance that the attitude of his hearers is responsible for the disaster, whenever it comes. He clothes that conviction in imagery which suits disaster.

One element of this prophetic language is an emphasis that the disaster is near. This "nearness" is not meant to be a prediction of calendar time, but is meant to suggest the haste with which a person should repent. The threat of punishment for sin is all the more fearsome, when the sinner is confronted with the possibility that his punishment could be at hand. Indeed, swift and sure punishment is the logical answer to sin. That the punishment does not occur as immediately as the prophetic words suggest does not indicate that the prophet is in error; punishment will come in God's good time, but it is for the sinner to realize that his sinful self should not be surprised if punishment follows immediately or soon on sin. And this is precisely what the prophet was anxious to convey to the careless sinner.

To be more specific about Jesus' response to his disciples, we can say that, without predicting the time of the destruction of Jerusalem, Jesus did give some signs: they are signs of activity which precede a massacre, signs which one who knows war knows how to read. Jesus did not, however, give a date for this destruction.

Jesus, however, went beyond his disciples' questions about the time and signs of the destruction of Jerusalem; he spoke of the destruction of this entire age, of which Jerusalem's tribulation is only a part. Jesus gave even fewer concrete hints about the when and signs of the end of our world, of "this age." But he did want to link the destruction of Jerusalem with the end of the world, for the destruction of the one is inextricably linked with the destruction of the other, as part is linked to whole. In brief, the sinfulness which causes the destruction of Jerusalem is symptomatic of the disease which will bring about the destruction of "this age." The satanic control of this age will dominate Jerusalem to the point that it will be destroyed in punishment, a prelude to that destruction to come by which the entire kingdom of Satan will be eradicated. The very imagery of this world prediction suggests the profound wrenching of nature, as though its very self is being cleansed with unremitting power, until a new age, "the age to come," takes its place.

Jesus did speak about the destruction of Jerusalem, and about the end of the world; in this he addressed his disciples' questions in prophetic fashion. But his concern lay elsewhere than in prediction. He was concerned with the reactions of his disciples to the eventual results of Israel's sinfulness, whenever these results shall happen. Jesus would not be with his disciples in that time of suffering, as he is now. Indeed, there will be much suffering in store for his disciples, suffering which is not directly related to the destruction of Jerusalem, yet suffering which should attract and hold their attention, for in it they will be severely tried. Thus the words of Jesus are as much meant to encourage his followers as to predict future destruction. His two main thoughts are "watch!" and "persevere!" For Christians, the exhortation to fidelity in this Temple speech is of the greatest value. Predictions of calendar moments are longed for, but God clearly is not providing them. But what he wants to give, he does—a call to those faithful to him to stay true, to persevere, to watch!

One cannot leave the Temple area without one more look at the eastern wall. After the time of Jesus, his followers gathered there, strengthened by the Holy Spirit and attractive to so many Jews who came onto the holy esplanade of the Temple. The ultimate separation between Judaism and Christianity is not yet visible in the public lives of these Jews, the first Christians, for, to Jew and Christian alike, the dispute is over Jesus, not over the one and only God. Here the first Christians were accustomed to gather till they were driven from Jerusalem. It was very near here, more precisely in the area of the Court of the Women due west of the eastern wall, that Peter and John cured a lame man and professed to all that they did this "in the name of Jesus Christ." By doing this they made all aware that the figure of Jesus had not been done away with by crucifixion; he lives to cure and awaits faith in himself yet, a faith which he sorely longed for in his life on earth and still seeks, now through the instrumentality of his disciples. The call to repentance now includes a call to repent of the killing of Jesus; with that call to repentance we hear the assurance of God's prized friendship for all who ask for it, who "call on the name of the Lord for salvation."

The Upper Room

The Upper Room

Last Supper

Just three minutes' walk from the present Zion Gate of
Jerusalem, the gate which leads out of the southern wall of
today's Jerusalem, is the site considered since the time of the
Crusades as the Upper Room. In this simple room, where the
practiced eye can see signs that the room has been used as a
mosque, took place three events which have become
foundational events for Christianity: Jesus' Last Supper, his
appearances to his disciples after the Resurrection, and the
outpouring of the Holy Spirit on about one hundred twenty of
Jesus' followers at Pentecost. Let us understand why these three
events are so significant to Christianity.

Passover and Unleavened Bread

For centuries Jews had been commanded to present themselves
for worship in Jerusalem; more specifically, the Law of Moses
orders all Israelite males to come to Jerusalem three times a
year, to celebrate the Pilgrim Feasts (See above, 195). Thus, the
Gospels say that Jesus went to Jerusalem for the Feast of
Passover, the feast which commemorates that singular salvation
of Israel from Egypt. The blood of the lamb, placed on the door
of each Israelite home in Egypt, kept away the Angel of Death
sent by Yahweh to kill the firstborn male, human and animal, of
all living in Egypt; thus, the blood of the lamb on wood made the
Angel of Death "pass over" or "pass by" the houses of the
Israelites. This saving of Israel is, therefore, appropriately called
the "Passover."

We can imagine that the compliance with Mosaic Law to
honor the Passover meant that Jerusalem would be filled to
overflowing with devout and obedient pilgrims, come to
celebrate, each in his own family and friends, the dinner which
resembled so closely the last dinner their ancestors had before

leaving Egypt and slavery forever. We find Jesus, then, directing his disciples to a unnamed friend who would provide for Jesus not just a space for celebration, but an entire room, and a choice room at that, since it would be an upper or second story room. Only relatively few pilgrims to Jerusalem would have a Passover feast in such privacy as Jesus and the Twelve enjoyed.

The Gospels often refer to this time Jesus was in Jerusalem as the time of the Feast of the Unleavened Bread. This was the name given to the celebration of the first harvest of spring. It was a time of great joy and gratitude for the winter's abundant growth, and of prayer that the next harvests be as generous. Since this harvest occurs in the spring, it eventually was celebrated just at the time of the celebration of Passover. Moreover, offering and eating of bread made from the newly harvested wheat characterized the harvest feast as an annual day of thanks. No yeast was used to make this bread, and so the feast has the name of the Feast of Unleavened Bread. Coincidentally, the bread baked by the Israelites fleeing Egypt at Passover was also baked without yeast. Thus, in Jesus' time, when the two feasts of Unleavened Bread and of Passover were celebrated at the same time, one ate only unleavened bread or bread made without yeast. One should remember, however, the different meanings in these two breads: the unleavened bread of the harvest symbolized the gift of wheat from God with no admixture of a foreign substance such as yeast—it is pure gift, unadulterated by human interference; the unleavened bread of the Passover symbolized the tearful journey begun in haste which will involve the wandering over the desert for forty years.

Last Supper in Matthew and Mark   *Mt 26:17-35;*
Mk 14:12-31

The Gospels of Matthew, Mark, and Luke place the Last Supper of Jesus with his disciples in this context of feasts. For Matthew, Mark, and Luke, the Last Supper is a Passover supper, eaten at the time of the Feast of Unleavened Bread. Being aware of this context for Jesus' Last Supper gives meaning to this dinner; it is all the more striking that John does not present Jesus' Last Supper as a Passover meal, and thus does not invoke the meaning of Passover as background to Jesus' final meal on earth with his disciples. It is only right, then, to expect that John will treat Jesus' Last Supper differently from the other evangelists; thus, we consider the two versions of the Last Supper separately.

If we consider Jesus' Last Supper to be a Passover supper, we can appreciate how little the synoptics have told us about what went on at the meal, for the traditional Passover meal involved much more than the few details given us by the Gospel reports. Clearly, the Synoptics have selected material from this dinner which they thought highly meaningful for their readers; it is to this material that we now turn our attention.

Matthew followed Mark very closely so what can be said for one is said for the other. Mark leads us into the Last Supper at the point where Jesus, well into the meal, suddenly and abruptly set a mournful tone by saying that one of his own Twelve would betray him. The reader had been prepared for this betrayal just a few moments earlier in the story which reported that Judas agreed to watch for the moment when he could hand Jesus over to the authorities—when the crowds would not be present to defend Jesus. But for all that preparation, the announcement of the betrayal, and that the betrayer was right in this very room, is chilling and saddening for those who love Jesus. The announcement itself does not come as news to the reader; Mark was concerned rather to convey the mood which dominated the Last Supper and soured it for everyone.

As in so many other places in the Gospel structures, so here an awareness that "scripture is being fulfilled" permeates the story of betrayal. All these happenings, even down to minute details, were in some deep sense already spoken of by God through his prophets; it was always there for those to read who knew how to read it.

What a sharp turn in mood is established, then, when the next moment in the story telling tells us that Jesus' death would be a death out of love for us. Such a contrast between Judas, who sacrificed a human being, and Jesus, who sacrificed himself lest others should suffer! Mark intentionally emphasized this contrast by putting these two persons opposite each other in quick sequence.

By announcing that Jesus' Last Supper is a Passover Supper, Mark, and Matthew and Luke following him, wanted us to interpret Jesus' death as a death by which believers were freed from the slavery, ignorance and sin symbolized by Egypt to reach the land of freedom, wisdom and holiness symbolized by Israel. The blood of the lamb, which warded off the Angel of Death, was now Jesus' blood; the slaying of the lamb was the means by which we avoid death and enjoy the happiness of God's life. Thus, what was eaten, the food of Passover, was now identified as the body of Jesus, the body which, slain tomorrow, provided the blood which protected the believers from death. By interpreting Jesus' broken body this way, Mark and Matthew and Luke want their readers to see Jesus not simply as a just person treated unjustly, a martyr who preferred death to backing down from his representing God to the people of Israel. Jesus was a martyr, a witness to the Father and a person treated unjustly by evil forces, but he was the one and only one whose blood allows us to live, to go free, to reach the land of rest, of peace, of freedom and holiness, of wisdom.

When Jesus looked into the cup, however, he suggested a further interpretation involving blood. The wine was identified, not as wine of the Passover, but as blood of the new covenant. To refer to blood in this way was to recall the pouring of blood by Moses as a way of confirming the covenant between God and Israel, an agreement whereby each partner dedicated all he has to the good of the other (Ex 24:4–8). The ancient prophets had talked of God's intention to strike a new covenant with Israel, a covenant to replace that which Jesus' ancestors had so often broken (Jer 31:31–34; Ez 11:17–20). Now, with the outpouring of Jesus' own blood we have the formal confirmation of God's new willingness to be Our God, with all that this means for the assurance of our happiness, and the appeal that we willingly become "My People," devoted and loyal to him. Thus, the Gospels remind us of the significance of Jesus' death as the deepest fulfillment of what was intended by the Passover and by the pouring of blood at the making of the covenant.

Finally, Jesus made clear that his blood was to be poured out for *many,* which in Aramaic means *all who will accept it.* Matthew added that it would be poured out for the forgiveness of sins. In specifying the blood of Jesus as effecting the forgiveness of sins, Matthew reminded us surely of the many institutional sacrifices offered systematically in the Temple as petition for forgiveness of Israel's sins, especially of that sacrifice on Yom Kippur, when the high priest entered God's private chamber to ask forgiveness of Israel's sins by pouring blood before the merciful throne of God. This blood has its meaning in this, that it represents not death, but life. Ancient Israel believed that life was contained in blood; to lose one's blood was to lose one's life, as anyone could see. Thus, what the high priest presented to God through sprinkling of blood was life, the life of Israel rededicated to keep union with God. Jesus' pouring out his blood was a sign of that life which he, for us, gave back to God, after we have spent our lives in service of other gods. Jesus' giving his blood was a plea that we join with him in making his outpouring our outpouring, his dedication of his life our renewed dedication of our lives to God.

But there is another suggestion in Matthew's identifying Jesus' blood as blood for the forgiveness of sins. It is that Jesus was fulfilling the role of the Servant of Yahweh spoken of by Isaiah so many centuries before the coming of Jesus. This anonymous Servant, spoken of in the Book of Isaiah, chapters fifty-two to fifty-three, was one who gave his life for the benefit of others. More correctly, this Servant, while innocent, suffered, and his suffering was so well received that it took the place of the suffering others deserved to undergo, but now will not have to endure because of the generous acceptance of suffering by the Servant. Mark had earlier noted Jesus' words that he had "come, not to be served, but to serve and to give his life as a ransom for many" (Mk 10:45). The blood of the Eucharist thus commemorates that bloodshed by which the innocent, loving the Lord God, endured suffering which belonged to others who deserved it. And by this blood we would no longer need undergo the suffering we have merited.

Multiple, then, are the meanings offered the disciples and the reader as Jesus identified the bread as his body and the wine as his blood. All these meanings or interpretations are meant to help us understand the significance of the death Jesus would undergo the next day and the abiding significance of the eucharistic celebration we enjoy each Sunday.

As Jesus brought to a close his reflections about the food and drink of this Passover meal, he accentuated the mournful circumstances of this dinner—never again would he eat this kind of human meal. Brief as this statement is, it cannot fail to impress the disciples and the reader, for with it was the acknowledgment that the friendship of Jesus with his contemporaries was ended by futile and destructive anger and jealousy. Life as they had grown to know it was finished; this was the last moment of that life.

It is noteworthy, however, that while Jesus admitted that his life with the disciples was at an end, there was hope that they all would eat again together in the kingdom of God; there will be reunion and the joys of renewed life together in the time of uninterrupted and full joy. Thus, the Eucharist celebrated each Sunday recalls, as St. Paul says, the separation from the Lord till he comes again (1 Cor 17:26). The Eucharist is a reminder of a

death, but also of a future life together, whenever the precious
time for it is allowed to begin.

The language of the Last Supper is terse, but for all that it is
intense. From the meaning of the bread and wine the author
turns to another painful moment of that dinner: Jesus showed his
awareness of the weakness of Peter and the others as it would be
clearly revealed when Jesus was trapped and apprehended. Mark
is extremely clever in his presentation of this dialogue between
Jesus and Peter; Jesus quietly insisted his expectation would be
fulfilled, while Peter, eventually claiming himself to be better
than the others at the table, was allowed to have the last word:
you will see that I will remain faithful even it if means my death!
The last word was Peter's, as though the last word were the
truth! Jesus was willing to let actions decide who was right.

We stand in this room, traditionally noted as the Upper
Room of the Last Supper. What words of profound meaning, what
words of prophetic tragedy and betrayal echoed around these
walls. Ultimately, it was the moment of parting, and the presence
of death was in the room. It is noteworthy that Mark, and
Matthew with him, has centered the extreme generosity of Jesus
for others between the hardness of Judas and the selfishness of
Peter, as though these two companions of Jesus might help
reflect even more brightly the one person who spent himself in
love in the midst of so much hatred and weakness towards him.

Mark, and Matthew with him, has centered the extreme
generosity of Jesus for others between the hardness of Judas and
the selfishness of Peter, as though these two companions of
Jesus might help reflect even more brightly the one person who
spends himself in love in the midst of so much hatred and
weakness towards him.

Last Supper in Luke   *Lk 22:7-38*

In the portrayal of the Last Supper, Luke differs from Mark and
Matthew both by changing the order of events and by adding
teachings of Jesus pertinent to this moment. Luke begins the
supper with Jesus' words that he had for a long time been eager
to celebrate this dinner with his disciples, and the reason for this
eagerness was his awareness that this dinner would be the last
till what it signifies would be fulfilled in the kingdom—only then
would Jesus eat again with his disciples. Indeed, until the

kingdom comes Jesus would not drink wine again with his friends.

Having set the mournful tone of this meal, which leads into events of great pain and sorrow, Jesus now pointed out the new identity of the bread and wine which we have already learned from Mark and Matthew. Luke, however, adds the command, "Do this to remind yourselves of me." In these words the habitual practice of the Christian communities was grounded and given meaning—in doing with bread and wine what Jesus did we recall the Jesus of this Upper Room.

Unlike Mark who had begun the Last Supper with the announcement of Judas' betrayal, Luke now has Jesus announce the presence of the betrayer. But the painful sadness afflicting everyone at the table became an opportunity for teaching a hard lesson to learn. Indeed, Luke proceeds to this lesson without ever identifying the betrayer. The lesson is one which is fitting in this context, for it centers on "greatness." Having heard how Jesus achieved his greatness, it can only follow that greatness for anyone was achieved by service of others, by acting as the youngest or the servant. The lesson is difficult to learn because the usual definition of greatness involves "lording it over" others. Jesus took this precious moment, as he showed his greatness through service so that his disciples must understand what true greatness is.

With perceptive logic Jesus next indicated the reward for those disciples who remain faithful in trials, presumably the trials about to begin, but including the trials the disciples would undergo in the years to come, when they practiced the deeds of service which merit the title of "greatness." Indeed, in anticipation of their fidelity Jesus now declared them participants of the kingdom to come. With a particularly Jewish flavor, he indicated this participation as that of eating and drinking in the kingdom with him and as that of sitting on the thrones of Israel as judges. This latter image was meant to remind the reader that one of the ways in which Israel had envisioned its glorification after centuries of humiliation and slavery was the placement of Israel as judge over those who had caused it so much suffering, enslavement and death. This role of judge over one's enemies who had unjustly condemned God's beloved was promised now to Jesus' friends who, in their turn, would suffering much, even death from their enemies.

At this point Luke placed the words of Jesus' awareness of

Peter's imminent denial. Jesus' prayer—that Peter may not fail totally, but, on recovering, be a strength to his fellow disciples— is a sign of the preeminent role Jesus saw Peter exercise among the remaining Eleven.

The final teaching Luke gives here concerns the difference the disciples would soon notice between life with Jesus and life when he is ascended. Earlier in the Gospel, Jesus had sent his disciples on a preaching tour for which, he said, they needed no purse or haversack or sandals; they would, in other words, be welcomed by their hearers and be well taken care of (Lk 9:1–6). No more! The tide of favor was against Jesus now, and against those who would represent him; now one would have to provide for and defend oneself. Scripture had said, "he let himself be taken for a criminal" (Is 53:12); Jesus interpreted *he* as about himself and, since he was now a criminal, it was clear how inhospitable would be all those who once might have received Jesus' disciples with kindness.

Luke, then, preserved in his own way what Mark had told about Jesus' Last Supper, but he included it in a different order to teach the disciples lessons which would be very relevant in the near future. Jesus' Last Supper, then, increasingly became a moment of separation when Jesus more and more looked to the needs of his disciples in the time when he would be gone. It was natural that the Gospel writers, aware of the situations of their audiences some thirty to sixty years after the lifetime of Jesus, should orient this farewell moment to instruct their readers. With the good of later Christians in mind, John devoted himself mainly to lessons for the future. To his Gospel story of the Upper Room we now turn our attention.

Last Supper in John   *Jn 13-17*

If we consider first what the Gospels of Matthew, Mark and Luke contribute to our understanding of what happened in the Upper Room that night before Jesus died, we are struck all the more by the contribution John makes concerning Jesus' Last Supper. Whereas the Synoptic report is at most half a chapter in length, John's report extends over five chapters. Most significantly, however, we become very aware that John does not tell of Jesus' statements about bread as his body, wine as his blood. Indeed, should one look for teaching about the Eucharist in John, one

would have to turn to a speech Jesus gave in Galilee, not in
Jerusalem, and in the Gospel, as early as chapter six. (See 33,
38.) Finally, we are not certain that John regards the Last Supper
of Jesus and his disciples as a Passover meal.

Such differences between John and the synoptic writers only
whet our interest and so we investigate the manner in which
John chose to present the meaning of Jesus' last calm moments
with his disciples. Since John's presentation is so long,s49we
restrict ourselves here to a rather limited representation of
John's report.

The five chapters dealing with Jesus' words and actions at
his Last Supper can be divided into two uneven parts. First, there
are the two accounts of Jesus' washing his disciples' feet and of
the announcement of the presence of his betrayer. Secondly,
from the end of chapter thirteen to the end of chapter seventeen,
there is a long discourse of Jesus, occasionally punctuated by
questions of his disciples but clearly dominated by Jesus' final
thoughts about his disciples and their future needs.

Washing of the Feet

In reading the bulk of chapter thirteen, we are again aware of
two constant themes of John, that Jesus was in absolute control
of everything that would happen to him and that what happened
to Jesus brought to completion what his Father had long ago
said would happen to his beloved Son. Jesus exhibited his
control by showing he knew what was to happen before it
actually happened. Nothing was a surprise to Jesus in John; in
this way John argues away the claim that Jesus was ultimately
conquered by his enemies, was impotent and ignorant, as the
crucifixion might suggest. Similarly, the correspondence between
so many of Jesus' acts, words, and circumstances of life and the
words of God in the Jewish Scriptures argues favorably for Jesus
in his defense. From John's study of the Scriptures, God clearly
looked forward to Jesus and very clearly loved Jesus and
encouraged belief in him; to thwart Jesus was to reject the goal
of God's words in the Jewish Scriptures.

Jesus, aware that he was at the end of his life, chose to teach
his disciples a lesson in service, something comparable to what
Luke had presented in his account of the Last Supper. In John,
however, Jesus not only taught by word, but also taught by a

symbolic action: he washed the feet of his disciples—he who was acknowledged to be the greater did a servant's work. No doubt, the crucifixion of Jesus was to be understood as a similar type of service, the greater humiliated in pain for the lesser, and in this humiliation the crucified showed his true greatness. But Jesus was also concerned that his disciples understand how central this acceptance of service to others was to the way of life Jesus thought would best lead to happiness. His concern here was as much to teach about the future of his disciples as to interpret his death.

This book is not intended to give exegeses of individual scriptural verses; but one verse, Jn 13:10, is such a sore point to the reader of John's account of the Last Supper, that I will turn to it. "No one who has taken a bath needs washing, he is clean all over." To understand this sentence, we must understand that here, as elsewhere in John, there is more than one level of interest being attended to. On the one hand, Peter resisted Jesus' washing his feet, and this resistance is on the level of what we might call natural interaction—indeed, few healthy people want their feet washed by anybody at any time. But Jesus interpreted this resistance as a way of opposing his will; once Jesus spoke his mind, Peter naturally said he was willing to be washed totally by Jesus, that he would, in other words, do nothing to harm his union with Jesus.

But Peter's willingness to be washed totally, "feet, hands and head," led Jesus to another thought, to another level, in which he indicated Peter needed no such total washing, for he has already taken a full bath. This "bath" is the bath of Baptism, the bath of total giving of oneself to Jesus. Jesus was for the moment not concerned with washing Peter's feet as a sign of himself being great because he acted as Peter's servant. Rather he wanted to affirm in a rather sophisticated way that Peter's commitment of faith to Jesus had been like a bath that washed Peter clean totally—Peter, and all like him. But not all the disciples can be described this way. In this way of looking at things, there was one who is unclean, the betrayer. We have moved from washing feet which needed washing, since people had just come from the dusty roads of Jerusalem, as a sign of greatness to an affirmation of the cleansing nature of faith in Jesus, which for a long time before 95 A.D. had been expressed publicly by the bath of Baptism. John, in short, was eager to take the opportunity to build one lesson on another in chapter thirteen. The lesson of greatness through service is the basis for further teaching that the baptism washes one totally.

Presence of the Betrayer

The second element of chapter thirteen brought to our attention is Jesus' announcement of the presence of his betrayer. As in the other Gospels, this is a moment of great confusion and sadness as each disciple searched for the meaning of Jesus' words. It was to the Beloved Disciple that Jesus revealed the identity of the betrayer, for the Beloved Disciple was reclining next to Jesus. One reclined on one's left elbow at such a dinner as this, for everyone used only the right hand in eating and serving, and had only to lean backward to have his ear only a few inches from Jesus' softly whispered words.

With the identification of Judas as the betrayer and his departure, Jesus acknowledged that the moment of his glorification has begun. The image he used for himself was that of "the Son of Man," the personage described in the Book of Daniel as the one who would be glorified and made judge of his enemies after a period of suffering. Jesus sees that his glorification has already begun as he was about to pass, through the decisive hands of Judas, into his long-awaited period of suffering. Indeed, as Jesus notes, this suffering will bring him God's praise, and soon; thus, John asks the reader to look beyond the suffering of the next few hours to the entrance of Jesus into the life of "that age" which replaces the world we know now.

With the accounts of foot washing and betrayal, then, John completed the incidents he wished to call to his reader's attention within the story of Jesus' Last Supper. Now he began the long discourse of Jesus.

Last Discourse of Jesus

In one sense the message of Jesus' long discourse in the Upper Room is simple. Jesus was deeply concerned to assure his disciples of his abiding love for them even though he no longer would be able to stay with them. In another sense the speech is difficult because it is difficult to grasp the fullness of intimacy Jesus promised to maintain in a variety of ways while absent from his friends.

From a group he knew with certainty would be thoroughly without hope Jesus asked for trust that his going meant a going to prepare a place for each of them so that they could all be together again. To a group whose faith in Jesus' relationship with God would be severely tested, Jesus pleaded for faith that "I am in the Father and the Father is in me." To a group unsure and disconsolate Jesus promised another Advocate, who would follow up on all that Jesus had said and done, and he promised that he would not leave them orphans, but would come back to them—"you will live... I in my Father, you in me and I in you." Indeed, to a disturbed people Jesus gave peace, which the world could not give. If only the group would remain in Jesus, it would be alive like branches in a vine and be fruitful. To a bewildered and shaken group of friends Jesus offered a way of looking at the events to come, a way to pierce what was otherwise confusing and frightening: Jesus would suffer out of obedience to an already conceived plan which was thoroughly wise, for it was rooted in the Father; Jesus was never to be forgotten as innocent of all wrongdoing, as his enemies and the world in general would insist. Contrary to all public and official statements, Jesus was the one who was right and they are the ones who are wrong. Jesus was to be remembered as the one who "came from the Father" and "now leaves the world to go to the Father"; to think of these last hours of Jesus in any other way is to refuse the truth of Jesus' reality.

The long speech of Jesus revolves, then, on a multitude of appeals which are ultimately reduced to trust in his protective love for the disciples and in the convictions they held about his belonging to the Father. But there was another element woven into this extensive and final discourse which was as much a legacy of Jesus as was his word of consolation. This element consists in his call to love one another, while he is absent, to be fruitful branches continuing that love which flows to them from the vine. Indeed, Jesus' friends are known as such because they love others. It is surprising to many that John, quite distinct from other Gospels and most all the rest of the New Testament writings, did not explicitly speak of morality except for the command: "Love one another, as I have loved you." Whatever the reason for silence about other moral stances, John accentuated the love of disciples for one another, and this accentuation was one of the last things on Jesus' mind as he left his disciples.

Resurrection Appearances   *Lk 24:36–49; Jn 20:19–29*

Two gospels tell stories which happened in a room, behind
closed doors. These incidents are appearances of Jesus to his
disciples. The stories themselves never identify the room where
the disciples met Jesus risen, but they strongly imply that—since
the Acts of the Apostles noted that the disciples returned after
Jesus' Ascension to "the room where they had been staying" and
that Pentecost occurred in a room they met in—all these events
occurred in the same room, the Upper Room made memorable
by the Last Supper. Accepting this assumption as at best
probable, I consider at this point both the two resurrection
appearances of Jesus and the Pentecost event; they contribute
ever more to our realization of what this simple room has to
share with those who enjoy union with the Lord and his Spirit.

Resurrection Appearances in Luke   *Lk 24:36-49*

Luke has three stories about Jesus' Resurrection from the dead;
the third took place in the room where the disciples were
gathered. In that room Jesus took great pains to convince his
followers that it was he, not some kind of ghostly image of
himself, which they saw—and heard and touched and watched
eat. Behind this insistence is an apologetic or defensive
intention, that we should have no doubt that the full Jesus rose
from the dead. The Resurrection from the dead was mystifying
enough without people drawing the conclusion that only the
spirit of Jesus was alive. No, forever Christians know that the full
Jesus of Nazareth is risen. Moreover, the identity of the risen
Jesus is precisely that of Jesus of Nazareth. It is Luke who makes
clear, both in the Resurrection appearances and in the
subsequent Acts of the Apostles, that the risen and worshipped
Christ is Jesus of Nazareth, whom everyone knew from his words
and actions, and from his death. One who reads Luke's writings
cannot separate the risen Christ from Jesus of Nazareth, for the
risen one is simply Jesus risen. For the content of Jesus risen,
then, we go to the story of Jesus before his Resurrection, not to
some speculation of what the risen one must be like apart from
the reality—the only reality we should use—of the life of Jesus of
Nazareth.

   In this final appearance Luke looks beyond the moment of
the disciples' joy at the presence of their Master, come through

the horrors of his death. Luke tells us that in this room Jesus
spoke of the necessity, revealed in Scripture, that the disciples
preach salvation in the name of Jesus to the ends of the earth as
his witnesses. Thus, the saving plan of God was not thwarted by
the Death, Resurrection and Ascension of Jesus, but continued by
Jesus working in and through his disciples who witness to him.
Nothing would stop God's offer to forgive and bless, no matter
what men did to Jesus. Within this room the disciples should
wait for that gift, that promised blessing which would start them
out as witnesses of Jesus; from this room, from this city of
Jerusalem the plan of God would push on to invite all to call on
the name of Jesus to be saved. However distant in time or place
the message about salvation travels, the message itself, Luke
insisted, is rooted in Jesus of Nazareth who was mighty in words
and deeds, who should not have been put to death and was
raised to prove it.

Resurrection Appearances in John   *Jn 20:19-29*

But the Upper Room was not only the site of resurrection
appearance in Luke; John, too, recalled the coming of Jesus to
this room after his death and Resurrection. John, like Luke, told
a story which contains many precious aspects.

On the day of his Resurrection Jesus appeared to his
disciples gathered in the Upper Room; Thomas alone was absent.
It is this appearance of Jesus which enshrined for John the
Evangelist the supreme gift of Jesus to his disciples, the gift of
the Holy Spirit. It was for this Spirit that the entire Gospel of
John had waited and looked forward to; it is the risen Jesus who
can give the Spirit, as he breathes on his disciples—much like
God who gave life to Adam by breathing his breath into the
"slime of the earth" (Gn 2:7). Thus, the Upper Room in John is
the site of the Spirit, with whom the final elements are associated
in the Jewish Scriptures which bring this world "which does not
know God, which cannot comprehend or overcome him" to an
end. It is not unpredictable, then, that with the gift of the Spirit
was given the gift to forgive sins. As God breathed his Spirit once
again, God revealed his eagerness that nothing separate us from
him again.

The Gospel of John felt it important to emphasize that the
full Jesus rose from the dead; thus, in John, too, Jesus ate

normal, human food to underline the full reality that stood before the disciples. It was the Jesus of three days ago who stood before them now.

The one disciple was absent from this meeting, Thomas, doubted the reality of the risen Jesus; the reports of eyewitnesses did not move him to belief. There is no doubt that, for the Evangelist, Thomas stands for all those who are not eyewitnesses of Jesus' life, death and resurrection, for all those who must depend on the preaching of others to bring alive to them the reality of Jesus which they themselves have not seen and touched and heard. Jesus obliged Thomas by appearing again when Thomas was present and by fulfilling the criteria Thomas demanded for his act of faith in the resurrection of Jesus. Jesus went to such lengths only to show how unreasonable Thomas's refusal to believe the "preachers" was. Unreasonable? Was Thomas's unbelief unreasonable? For John it is. Or better, if we had seen all that Jesus had done, as had Thomas, and had read John, as the reader has done, Thomas and the reader should be expected to believe; to the believing evangelist, the evidence for belief is overwhelming. The resurrection is another, and the greatest, indicator that Jesus is the Christ, the Son of God, through whom we have life (Jn 20:31). The resurrection is a sign by which faith is excited and continued. For the evangelist, it matters little in the long run whether one is an eyewitness of Jesus risen or not. Ample evidence offered to eyewitness and hearer alike to encourage belief and make believing a reasonable act. Blessed, as blessed as those who have seen, are those who have not seen and yet believe. This Upper Room is silent witness to this conviction.

Finally, Thomas in this room confessed Jesus to be "my Lord and my God." Most scholars agree that originally John ended here; chapter twenty-one, although considered an inspired part of Scripture, is an addition by another author. The addition has valuable stories, but obscures the finality and triumphant confession of Jesus' identity desired by the author of the first twenty chapters. John's entire goal had been to affirm the identity of Jesus. It is his hope that the profound confession of Thomas, that Jesus is his Lord and his God, be the final words of the reader of the story John has woven as his Gospel or good news. The Upper Room reminds us of this hope, that we too can affirm, with Thomas, that Jesus, though unseen and unheard and untouched by us, is surely our Lord and our God.

Pentecost   *Acts 2*

Besides being the site of Jesus' Last Supper and the supposed site of Jesus' appearances to his disciples after his Resurrection, the Upper Room has been traditionally the place filled by the Holy Spirit at the time of the Jewish feast of Pentecost. Let us consider for a few moments the understanding of Pentecost suggested by St. Luke, who, in chapter two of his Acts of the Apostles, relates the Pentecostal outpouring of God's Holy Spirit on one hundred twenty or so disciples of Jesus.

That God shares his Spirit with human beings is the most intimate sharing God has ever offered to his creatures. It was to this sharing that Jesus dedicated his life and it was to release the Spirit that Jesus died and rose to the right hand of his Father. The new intimacy with God through a most profound sharing of his Spirit is really the beginning of that age which, in Jewish hopes and longing, was called "the age to come." Nothing more intimate to the Father could be shared with human beings, and so with this sharing began "the final age," the last stage of that long effort by God to repair what Adam had done, to save us from domination by evil, to snatch us from the clutches of eternal death, so that we may live as fully one with God as possible.

According to an understanding of the Jewish Scriptures, God created by breathing his Spirit into clay and making it live. The word *spirit* comes from the Latin word *spiritus* for *breath.* In other words, God gave life from himself to something not alive of itself by breathing life from himself into it. For centuries Jewish prophets had foreseen what could be the most profound intimacy with God and talked of it as a new "breathing of God's Breath [Spirit]," and the living creature would live by virtue of that breathing of God's life. Luke, like so many others of the New Testament period, believed he was living in this new and final age of God's new, life-giving Breathing. But because Luke had certain limited goals in writing the Acts of the Apostles, he chose to emphasize one aspect of this new breathing of God: that it gave strength and wisdom so that human beings may be outstanding witnesses to the opportunity for salvation and intimacy with God that God now wanted to offer everyone. Thus the story of Pentecost, while indicating that the long-awaited moment of new life through God's Spirit had now arrived, stressed the impact of that new breathing in its ability to give strength and wisdom to the ones chosen to witness before an often hostile and skeptical world. In other words, whereas Paul stressed the profound unity or intimacy we now share with God through his new creation of us, Luke, to serve the purposes of his book of witness, showed the qualities the witnesses enjoy because of this same breathing of God.

That Luke associated the breathing or outpouring of God's Spirit with the Jewish feast of Pentecost may be intentional. For the Jews, Pentecost meant two things: it was the time of harvest and it was a memorial of the giving of the Law to Moses which finally brought to realization the intention of God that "he would be their God and they would be his people." It is often said that Luke wanted his readers to understand that, as Pentecost brought to conclusion the harvest begun with the feast of Unleavened Bread, temporally coincident with the feast of Passover, so the outpouring of the Spirit brings to completion or fulfillment the purposes for which Jesus died and rose. What is underlined in calling this outpouring of the Spirit *Pentecost* is the tight bond between what happened to Jesus at Passover and God's gift of the Spirit.

It is also often noted that Pentecost, which means *fifty* in Greek, and indicates fifty days between the beginning of the spring harvest and its completion, calls to mind what happened fifty days after the Israelites fled Egypt in the famous exodus ordered by God. Fifty days into the desert brought the Israelites to Mount Sinai, to the moment when God formally became the God of Israel and Israel became God's People. This moment, long-awaited and planned for by God from the moment of his dealing with Abraham, was the beginning of the fulfillment of God's plan to save all mankind through Israel, the light of the world. Against this understanding of Pentecost, it is easy enough to perceive what Luke had in mind by noting that the Spirit was poured out during the time of "Pentecost." Indeed, God has again formed the People of God; this time, he did this forming by sharing his Spirit, which is a deeper sharing than is the sharing of his mind through Law. It is the realization that God has formed his people on the analogy of what he did earlier at Mount Sinai that caused people to refer to Pentecost as the "birthday" of the Church.

Pentecost, then, sets a context by which we can better understand the significance of God's gift of the Spirit, who is the flowering of Jesus' death, the Spirit is the bond by which those who believe in Jesus become the people of God. But there is something more to be said about Luke's handling of this event, something which brings out the peculiarity of the gift of the Spirit to those designated "my witnesses."

When Peter heard the suggestion that he and his friends spoke about the wonders God has wrought "because they have drunk too much wine," he embarked on a speech meant to give the true cause of their witnessing. The bedrock of Peter's explanation is the series of verses cited from the prophet Joel. In this citation Joel speaks of a cause and its effects. The cause is God's outpouring of his Spirit in the last days. The effects of that cause are unexpected and marvelous speech about God from even the least of human beings, and wonders in nature. Peter's intention was to argue in reverse: if God's Spirit at some future time is to cause praise of God and wonders in nature, then, since people are praising God and wonders of flames like tongues, of sound like a wind, have occurred, we should conclude that the Spirit of God is the cause, that the Spirit of God, promised so long ago, has finally been poured out. In this form of logic Peter argued that the true cause of their speaking God's wonders was the Spirit, promised by God through Joel.

But Peter was not satisfied with simply explaining that the outpouring of the Spirit made understandable the disciples' wondrous proclamation about God. He included in his citation from Joel the words: "All who call on the name of the Lord will be saved." But the citation does not support an argument that the Spirit has been poured out; rather it proclaims an effect of the outpouring of the Spirit. That is, if the Spirit has indeed been given, it follows that anyone who calls on the name of the Lord can be saved. In other words, God pours out the Spirit as a sign that he is now willing to offer salvation to anyone who will call on the name of the Lord. Whatever God's attitude was before this event, it should now be known that he is willing to save all who call on the name of the Lord.

Thus, Pentecost becomes a sign of the most tremendous opportunity offered to the world since creation: God is willing to forget what Adam did and ready to offer his salvation. The new age, the age to replace this one of sin and death, has come!

But Luke has more to say, for he must clarify certain elements of this marvelous sentence: "All who call on the name of the Lord will be saved." Peter concentrated on a rehearsal of the life, death, resurrection and ascension of Jesus—presumably to move his Jewish audience to repent for the unjust end they put to Jesus' mission from God. But Peter also told the story of Jesus so that we can be convinced, according to the logic of the first century A.D. Israelites, that Jesus is the Lord, that it is therefore the name of Jesus we should call on for salvation. True it is that, when Joel spoke his prophecy about the outpouring of God's spirit, he understood "Lord" to be Yahweh, that it was the name Yahweh one calls on for salvation. But it became clear to Luke and to Peter that what was really meant is that, when the Spirit is given, one should call on the name of Jesus for salvation, as people in the Gospel had called on Jesus for healing and were healed. Peter's ultimate goal, then, is to present his audience with the reality that the Spirit of God has been poured out and that, in the light of this outpouring, we can now call on the name of Jesus and be assured of salvation. Above all else, Jesus' resurrection and ascension, witnessed by the disciples, revealed the reality of Jesus' identity visible to those who could grasp it during his mission in Galilee: Jesus is Messiah and Lord. To whom do the promises of Scripture apply if not to Jesus? He must be the Messiah and Lord promised by these Scriptures; as such, it is upon his name we call now for salvation.

Peter has explained a fundamental understanding of the outpouring of the Spirit as it related to the preaching which now began in Acts concerning belief in the name of Jesus. But Luke clarified more than just the identity of this "Lord" of Joel, upon whom we call for salvation; Luke further opens the door to the reality that the "everyone" who calls on the Lord's name will be precisely this: *everyone.* Clearly this term includes all Jews and all Gentiles; this will be a major theme throughout the Acts of the Apostles and a fundamental principle of the Church: *everyone!*

Luke also clarified what *to call upon the name of* meant in the Christian context: it referred to baptism, the formal, public profession of faith that Jesus is the one through whom salvation is given by God. Further, Luke made clear that *salvation* is specified as *forgiveness of sins* which leads to "the gift of the Holy Spirit." Thus, Jesus would go beyond those physical and psychological healings by which people during his public life enjoyed aspects of that wholeness called *salvation.* Now, we will enjoy the fullness of wholeness as the essence of that wholeness—forgiveness—is granted.

This forgiveness, the effect of repentance which calls on Jesus' name for forgiveness and the Spirit at the time of Baptism, results in the fullest willingness to live out the will of God. This will is expressed most fundamentally in two formulas: You shall love the Lord your God with all your heart and mind and soul and strength; you shall love your neighbor as yourself. And it is precisely the living out of these two commandments—together with the affirmation that Jesus is Savior—which the final lines of chapter two of Acts address. In short, though the actual description of the outpouring of the Spirit is restricted to a few lines at the beginning of Acts two, Luke cannot convey the fullest meaning of that outpouring until he can explain that salvation is to be given "in the name of Jesus" and show the concrete results of calling on the name of Jesus: the fullest love of God and love of neighbor. Pentecost, then, gives the best proof that the desire of God that he be loved and that our neighbor be loved—that this desire has finally been fulfilled. Once Luke showed this to his satisfaction, he left the subject of Pentecost to move to the next witness Jesus' disciples would give. Pentecost, then, began within these four walls, but lives in the hearts and actions of all who are willing to call upon the name of the Lord Jesus for salvation.

Via Dolorosa

V*ia Dolorosa*

After Jesus was captured in the garden on the lower slope of the Mount of Olives, the Gospels tell us that he was tried by the high priest Caiaphas and by Pontius Pilate; added to these trials is an informal trial before Annas, a former high priest and father-in-law of Caiaphas, and, as Luke alone reports, a trial before Herod Antipas, Rome appointed ruler of Galilee and Samaria. Associated with these trials were various abuses Jesus underwent—slapping, spitting, taunting, mocking, crowning with thorns and, eventually, the scourging by which a prisoner was prepared for crucifixion.

An old tradition says the palace of the high priest is under the present Armenian Church of St. Savior, just some yards north of the site revered today as the Upper Room or Cenacle, and very near to the southeastern wall of present Jerusalem. The other events of Jesus' hours between his capture and his crucifixion tradition places in the area just north of the present Temple grounds. More specifically, if we were to proceed a little over a hundred yards westward on the road from St. Stephen's Gate, we would stand near or under an arch stretching above and over the street; this arch for a long time was thought to be the arch on which Jesus stood while Pilate spoke to the crowd the famous words, "Behold the man!" The area on either side of this arch and stretching eastward from the arch is the site of Fortress Antonia, the place where Pilate and his soldiers lived during the Feast of Passover.

Very near the arch is a door of the Convent of the Sisters of Sion. Beneath the convent is a pavement which some have identified as part of the area where Jesus was tried by Pilate. It is called in the Gospel of John *Lithostratos,* which means *stone pavement.* Here we can see ridges and etchings and marks deciphered as a game which Roman soldiers were wont to play, a game in which their prisoner was mocked for his claim to be a king. In this underground area, we have a sense of what the Roman quarters of the fortress may have been in Pilate's time, as we peel off the centuries of building over the destroyed fortress. The fortress Antonia, as the Romans called it, was meant to sit ominously at the northwestern corner of the Temple grounds, to remind Jews milling about on the Temple platform that the Romans were watching their every move lest revolt break out. Indeed, if this is the area of Jesus' trial before Pilate, it is also the area of his crowning with thorns, of his scourging and of his first steps on the way to Calvary, due east of here.

Luke, as mentioned earlier (See 229), tells of Pilate's attempt to shift the trial of Jesus into Herod Antipas's hands; after all, Jesus was from Galilee, where Herod ruled. Near the Convent of the Sisters of Sion and near the arch stretching over the road mentioned earlier are the supposed ruins of the palace Herod Antipas used. However, it is more reasonable to look for Herod's Jerusalem residence at a point just south of the Jaffa Gate and of the site pointed out today as David's Tower.

But with the suggestion that the residence of Herod Antipas lay on the west side of old Jerusalem near the Jaffa Gate, we must give fair account of a position held by many reputable scholars, namely, that here too, near the Jaffa Gate—and not in the area of the Convent of the Sisters of Sion—was the praetorium of Pontius Pilate wherein Jesus was tried. In this view, Jesus would have been tried, beaten, and led to Calvary from an area due south of the Basilica of the Holy Sepulcher—rather than from the area of the Convent of the Sisters of Sion located due east of the basilica.

Trial of Jesus   *Mt 26:57-68; Mk 14:53-65; Lk 22:54-71; Jn 18:13-24*

Shrouded in the secrecy nighttime afforded, the high priest, and his father-in-law, the powerful former high priest Annas, strove to formulate of a charge which could justify the death of Jesus. The high priest, Caiaphas, had earlier noted the advantage of Jesus' removal: if he did not go, he might so rouse the people looking for political freedom that the Romans would turn their might loose on the leaders of Israel and on their people. Better that one die, than that all suffer (Jn 11:49–50).

For many months various religious leaders of Israel had crossed paths with Jesus, sometimes intentionally, most often in Galilee, but in Jerusalem as well. The gospel stories usually conclude such meetings with the explicit or implicit affirmation that Jesus grew ever more to be their enemy. Matthew and John are particularly willing to provide a picture of intense acrimony between Jesus and other religious personages; the offer of betrayal in Jerusalem was a welcome offer to the ears of those portrayed as the harshest of Jesus' critics.

Nor was the debate with Jesus grounded only on a simple disagreement about how to interpret the mind of God for the happiness of human beings. Not to mention other moments, Pilate himself is said to realize that the reason Jesus is handed over to him with the request that Jesus be crucified is jealousy. It is clear from such a statement as "Do what they say, but do not do what they do" (Mt 23:1–3) that Jesus not only presented his interpretation of the Jewish law, but also took the Pharisees and others to task for their hypocrisy—publicly. Not surprising, then, is the increasing animosity in the gospel stories, until it all came to a head in Jesus' tragic visit to Jerusalem for Passover. It is noteworthy that, at this point of Jesus' life the opposition by Pharisees and scribes was replaced by the most powerful figures of Israel, the priests and members of that sect whose theology the priests by and large supported, the Sadducees.

Given the obvious fact that the Gospel writers were loyal disciples to a Jesus who, they believed, was greater than any human being, it is not surprising that the tragic end Jesus had to undergo should be painted in vibrant colors; the enemy is truly enemy in the retelling of the story. This historical viewpoint results from the advantage of hindsight which knows a Jesus so clearly Son of God that he, unlike any human history thus far known, was raised from the dead. This historical retelling is further encouraged by the continued harshness of Jews towards Christians, Jewish or Gentile, in Israel and throughout the Mediterranean.

Yet sometimes a sympathetic portrait is drawn of a Jewish religious leader, such as Nicodemus and Gamaliel. Indeed, despite what happened to Jesus at the hands of the enemy, Luke for one is willing to tell how the early preaching of the Apostles considered this animosity towards Jesus an excusable ignorance—for in fact the Jews had not really known the full Jesus, the risen and ascended Jesus now seated at the right hand of the Father. Their deed, Luke contends, was ugly, but it was done in a climate confused both by individual pride and jealousy, and by uncertainty about what we should conclude about Jesus' identity from his words, actions, and way of life.

More moderate voices and stances to the contrary, the leaders of Jerusalem eventually reaped the fruit of their plotting and forged an accusation which, though knowingly false, gave some legitimacy to their act of handing Jesus over to Pilate. On the one hand, they satisfied themselves by assuming that Jesus agreed to their question, "Are you the Messiah, the Son of God?" On this assumption they thought Jesus a liar in most seriously making a connection between God and himself which did not exist. Moreover, they could not reject the clear challenge of Jesus to their question when he retorted by putting to them the fearful image of the Son of Man who sits in judgment on all God's enemies. On the other hand, they satisfied themselves by creating an accusation that could not help but disturb Pilate. Though the Jewish leaders understood that Jesus had no political pretensions, they won the day against both Pilate and Jesus by accusing Jesus of claiming himself to be king of the Jews. Rome never failed to handle people who were self-proclaimed kings.

Jesus before Pilate   *Mt 27:11-25; Mk 15:1-15; Lk 23:1-25; Jn 18:28-40*

Ironically, Pilate knew that he was being used, but he could not stop the fire or rage lit against Jesus. History has left a record that Pilate was often a ruthless man; this situation was no exception, for, to the ruthless, it is satisfactory to calm rage by sacrificing only one life. Pilate gave the word and Jesus was taken away to be prepared for horrible crucifixion by the accustomed whipping, which should so blunt his senses that he would not feel the extreme pain crucifixion by itself would cause.

Before leaving the figure of Pilate and the trial he conducted, one or two more comments about particular Gospels should be made. Let us look first at John, then at Matthew, for each has a very particular insight to contribute at this point of their stories.

John on Pilate

All the Gospels tell their stories of Jesus before Caiaphas and Jesus before Pilate so as to emphasize the innocence of Jesus. Part of this emphasis is to underscore Jesus' intimate relationship to God, whether it be under title of Messiah of God or of Son of Man who would exercise God's traditional role of judge of the world and condemner of the unjust. All the more poignant, then, was the willingness to go so far as to prefer Barabbas, a murderer—whether as a revolutionary or as a thief is immaterial—to Jesus, the Beloved Son of God.

John is willing to consider the false accusation made about Jesus that he claimed to be a king. Here John goes further than the other Gospels to affirm the role of Jesus as king of a kingdom not of this world. Not only did Jesus here clearly define his royal nature as distinct from political kingship, but he opens the mind of the reader to think of the extent of Jesus' rule over a world so distinct from that of the Caesars, of Pilate, of Herod. It is the world of the Father and of his love and justice where Jesus rightly plays a central role. Jesus admitted to this kind of kingship and continued with the statement that he admitted it because he came into the world precisely to give witness to the truth—and his kingship is the truth.

Pilate's famous response, "What is truth?" highlighted the theme of the Gospel's witness, that Jesus is the key to truth, to all truth that matters in life, and that a life without the truth or in doubt about it is not really life at all, but rather a subsistence without the happiness for which any human being is made. As John says, to know Jesus as the one through whom God sends his blessings is to begin to have the life which lasts forever, which cannot be touched by that reality whose most visible representative is death.

But this witness to a kingdom not within the normal experience of men and to himself as truthfully king and judge was not the end of matters before Pilate. One could say that it was inevitable that the identification of Jesus as Son of God should once more be affirmed before Jesus is led off to crucifixion, and it does appear. In John, unlike the other Gospels, the sonship of Jesus as Son of the Father or Son of God is heavily argued; Son of the Father is the most profound pre-Resurrection expression of Jesus' identity. This title allowed Thomas to call Jesus, after his resurrection, "my God," for Son of the Father is used consistently throughout the Gospel as a way of showing Jesus' equality with God—even though the distinction is carefully drawn between the Person known historically as God or Yahweh and the person who walked the hills of Galilee. It is this expression of Jesus' identity which caused Pilate to fear the most; it is this expression of Jesus' identity which moves the reader to ever deeper loyalty to the King about to be crucified.

Matthew on Pilate

The comment I wish to make about Matthew's story of Jesus
before Pilate is of a different order; it has to do with the
astonishing statement of the "people" that "his blood be on us
and on our children" (Mt 27:25). This statement, though only of a
few words' length and mixed in with so many other factors
contributing to the sadness and pain of the moment, actually has
a significant function in the working out of a main theme of
Matthew. Let us consider first the context of the statement, then
its relationship to other key elements of the Gospel.

If it is true, as many scholars claim, that Matthew had Mark
as one of his sources for his Gospel, we are all the more struck
by the statement of the people that "his blood be on us and on
our children," for nowhere in Mark is this reported, nor is it for
that matter part of any other New Testament work. The
statement is all the more notable because nowhere else did the
people contribute so significantly to Jesus' death. It should also
be remarked that, once they made this statement, the trial of
Jesus ended quickly and the steps to crucifixion, already outlined
in Mark, are described; it is as though all can proceed as
expected, but only after the people explicitly took their position
about this condemnation to death, "his blood be on us and on
our children."

And what precisely is meant by the people's willingness to
have "his blood on us and on our children?" The trial of Jesus
had come to a momentary and awkward standstill; the only one
who could give the death order, the representative of Rome,
could see no justification for condemnation. Indeed, he
symbolically washed his hands of responsibility, both as a sign of
his inability to kill Jesus justly, and as a sign that he would send
Jesus to death only at the insistence of the crowd in Jerusalem;
somehow, Pilate thought he could give the death order without
taking the responsibility for it. It is at this point that the people
intervened; they would assume the responsibility, if that is what
made Pilate hesitate to condemn Jesus to death. In fact, they
were so convinced that Jesus should die that they promised that
their children, too, would assume responsibility for what
happened to Jesus. Assuredly, the people who shouted out this
acceptance of responsibility did not think they were accepting
future punishment from God for Jesus' death. But the believer,
knowing what happened between the death of Jesus and the
writing of Matthew about 85 A.D., especially the resurrection of

Jesus, the spread of belief in Jesus and the destruction of Israel in 67–73 A.D., the fall of Jerusalem in 70 A.D., and of Masada in 73 A.D., can only see the bitterest foolhardiness in this statement.

Indeed, this statement about willingness to take the punishment for a wrong judgment of Jesus was the culmination of the rejection of Jesus shown throughout his public life. Matthew and Mark recounted Jesus' parable about the vineyard owner who, deprived of the profits of the vineyard by his workers, sent one representative after another to seek what was his due; eventually he sent his son, only to lose him as well. Matthew is much more explicit in its assessment of what would happen to those vineyard workers when the master of the vineyard (Israel) himself came: "the kingdom of God will be taken from you and given to a people who will produce its fruit" (Mt 21:43).

It is important to notice that with this parable is interwoven the description of Jesus as the stone rejected by the builders, yet the stone which is chosen by God to be the keystone. Thus, the failure of the vineyard workers is that they did not return to God the produce fitting to God's vineyard, produce which flowed from acceptance of Jesus' teaching, the teaching of the keystone.

The people's rejection of Jesus before Pilate was the final, definitive rejection foreseen by this parable of the vineyard workers. Their continual disobedience toward the vineyard owner culminated in the acceptance of responsibility for the rejection of the owner's son, the keystone to God's plan of salvation. But not only does the cry before Pilate sum up the responses given throughout the Gospel; it also opens the way for Jesus' significant command to his disciples after his resurrection: to go to all nations, to form a people from all peoples who will give to God what is his due. One should not forget how forcefully Matthew put Jesus' words about his being sent only to the house of Israel; eventually, Jesus cures a non-Jewish mother's child, but only after it is made abundantly clear that his serious intent is to save Israel. No later judge, looking at the heavily Gentile composition of the churches of the Mediterranean in 85 A.D., could say that Jesus came only for the Gentiles; the Gentile mission is somehow the result of Israel's rejection of Jesus who, Christianity insists, came first for Israel.

In the trial before Pilate, then, can be seen themes very central to the Matthean and Johannine arguments; even in this sad moment, ringing defenses of Jesus and his identity are argued—as will be the defense of a belief in Jesus professed in the communities so many decades after Jesus' death.

We must recall for a moment the painful humiliations and the physical sufferings of Jesus during these miserable hours. Ridicule and mocking were meant to cause mental anguish to Jesus; behind all this for many was an anger which had simmered for a long time, and was finally released in a brutality. Slappings and crowning with thorns were further forms of pain meant to dehumanize the prisoner. Finally, the scourging with whips, probably leather cords with metal pellets fixed into the end of each cord, was a terrible punishment in its own right, even though it was considered as preparatory to quiet further pain. One can appreciate the pain of scourging, when we realize that by scourging the prisoner's senses are to be dulled to a significant degree and his strength greatly sapped lest he have to suffer the horror of crucifixion in full consciousness and without a "prior sedative." What a form of mercy!

Jesus before Herod   *Lk 22:8-12*

We must consider Herod's trial of Jesus under the heading of humiliation. As mentioned earlier, Pontius Pilate sent Jesus to Herod Antipas, son of Herod the Great who slaughtered the children of Bethlehem,, because Pilate was looking for an excuse not to have to deal with Jesus and because Herod was the legal authority under whom Jesus spent his preaching career—let Herod handle this problem! But as Herod tried to handle Jesus in a judicial way, it became clear that Jesus offered him no cooperation. Soon the Herod trial is allowed to turn into a forum for humiliation of Jesus; he was even dressed in colors meant to taunt him for pretending to be a king.

No matter what responsibility the Jewish authorities assumed for Jesus' death, only Pilate could give the order, if death were the desired punishment. The Gospels and later tradition show a certain understanding of Pilate's quandary as they underline the role of Israel in this death.

Carrying the Cross   *Mt 27:31-33; Mk 15:20-22; Lk 23:26-32; Jn 19:17-18*

In the process of crucifixion, the prisoner must carry either a small cross with the bill of charges or the crossbeam of the cross to execution site. The longer, upright beam would already

be in place. Jesus, then, began his walk to Calvary, the place of
execution outside the city's walls. The Scriptures tell us of two
incidents along this bloody route of the prisoner: he was deemed
so feeble that someone had to be enlisted into carrying the cross
for him, and Jesus spoke to a group of women he encountered
weeping for him in his terrible plight. Each of these moments
deserves reflection.

Simon from Cyrene   *Mt 27:32; Mk 15:21; Lk 23:26*

The Roman soldier's calling on Simon from Cyrene, on the north
coast of Africa, is mute witness to the depth of suffering Jesus'
system has undergone; Jesus could not move even the equivalent
of three blocks without another person's help. But Simon also
offers a concrete example of the rule which lies behind a
teaching of Jesus in his Sermon on the Mount. Then Jesus had
encouraged his disciples to go two miles, should they be forced
to go one. Jesus was referring in this teaching to the situation in
which, according to Roman law, a soldier on duty could legally
demand the help of any bystander he chose to help him fulfill his
duty; this included carrying heavy burdens. Thus, according to
the known law of the times, Simon was legally ordered to help
Roman soldiers fulfill their duty of crucifixion; indeed, Simon
helped for a distance quite short of the one mile maximum
dictated by law.

This Simon was the father of Rufus and Alexander; Rufus was
most likely the Rufus to whom Paul sent his best greetings in
Rome and whose mother was "like a mother to Paul" (Rm 16:13).
Cyrenians, together with Alexandrians, formed a synagogue in
Jerusalem, after being set free from an imprisonment in Rome
which began about 63 B.C. Thus, it is thought that this
crossbearer of the Lord's cross had relatives in the Christian
church who were known to Mark and to Paul; that is why Mark—
and Matthew and Luke after him—and immortalized his special
act and his name.

Jesus and the Women of Jerusalem   *Lk 23:27-31*

A second event which took place along the route to Calvary was
the meeting between Jesus and certain women. Luke notes that
Jesus was followed by a great crowd, that a part of this crowd
was made up of women who beat their breasts and lamented

over the suffering prisoner. Such activity by Jerusalem women was not uncommon; these women tried to offer whatever assistance they could in their awareness of the terrible suffering anyone on the way to crucifixion must be enduring.

Seeing these women weeping for him caused Jesus to affirm again the reality of a tragedy which would visit all Jerusalem, including these women. Sympathetic as they were with another's suffering, they should understand how much suffering was in store for them; if they did, they would weep equally for themselves, so great would their suffering be. Another measure of their grief would be their counting themselves fortunate if they have no children; these children would surely die, and their death would only serve to increase still more the pain of these women. Such would be the suffering of the Jerusalemites that they would ask that mountains fall on them and hills cover them; better such an end than to have to endure the greater suffering in store for anyone in Jerusalem when the Roman armies come.

One should remember that the prophet Hosea had used the same imagery of mountains and hills when he described the punishment to fall on Israel in an earlier time for another refusal to obey the will of God (Hos 10:8); better to die under mountains and hills than to suffer the punishment to result from Israel's worshipping of false idols. The rejection of Jesus is one more act against the good God, and the punishment for this will make death under falling mountains appear the easier, preferred suffering.

If, indeed, the sight of another suffering brought the women to tears—this was described as the time of green wood—what would be their weeping for themselves—a time of dry wood? If the women weep when it is not their own punishment for which they weep, what would they do when it is time to pay the price for their own sins?

At first, it seems that Jesus, or the gospel writer who portrayed Jesus, was ungrateful for the sympathy offered him by these women. But actually Jesus, here as in his entire life, would rather awaken awareness of sin and forgiveness in the lives of others than seek sympathy for himself. Indeed, this principle explains the relatively small writing to stir up the grief of Jesus' contemporaries for Jesus as opposed to the much longer writing to encourage his contemporaries to repent and be saved. Jesus preferred to seek salvation of others than sympathy for himself. In this particular case of Jesus' way to Calvary, we might be misled by the women's weeping to think that the tragedy of Jesus was the greatest suffering; if only the women were aware of what would happen because Jesus is rejected! Then would they weep indeed!

The northeast district of old Jerusalem serves to recall the painful events occurring between the capture of Jesus in the Garden of Olives and his crucifixion next day. The events are those of condemnation, insult and physical pain. It is not clear to all scholars that these events must be tied to this area of Jerusalem; for many, the area just south of the Jaffa Gate is preferable as the true backdrop for the tragedy. Whatever the choice we make—and however difficult it is to imagine what things must have looked like that night—there is no difficulty in understanding the minds that created such pain for Jesus. It is not, ultimately, difficult to grasp the fear, jealousy and anger which motivated religious authorities of Israel to eliminate Jesus. He claimed to know better than anyone of any time the mind of God, an outrageous claim which could undermine tradition and transfer by obedience to him alone. Nor is it difficult to understand Pontius Pilate. He was basically cruel and insensitive; for him death was satisfactory if peace was its outcome. And it is not too hard to read Peter's reactions to a situation which he unexpected, despite his protest that he could handle any challenge to his loyalty to Jesus. Perhaps the one most difficult to understand of all these actors is Judas, accused though he be that money was his master. It is perhaps too simple to say that he betrayed Jesus for a sum of money, goodly though it be, and thus end an association which, at least, in its beginnings must have been satisfying; for awhile Judas had been willing to leave all things for Jesus.

But whatever be the character or situation of that night which we contemplate, we are asked to sense in it the tragedy of the good, our good, being rejected for the bad. These scenes tell the gospel reader about Jesus and his friends and enemies. They tell us something about sin as well; as such they speak very directly to the reader.

Site of the Crucifixion, Church of the Holy Sepulcher

Basilica of the Holy Sepulcher

Within the Basilica of the Holy Sepulcher lie two sites which, from the scientific point of view, are assuredly true to their names: the place of crucifixion of Jesus and the place of his entombment. Its obvious deterioration cannot diminish the realities the basilica contains. The visitor may feel disappointed, but here, more than anywhere else, we must distinguish between what surely happened in the small area now wrapped in the Crusaders' basilica and the sights and sounds to contend with. The visitor must use his or her imagination to the full here!

On entering the basilica we notice stairs on the right. These steep, small stairs lead up to a height of about fifteen feet; at this height is a chapel divided into two parts, Orthodox and Latin, with three altars. If we ascend to look at these three altars, we notice a hole, encircled by a star, at the base of the altar at the farthest left, the Orthodox Altar of the Crucifixion. To reach through this hole is to reach down to rock, the rock on which was raised the cross on which Jesus died.

On descending from the chapel platform over the rock of the crucifixion, we pass a large stone slab, revered as the site of the Pieta and the Anointing. Then we can round a wall of paintings on the left and go to the center of the rotunda. We look up to see the large cupola of the basilica; beneath the cupola and in the center of the round floor is a marble monument with many lamps and candles in front of its entrance. This monument stands over the shelf on which the body of Jesus was laid to rest. To reach this shelf, we pass through the low doorway of the monument, into a first chamber, then through a second doorway into the second and final chamber. Here, under a marble slab to protect it, is the shelf on which the body of Jesus was laid after his crucifixion.

If we could imaginatively take down the entire basilica with its monuments and paintings and lamps and mosaics and altars and sacristies and pillars, and remove the flooring of stone, we would stand between two places not more than thirty yards apart, with dirt and rock and grass under one's feet and the open air all around one. Such was the original form of this area when Jesus died and was buried here. Indeed, there was nothing of any significance here, except other burial tombs; the place in 30 A.D. could be described simply as a garden lying outside the city walls of Pontius Pilate's Jerusalem.

This area once was a quarry. One piece of rock, about fifteen feet in height, was left by the stonecutters because it rock was of poor quality—perhaps because it was broken by an earthquake or cracked during quarrying. This rock stood out in this "garden" space and gave the effect of a skull rising out of the earth. hence, it was called in the languages of the time *Golgotha, Kranion,* and *Calvary*—all of which mean *skull.*

The area was not protected by the city walls and was uninhabited. It was a place suitable for a burial ground and a garden for the mourners. It thus had a raised rock, ready for placing crosses on, and tombs nearby where crucified persons could be buried. Though it was unlikely that, since the crucified were such a miserable lot of criminals, they would have given much thought to preparing tombs for themselves.

Such then were the two points of this area before the time of Constantine's building the basilica (335 A.D.) meant to protect them. So many changes have occurred over the centuries that it would take a particular and long study to explain how things have evolved from a simple garden place to what we have before us today. One should only note that today's basilica includes at the end opposite to the tomb of Jesus, a chapel marking the area in which Constantine's mother, Helena, found the cross on which Jesus died.

Between the time of the death and burial of Jesus and the time of the building of Constantine's basilica, the Romans twice destroyed Jerusalem; the second time Hadrian built an immense Temple of Venus, with a statue in a large parklike area with buildings and surrounded by a wall, exactly in the area of the crucifixion and tomb of Jesus. Constantine's architects would have had a large job on their hands as they replaced one massive shrine with another. Indeed, some of the remains from the Roman shrine were used to build Constantine's basilica.

Today's basilica is a place where three communities—

Greeks, Armenians, and Latins, have rights and allow other Christians to have liturgies here. The Latins, that is, Roman Catholics and Uniates represented by the Franciscans, the Greek Orthodox, and the Armenian Orthodox, have residences here, control certain chapels and succeed one another, by turn, at night and by day in praying their own forms of liturgy. The others, Copts, Syrians or Jacobites, and Abyssinians, are allowed a presence and times for their liturgies which are much more limited than those of the first three mentioned. But it is important to realize that each of these groups has rights, often defended with blood; because of the history of Christian struggles associated with professions of contrary or contradictory beliefs, there is at best reluctant cooperation among them. The standoff which characterizes the existence of the six religious groups accounts in the main for the present condition and situation of the basilica. To understand these relationships is to grasp better why the basilica is in such disarray and is the heir of such varied forms of religious art, prayer, decoration and dress. One cannot have narrowly Western expectations here!

Death of Jesus   *Mt 27:33-66; Mk 15:22-47; Lk 23:33-56; Jn 19:17-42*

The important things is the unity of so many at the place here Jesus died. Here ends the struggle of Jesus to reach Calvary, begun at the order of Pontius Pilate. Here Jesus was prepared for death, stripped of clothes, nailed to the beam which he tried to carry. Then the beam was hoisted up to and fitted on the vertical beam wedged into the rock called *Skull.* Here Jesus was offered a drugged drink to further dull his senses to the terrible pain of crucifixion. And here he breathed his last and died. Here his dead body rested on his mother's lap, tradition insists, and here he was, finally, prepared for burial.

The Meaning of Jesus' Death

The New Testament encourages us to think of the death of Jesus in three major ways. First, his death took away our sins; secondly, the crucifixion was unjust; thirdly, Jesus is a model for his followers in this moment of life. Let us spend a few moments in consideration of these New Testament teachings.

Removal of Sins

St. Paul most thoroughly presents this understanding of Jesus' death, so it is to him we turn for enlightenment here. Without explaining each step in his own arriving at the belief that Jesus' death removed sin, Paul consistently explains Jesus' death in this fashion and thanks God profusely for this unique gift. Paul suggests many ways by which to understand this achievement of Jesus or us, but they are all written so that we can better realize the love behind his tremendous accomplishment, an accomplishment which, ultimately, no one of us deserved, which is purely and simply a gift from Someone who owed us nothing. Having learned of what has been done for us, we breathe an immense sigh of relief, for in realizing what has been given us, we also realize what our fate might have been, if God had not intervened. In what ways does Paul try to help us realize the truth about our future?

Reconciliation

It is not surprising that Paul resorted to images which made an impact on the people of his time and on himself. Paul called Jesus' death a reconciliation. In saying this, he counted on our understanding of this human experience. Imagine an initial union between two friends, then a painful separation, finally a reunion which ends the tragic separation and allows the freshness of friendship and happiness again. Whoever has experienced this sequence of moments can apply them to one's relationship with God and realize that it is solely through the death Jesus freely chose that we have friendship again with God. But the death of Jesus can be appreciated only if we appreciate friendship with God; we appreciate one gift if we realize the eternal value of another—union with God forever.

Perhaps it is not altogether clear why Jesus had to die that reconciliation with God become possible. Yet, on the level of human relationships, there some dying is usually involved as the sometime friends must try to overcome themselves and offer each other renewed friendship. From this perspective Jesus' dying represents in hope each person's willingness to die to that which used the rupture of friendship with God.

But we must mention another element of reconciliation. As we said above Jesus can represent us as we die to that which cost us God's friendship. But Jesus also represents God, and from this perspective Jesus is doing something usually not evidenced in human relationships. Ordinarily, when friendship is lost between two people, it is the guilty one who should initiate the forging of new friendship, at least by apology. Yet, as St. Paul puts it so well, "while we were still enemies to God, he gave his only Son to die for us." It is God who, in the death of Jesus, buries his justified anger with us and seeks our love by offering us his, even though we do not even think to look for him.

Redemption

Another way of looking at what Jesus accomplished on the cross is through the analogy of redemption. For Paul's contemporaries, redemption meant that something is bought back for a price, something which originally belonged to its rightful owner but somehow fell into the possession of a foreign owner. The most common example of redemption in the Mediterranean as a whole is that of slaves who buy back their freedom; in this way, they are set free from slavery Israelites from Egypt as the exemplar of "setting free." In speaking of Jesus' blood as the price paid for our redemption, Paul is grounding himself in the Jewish belief that, though the world belonged to God, it had come under the possession of a foreign owner, Satan. God now frees his people from this domination which is to the ultimate harm of human beings, in order that they might return to the obedience to which they were originally called, for their fullest happiness. For Paul, as for Jesus, a human being is always servant of some master; ultimately, it is a question of serving God or Satan—man cannot, in the nature of things, claim to be free of both God and Satan; human freedom does not mean that. Thus, if one is dominated by power or master that would ultimately harm one; and if that servant could never free himself or herself on one's own resources—the servant can only rejoice to finally be free and in the service of the Master who will bring the servant to fullest happiness. This kind of freeing is what redemption is all about. God lost us, but then, seeing our being helplessly mired in the power of Satan to our destruction, pays a price—the price our sins demand—so that we might be freed from tyranny and find again the guiding love of our original Master.

One must realize in this context not only that God spontaneously came to our rescue—we were so lost that often we did not realize how enslaved we were to our ultimate destruction—but also that Jesus freely chose to be the price of our freedom. The cross, then, signifies freedom, but it recalls the price paid for it by someone who freely gave his life for our happiness.

Atonement/Expiation

Paul suggests a third way of looking at the death of Jesus as an action which seeks the forgiveness of our sins. This third way is best known as the way of atonement or expiation. For Jews, and for others as well, sacrifices offered in a holy place to God for various purposes was a way of life. Among such sacrifices was to be found both communal and private sacrifice offered in hopes that sins would be forgiven. The most famous sacrifice in this regard is the sacrifice of Yom Kippur, which means *Day of Atonement.* It is to a sacrifice like this that Jesus' death on the cross is compared.

One day a year the high priest enters the holiest room of the Temple, the holiest Temple of the world. In that room, in the time of Solomon until the destruction of the Temple in 587 B.C. was a box, the Ark of the Covenant. In that precious box were memorabilia of the Exodus, things which recalled the great mercy God showed to Israel when he called his son out of Egypt. From the way in which the box or Ark of the Covenant was adorned, we could see that the Ark looked like a chair or throne—and it was said that God sat on this chair or throne in the midst of his people. Even when the Temple was rebuilt and during the centuries down to the time of Jesus—when the ark had been lost or destroyed—the idea remained that in this innermost holy room God continued to dwell in some way. Thus, to ask God's forgiveness for the sins of the nation as a whole, the high priest entered this holy room once a year to perform an ancient rite the essence of which was the request for and belief in the forgiveness of Israel's sins. What did the high priest do in this sacred moment?

Some distance from the Temple building itself, an animal was killed and a bowl was filled with its blood. With this bowl of blood the high priest entered the Temple and made his way to the furthest room, the Holy of Holies. Once inside the room, the high priest sprinkled some of the blood about the room. In ancient times, when the ark was there, it also was sprinkled with blood. Then the high priest turned around and exited the Holy of Holies and the Temple until he came to the people awaiting him outside. Then the high priest now sprinkled the people with the blood from the same bowl.

What does this blood mean? An ancient tradition of Israel was the understanding that in the blood is the life of a being; experience had shown this to be verifiable, for to lose enough blood was a sure way to lose one's life. From this simple perception arose the conviction that the blood contained life; indeed, this conviction lies behind the ancient prohibition against spilling a human being's blood. Life, you see, belongs only to God, and the spilling of blood is taking a life into one's own hands instead of leaving it in the hands of God to whom alone the disposition of life belongs. To sprinkle blood, then, on God's throne and on his people is symbolic of a giving of life to God, for life is in the blood. The Yom Kippur ceremony, then, is really a rededication of life to God, and the giving of God's life to his people—through the symbolism of the sprinkling of blood, "in which is the life." It is not the death of the animal which is given to God for sins; it is the promise of life for God which is symbolized as the blood is sprinkled on God's throne. And it is understood that God accepts this gift of life rededicated to him. From this Ark of the Covenant flows mercy and the rededication of God as God of this people. Indeed, the Ark of the Covenant is called, from this ceremony, the Mercy Seat or Throne of Mercy. Israel stands repentant before a merciful God; to him is given a life of devotion to replace that life of disobedience which characterized the days of the past year.

In using this ceremony to help understand what Jesus did on the cross, we have only to see the sprinkling of Jesus' own blood on a piece of wood even as the ark was made of wood; Jesus is victim who gives the blood as well as the One who does the sprinkling. It is his life which is given in this sprinkling, but Jesus hopes others will now join their lives to his as, one by one, people rededicate their lives to God as Jesus hopes they will. It is for this hope that he gives his life in blood; from this wood, as from the wooden Ark or Mercy Seat, will flow that mercy which wipes away all sin and death. In this imagery, it is not death which pleases God, but the life of rededication. Jesus stands for all mankind in this; it is God's hope that it is not only Jesus who lovingly dedicates his life to him.

Justification

But there is a fourth way of understanding the effect of Jesus' death, a way which is very important to the thinking of Paul in his letters to the Romans and to the Galatians. It is the way by which Paul thinks of Jesus' death as winning justification for us; by his death we can, if we believe, be called just. Behind these terms *justification* and *just* is an analogy to a legal trial. We must envision the following scenario: a person is absolutely guilty of a serious crime, and, on entering the judge's court, can reasonably, logically, expect only suitable drastic punishment for the crime. Indeed, everyone knows he is guilty and awaits full condemnation. At this moment, the judge, contrary to all logic, unilaterally declares the prisoner not guilty, or, to use Paul's term, just. This public declaration, contrary to what the prisoner deserves, is in every sense valid and legal; thus, society must honor the citizen as innocent, though the citizen, above all others, knows he is truly guilty.

Using this analogy to an improbable courtroom scene, Paul elicits from the reader a cry of wonder or gratitude that the fate owed the prisoner is totally changed. What one deserves, one does not get; and this wonderful change is due solely to the free choice of God. If we can enter heaven only if we are "just," we are made "just" by God's changing our reality.

Such, then, are metaphors Paul uses to try to convey both the adverse, even hopeless situation in which human beings were locked by their sins, and the overwhelmingly pleasing result of God's decision to intervene on our behalf to change things all around. All these metaphors—expiation, redemption, justification, reconciliation—are drawn from human situations and aim to help the reader realize how blessed he is to have the Lord as his God.

One other image the New Testament suggests the reader acquaint himself with to understand better what Jesus did on the cross: the image drawn by Isaiah in his fifty-second and fifty-third chapters of the servant who suffers out of obedience to Yahweh. This servant is so loyal to Yahweh and loves him so much that, even when Yahweh asks him, who has done nothing worthy of punishment, to suffer the pain which is punishment for the failings of others—this servant is so responsive to whatever the Master asks that he goes even to death "like a lamb before the shearers."

Jesus had often referred to himself as the Son of Man, that

imaginary character of the Book of Daniel, chapter seven, who, after suffering, would judge the world which condemned him. The image of the Son of Man was lacking in one respect; it did not clarify the suffering of the Son of Man before his glorification. It is the image of the Suffering Servant, used so plentifully during Christian Holy Week, which makes clear that the suffering of the Son of Man was not due to anything wrong he did; it is suffering which belongs rightly to others, but suffering borne by One who was willing to bear it, if that is what Yahweh wanted. And those who deserved the suffering go absolutely free! It is no wonder that the "News" Paul and others preached is forever designated as "Good News"!

Crucifixion Unjust

A basic theme of each Gospel is that Jesus was unjustly condemned to death. The Gospels, in particular, are determined from their very outset to so tell or retell the story of Jesus' public life that the reader should, when the time comes to tell of Jesus' capture and trial, be able to assert with impartiality and fairness that Jesus should not be condemned, that a sentence of condemnation is simply unjust. This purpose determines how stories about Jesus are told, for as each story adds its significance to those before it, a strong case is built by which we know Jesus to be anything but guilty of any or all the charges brought against him in various courtrooms in Jerusalem. More specifically, we should understand from the infancy of Jesus' life that he is destined by God to preach repentance, to be Messiah and Son of God, to represent God to one and all. His adult teaching is, upon reflection, making the law of Israel a more perfect reflection of the mind of the Lawgiver than anything taught so far. His miracles show a power to overturn the tyrannies of this world for which we could only hope, but never anticipate to see come from a human being.

This freewheeling and generous exercise of power justified the implicit claim of Jesus to be the One who most thoroughly understood what God thinks will bring human beings to the fullest happiness. Jesus is clearly the winner in any debate initiated by the religious leadership of Israel; his miracles suggest that not even the supreme power of Rome could shackle him, unless he permitted it. In short, once we come to the point of the narrative where Jesus is captured and put on trial, we should realize that Jesus is not guilty of any evil; on the contrary, the story has been so told that we have for long been led to another question than that of guilt. The question is not "Is he guilty?," but rather "Who is he?" Servant, Son of Man, a second Elijah, another prophet or the prophet who was to succeed Moses, Messiah, Savior? If Son of God, in what sense? Like David or the prophets or the angels or the whole of Israel—all of which were called at various times Son or Sons of God?

But not only is the entire gospel narrative aimed to argue that Jesus should not have been put to death. The moments of capture, trials and dying underline in various ways that Jesus is no criminal. Of particular importance to the Gospel writers was the opportunity to compare Jesus favorably with the Old Testament's own witness, in the Wisdom literature, that the just man suffers at the hand of the unjust, that suffering may not always be what human authorities want to call it, *just punishment.* Too often do human beings only later realize that suffering dictated by human authority can be unjustly imposed; what is paraded as evil before the crowds is at times quite the opposite. But because authority is trusted, the ordinary person simply shrugs his shoulders and assumes the authoritative statement is to be accepted as true; the Gospels so tell the story of Jesus' last hours that it is clear to one who knows the Old Testament that Jesus is precisely depicted as one of the Just who suffer injustice at the hands of this world's powers.

The just man of the Book of Wisdom, then, is an underlying image which is used to depict Jesus in his last hours. But there are many other instances we can recognize, if we are aware of the gospel tendency to show Jesus was guilty of nothing; indeed, the Gospels are hoping that, even if we are not consciously aware of the buildup, we will subconsciously know that Jesus is innocent.

Jesus as Model

Jesus is a model for his followers. Often enough the various writings of the New Testament speak of the sufferings and trials which Christians have endured for their belief in Jesus, are enduring and will surely have to endure for Christ. Jesus speaks of these moments for his disciples, indeed, for anyone who will "follow him." Other writings of the New Testament attest to the tribulations afflicting Christians as one generation succeeds another in Christian witness. Given the situation of Christians in the first century A.D., it is not surprising to find that scholars think that one of the major purposes of the entire Gospel of Mark is that of consoling and strengthening Roman Christians facing persecution and martyrdom. The bulk of the Book of Revelation is certainly aimed to give Christian readers the strength to exit this world victorious over the deadly attacks of Christ's enemies. Thus, in the massing together of individual sentences and entire books, we are forced to realize the constant effort of the New Testament writers to urge Christians to heroic confession of Christ.

In this encouragement there is a constant theme that the death of Christ is a model for the suffering Christian. Baptism is often used by Paul as the public ceremony which proclaims to all that one has died, like Christ. This death which baptism announces is to be a moral death, that is, a death to choosing what displeases God. But it also implies a death to the old so that God can live in us, so that we may live life with God by sharing his life.

This death to sin is particularly death to all which does not promote love of neighbor. One need only read Mk 8:31–38 to see how reflection on the death of Jesus can extend to the death of the disciple when he gives his neighbor that justice and love which God asks. Odd as it seems, charity and justice suggest death by the one called on to love and be just.

But particularly it is Jesus crucified who, by his conscious acts and his overall attitude, set an example for the Christian who must suffer for being Christian. Jesus on the cross is a Jesus who calls on the Father to forgive Jesus' tormentors. Jesus on the cross is a Jesus who gives his attention to one who asks for forgiveness and assures him of it. Jesus on the cross, moreover, is a Jesus who, though preferring not to die, throws himself unfailingly on the wisdom and love of his Father. He had preached God as Father to so many; now he was called on to live out what he preached, to trust the choice of his Father in a situation he would have preferred to avoid. Jesus, then, is a model not only of that death which is involved in obeying the commands of God to be loving and moral; he is also a model of the way we accept the will of God in all aspects of life, many of which we would choose to avoid if left to our own wisdom and resources. To Jesus, all life is in God's hands, not only the life of moral choices. Fortunately, our lives are in the hands of a God who is Father; knowing him to be Father assures us that our trust in his wisdom is not misplaced. It is the living out of this

conviction about God as his Father that is Jesus' great
contribution to us as he lies helplessly in pain on the cross.

When I sit in the Basilica of the Holy Sepulcher and realize
that here is the place where my Savior died for me, the
confession of Paul overwhelms me: "he gave himself for me;
while we were still God's enemies, God gave his Son for us."
Death is never pleasant. Here was death. It was a death for me.
And, though it does complicate things a bit more to say this, we
should always remember that, though we say Jesus offered
himself to God to make up for our sins, it was, more profoundly,
God the Son who willingly died before God the Father. It was
God, then, who—aware of my everlasting death—did for me
what I could never do for myself. Thus, in saying that Jesus took
my place, I must realize that God took my place, God the Son to
please God the Father. It was indeed a death for me, but also a
death which, in its deeper mystery, was necessary only because
of me. Such is the unpleasantness of this particular death. The
only abatement of my humiliation as cause of this death is the
memory of the depth of love God has for me, that he would do
nothing less than go to a terrible death for me, if that would help
me. I caused a very unpleasant scene here; but I know for sure
now how loving God can be to me.

Jesus Risen   *Mt 28:1-10; Mk 16:1-8; Lk 24:1-12; Jn 20:1-18*

Not very far from Calvary, the place of ignomiy and intense
suffering, is the site of glory and eternal joy. Jesus was hastily
wrapped in cloth; the intention of those who did this was to lay
him to rest on Friday before sundown, when the Sabbath began,
and to return to the tomb at the first daybreak after the Sabbath
was over, Sunday, to complete the anointing and wrapping of the
body for burial. Thus it is reasonable that the first awareness of
the Resurrection occurred when people came to the tomb after
the Sabbath; for no one saw Jesus rise. Then was the discovery
made and the explanation given that Jesus was no longer dead,
but now lived the life of eternal union with God.

Apologetic Character

It would not be surprising if we underline the defensive tendency
of the Gospel stories about Jesus risen; even for believers the
resurrection from the dead needs to be made reasonable, as far
as this is possible. Hence, the Gospels will not depict a scenario

in which people discover an empty tomb and then reason on their own to a conviction that Jesus is risen. No; rather divine messengers are sent to proclaim the Resurrection, memories of Jesus' firm predictions about his Resurrection are recalled, Jesus himself eats before his disciples, allows himself to be touched, performs actions which can only be interpreted as this —he is alive!

Resurrection as Fulfillment of Old Testament

One of the main thrusts of New Testament treatment of Jesus risen is to argue that the Resurrection was foretold by God in the Jewish Scriptures. For people of the twentieth century A.D. an attempt to show that Jesus fulfills an Old Testament quotation is a weak, even unimpressive argument. Yet, if we would appreciate the New Testament as a document of its own time, we must realize how the people of the first century A.D. prized the argument that Jesus fulfilled the Old Testament; indeed, the more times they could relate him to the Old Testament, the more binding and convincing they considered their argument.

Thus, besides appearances of Jesus himself and angelic witness, Christians argued with Jews throughout the first century A.D. as to the reality of that Resurrection and to its implications. For, while the number of eyewitnesses to Jesus in his risen state are few and limited, the meaning of his Resurrection is open to all who will trust the testimony of the eyewitnesses and apply the Old Testament expectations about the one who has risen to Jesus, the one and only one who actually is risen.

Let us take a moment to be specific about this relationship between Jesus risen and the Old Testament. In one of the psalms of the Old Testament, David who, everyone in first century A.D. Israel presumed, was the author of all the psalms, says this: "You [Yahweh] will not abandon me to Hades; nor allow your holy one to experience corruption." (Ps 16:10.)

Abandon here means *leave forever*; thus, the *me* not abandoned is the author of the psalm who will, after entering Hades or the realm of Death, leave it; he will die, but not experience corruption. Now this sentence is clearly in Scripture; since God clearly said it, he must have intended that it be fulfilled. But could it really have been said about David? David, everyone knew, both died and remained dead. So, though the psalm seems to refer to its author, it really is not. Perhaps then it is speaking about a part of David, a descendant of his. Well, Jesus is a descendant of David! And now comes the testimony of the eyewitnesses: we have seen him risen, him who was dead.

So, we put together the two arguments: 1. somebody is to die, but not stay dead, somebody who is a descendant of David; 2. we know that Jesus, a descendant of David, died and is risen. Therefore, we know Jesus to be the one and only candidate for fulfillment of the psalm. But to say this is to admit that God had long ago foreseen and planned for this Resurrection, that Jesus must be contemplated in this most intimate relationship with God which no other person has ever enjoyed. Moreover, if the psalm is really talking about Jesus and about his Resurrection from the dead as something to be expected, then he qualifies to be called "Messiah," for Psalm 16 was considered a psalm about the Messiah who is, among other things, expected to be a descendant of David. In short, if the eyewitnesses can be trusted, it is Jesus who brings the expectation of Psalm 16 to completion and Psalm 16 shows that what is claimed for Jesus was already long ago foretold and shows that he is the heir of the promise made to David, that the Messiah would be his descendant, a Messiah who would rule forever. In this way the Christians argued that belief in Jesus was justified; in this way they gave him his first meaning.

Perhaps a second example is in order. Psalm 110 begins with the words: "The Lord [Yahweh] said to my Lord, 'Sit at my right hand . . .'" Ps 110:1. Again, David is considered the author of this psalm, so clearly *my* in the first line refers to him. If, however, the first mentioned *Lord* is Yahweh or God, then who is the *Lord* mentioned secondly in the same line? It is someone who will sit at God's right hand, but it is not David, for David refers to him as his "Lord." Well, who qualifies to be David's Lord, that is, who can be said to "sit at God's right hand?" At this point, Christian witness testifies, first, that Jesus has entered the age in which one can sit at the right hand of the Father, the age beyond death, and secondly, that Jesus has ascended to the right hand of his Father—certain Christians, the essential eyewitnesses, have seen this ascension of the Risen One. Jesus, therefore, qualifies to be David's Lord, for he alone is known to have been taken by God to God's right hand.

Thus, it is argued, Jesus is fulfilling what Psalm 110 expected, and Psalm 110, as fulfilled, bestows its own witness that Jesus is Lord. Once again, then, eyewitness and words of Scripture join forces to indicate that what Jesus has done completes Scripture and that Scripture foretold what Jesus would do and gives meaning to this Jesus; he is, as God indicated through the psalm, Lord of David.

Such then is the defensive or apologetic strain running through New Testament accounts of Jesus risen from the dead. But there are other directions the New Testament follows in its attempt to penetrate the meaning of Jesus' Resurrection. Let us spend a few moments considering these.

Resurrection as Vindication

A theme taken up by more than one writer of the New Testament is that Jesus' rising from the dead is sure proof that Jesus was never guilty of any of the things he was accused of; rather, the Resurrection, which occurs through the power of God, shows that Jesus must have been pleasing, very pleasing to God—otherwise, why did God intervene for the dead Jesus? Thus, though other events of Jesus' life could argue to the positive relationship between God and Jesus, the Resurrection is the greatest of all these events; Jesus never should have been put to death on the score that "he was not from God."

Resurrection as Restoration of Mankind

Another way of understanding the Resurrection is to see it as God's way of setting on track again what human powers for a moment had derailed. The plan of God was that Jesus would save mankind. This plan was momentarily obstructed, when the Savior died. But the plan was reactivated with the Resurrection of Jesus from the dead; now he could again be Savior—this time he saves from the right hand of the Father all those who call on him for salvation. Jesus will work through human witnesses, as he did once or twice in Galilee when he sent his disciples to preach the kingdom for a few days; but it is the living Jesus who actually does the saving, who is actually Lord of all communities till the end of time. He will be with his disciples to the end of the world.

Resurrection as Forgiveness of Sins

Another aspect from which to search for the meaning of the Resurrection is that which begins with Jesus' wiping away of sin. If going to death eliminated for us the debt we owed for our sins,

Jesus risen is the result of sin forgiven. We will look like him, after we have died with him to all disobedience to God. Jesus has gone before us who have been freed from sin; we will follow him, freed from the effects of sin, the worst of which is death forever, but others of which are corruption, lowliness, imperfection. Jesus has crossed to the new age; we will—glorious, exalted, perfect—be drawn in his wake, through death to unending life. What he now looks like gives us an idea of what we will look like.

Necessity of Resurrection

The Resurrection of Jesus is to be considered a necessity. Jesus had to be raised from the dead, of course, because God said through the Old Testament writers that he had planned the saving of the world in this way. But the necessity runs more deeply. Jesus had to rise because of his unremitting love for his Father. To understand this, we should reflect for a moment on the effects of love. God, in the beginning, created; it was his love that made him do it. From Goodness or Love can proceed only life; it is from Hatred or Evil that death or separation proceeds. If we separate ourselves from God by hatred or disobedience, we separate ourselves from the source or font of life. But if we love God, unite ourselves to God, then we must necessarily live—from such a union of love can proceed only life. Thus, although Jesus died, and all the fury of enemies—death, human opposition, Satan—were allowed full exercise over him, Jesus, because of his love for the Father, could not remain dead. Love simply will not allow death forever. Jesus had to rise from the dead. Such is the inexorable logic of love.

The Resurrection from the dead means that Jesus continues to live. However, it is important to understand the quality of life he enjoys. Many societies and cultures professed belief in an afterlife, but the Judaeo-Christian tradition emphasizes that the only life-after-death worth living is life with God. Thus, to rise from the dead, in Christian expectation, is to rise to uninterrupted intimacy with one's God. To live forever, but without God, is, in the Christian way of thinking, its own kind of hell. Thus, when we speak of rising from the dead, we understand that this rising is coming to life with God.

Peculiar to Jesus' way of risen life with God are two qualities ascribed to him. First, Jesus sits at the right hand of the Father. Jesus is in glory and, in glory, he reigns as King, after the fashion of ancient kings who were pictured at the right hand of divinity. This picture of Jesus at God's right hand is meant to encourage the Christian who should be inspired by the greatness of the one to whom he has dedicated his life.

But, as risen, Jesus also performs certain functions. For instance, he is the eternal high priest, the one who prays constantly for his people. He is also able to continue the mission given to him by the Father, a mission begun in Galilee, but continued throughout the Mediterranean and to the ends of the earth, through all time. Because he was crucified we might think his work was abruptly and thoroughly ended. But he lives, and clearly Jesus is the one who pours out the pentecostal Spirit, thus accounting for the opening of the floodgates of the Holy Spirit. It is Jesus who continues to call disciples, such as Paul, and it is Jesus who continues to cure the sick and to protect and guide his witnesses. It is Jesus to whom the Christian community prays, it is Jesus who is in their midst and it is Jesus who receives those who die in martyrdom for him. In the last time, it is Jesus who will judge all. And all this activity is grounded in the reality that Jesus lives, that death has no hold on him. He is the first to pass into that endless life promised to all who love God.

Jesus is alive. The first century A.D. Church tried to plumb the depths of this reality and concluded that Jesus lives by virtue of God's Spirit. What this means is best explained by considering the principle of life by which we know human beings to live. That is, something becomes human because two human beings cooperate to make it become human; thus it enjoys human life, rather than another form of life. But one of the limitations of this human form of life, a form of life which belongs to "this age," is that it will die. Thus, what we need, to live forever with God, is a form of life which will not die; this form of life cannot be conveyed, of course, by human beings who themselves are to live only for a limited time. It is for God to provide the means by which a human being can transcend the natural, human form of life. God does this by enlivening us with his Spirit, which conveys to us God's own life, which makes us live by God's own life. Thus, we can at the same time to live forever and to live in the deepest intimacy with God, for it is by his life that we now live after death. Jesus was the first to be "raised in the Spirit"; but he is only the first, having made it possible for all those who belong to him to live, eventually, by the very life by which he lives forever, by the life of God.

In all this there is a supreme gift of the very Spirit of God to

Jesus and to his disciples. But in the conviction of certain New Testament writers, that gift of life is already given to an ever increasing degree to believers even before they die. In some real, though mysterious way, believers, though still living in "this age" by virtue of the human life received at conception, are also sharing in the life of God as communicated by the real presence of the Spirit in themselves. It is that life from the Spirit which becomes, after death, the sole reason we live for God forever in eternity. Thus, what is promised in the resurrected life has already begun in life assigned to "this age."

Finally, Jesus risen is our hope. One need only see death occasionally to sense how much one's total being longs to avoid it, to escape from it, to hold on to life while possible. We are made to live, and though the New Testament does not, despite the occasional miracle, offer any hope of respite from the persistent grinding of life into death, it offers supreme hope that life—and death—lived in love of God will pass into life eternal, a life of total happiness. It is the supreme hope and the source of deepest joy, that joy that flows beneath all troubled waters of life in this age. Jesus' cry, "save me from this hour... take this chalice from me," that his God has forsaken him, is always followed by acts of trust and confidence. Beneath the most profound hope of all is belief that God loves me so much that, no matter how frail I reveal myself to be, he will bring me to eternal intimacy with him.

A last footnote about Jesus risen. One can try to bring out the implications of this grand and mysterious event of Resurrection—and we have tried to do that in these past pages. But there is another focus to use on this event. For this, we should look at Mary Magdalen. For all that the Resurrection of Jesus meant for her own life eternal, part of her joy at the Resurrection of Jesus is her knowledge that he is safe. Great saints have encouraged us to rejoice with Jesus for his sake, as friends would. Putting aside for a moment the meaning of Jesus' Resurrection for us, we are simply glad for him—and, like Mary, are very reluctant to see a friend go so soon after escaping from the bonds of death.

We have reason to rejoice for ourselves and for Jesus. Everyone benefits from love unhindered by evil of whatever kind; we share fully in the love of God for Jesus and of Jesus for God. We can only be grateful and joyful as we place ourselves before the tomb of Resurrection. Though we do not know what we will look like risen from the dead, we know that our total selves will rise—because we know how much God loves us and that he has placed us with Jesus; if Jesus is risen, we also will rise. Alleluia!

Index

Scriptural References

Other References